THE ATLANTIC CRITICAL STUDIES

JANE AUSTEN'S

Pride and Prejudice

Pulakesh Ghosh

ATLANTIC

PUBLISHERS & DISTRIBUTORS (P) LTD

Published by

ATLANTIC

PUBLISHERS & DISTRIBUTORS (P) LTD

7/22, Ansari Road, Darya Ganj, New Delhi-110002
Phones : +91-11-40775252, 23273880, 23275880, 23280451
Fax : +91-11-23285873
Web : www.atlanticbooks.com
E-mail : orders@atlanticbooks.com

Branch Office
5, Nallathambi Street, Wallajah Road, Chennai-600002
Phones : +91-44-64611085, 32413319
E-mail : chennai@atlanticbooks.com

Printed in India at Nice Printing Press, A-33/3A, Site-IV, Industrial Area, Sahibabad, Ghaziabad, U.P.

For

My Parents and

My Wife

Sangita

General Preface

The Atlantic Critical Studies are modelled on the study-aids available in England and America, among other places, and are primarily meant for the students of English Literature of Indian universities.

However, in consideration of the local conditions and the various constraints under which our students have to study—non-availability of relevant critical books, dearth of foreign and Indian journals, inaccessibility to good, well-equipped libraries, just to mention a few of them—the models have been considerably improved upon, both qualitatively and quantitatively.

Thus, while these studies are meant to be comprehensive and self-sufficient, the distinguished scholars who have prepared these study materials, have taken special care to combine lucidity and profundity in their treatment of the texts.

The Select Bibliography at the end, or References in the chapters are meant not only to acknowledge the sources used but also to help a student in the pursuit of further studies if he/she wants to.

Atlantic Publishers & Distributors (P) Ltd. believe in quality and excellence. These studies will only reconfirm it.

MOHIT K. RAY

Chief Editor [English Literature]
Atlantic Publishers & Distributors (P) Ltd.,
New Delhi

Contents

1 Jane Austen: Life and Works

Andrew H. Wright writes in *Jane Austen's Novels: A Study in Structure*:

> Jane Austen occupies an embarrassing position in literary history—embarrassing because never for a moment does she accommodate herself to the facile generations which are made about her contemporaries. Wordsworth and Coleridge can, though with some inaccuracy, be called Romantic; they were both born within five years of Jane Austen. But she is too little a writer to be called Romantic, too much a person of her time to be called Classic, too original and too great to be considered a precursor or apotheosis: she is, however much indebted to her literary forebears and coevals, unique. (1)

Jane Austen's life was neither long nor eventful. Jane Austen was born on 16 December 1775 at Steventon rectory in the county of Hampshire, and there spent her years of childhood and youth. Her father, George Austen, was gentle and strongly attached to his family; he occupied himself with the cares of his parish, his farm, and his pupils, and left a reputation for scholarship and literary taste which was supported in his day by his having prepared two of his sons, with other pupils, for Oxford, and rests more firmly on his quick perception of his daughter's gifts. Mrs. Austen was a country woman and busy gardener, with vital energy enough to carry her work through long stretches of ill health. Jane

Austen had no formal education, but her claim to be 'unlettered' is comic hyperbole. She was instructed both by her father and by her eldest brother James (more than ten years older than herself) who was a clergyman like his father, and became rector of Steventon after him. James' career—at Oxford, in his first curacy, and, when he succeeded his father, at Steventon—never carried him far from his sisters, and who played a constant if unobtrusive part in their lives. He dabbled modestly in letters. Edward was adopted, while a boy, by his distant cousins—Thomas and Catherine Knight of Godmersham in Kent—who brought him up to be their heir. His share in the family life became larger when he married and settled in a home of his own, to be visited often by his brothers and sisters. Henry, next in age after Edward, was thought by the rest to have been closest of all the brothers to Jane herself in sympathy and understanding. Cassandra, the most important of them all in Jane's life, yet remains the most shadowy. A strong and subtle sympathy bound these two together. 'They were everything to each other,' wrote the one of their nieces who had known them longest.

Outside this charmed circle Cassandra left a reputation for sterling sense—*Mansfield Park* was her favourite among the novels—and, in Jane's letters, as faint an echo of raillery as Henry's—"You are indeed the finest comic writer of the present age" (*Letters* 8). Francis was the next of the family, and the nearest to Cassandra in steady good sense. Last of all came Charles; like Frank, he was his father's pupil until he became a sailor, and like Frank, he was still tenacious when at sea of his share in family affections. Frank, as an officer, left a reputation for sound discipline and just consideration of others' claims; Charles, for the power of engaging affection.

The years at Steventon seem to stand apart from the latter half of Jane Austen's life; perhaps one may even perceive a difference between the first sixteen of them and the rest. The first recorded happening is her visit, with Cassandra, in 1782, to a connection of their mother, followed shortly by a stay of a year or two at a school in Reading. Perhaps they were "sent to be out of the way and scramble themselves into a little education," like Mrs. Goddard's pupils, for the rectory was full to overflowing, Cassandra was then ten years old, and where she went Jane must would go because she would not endure separation. By 1784 or 1785, they were at home again, ready to scramble themselves into a little more education. Mary Lascelles observes in *Jane Austen and Her Art*: "Of Jane's reading under these various influences there is no explicit record; but she must have been young when she made the acquaintance of the eighteenth century prose writers who so strongly influenced her style, and of Johnson, whose thought coloured her view of life—of Cowper, too, whose phrases lingered in her memory. Goldsmith was a favorite of those years; and perhaps she already enjoyed Crabbe; her liking for books of travel may have developed later; Scott was not yet above the horizon. For one kind of writing she seems always to have had an insatiable appetite: novels, good and bad, were all grist to her mill. Her enjoyment of what was absurd in current fiction must have begun to develop early..." (7-8).

The only claim to literary distinction in Jane Austen's ancestry is that Mrs Austen's uncle was Dr. Theophilus Leigh, a master of Balliol College, Oxford, and a noted wit. As a writer, Jane Austen began young, with private, comic burlesques of literary modes, written for family entertainment only. Perhaps it was the possession of a room of Cassandra's and her own that prompted Jane Austen to scribble her first mimicries of her fellow novelists. Some of them were pieces of serious, direct imitation; others, of outrageous burlesque. The author of the *Memoir* implies that there was a period of simple, nonsensical writing, followed by another of mocking mimicry. The authors of the *Life* notice a second stage in her literary education: when she was hesitating between burlesque and immature story-telling (*Life* 57). The order is of small importance; very likely these phases were not distinct; and what we have of this childish writing survives only in copies made several years afterwards. One thing is clear; there was a great deal of scribbling done before the end of those first sixteen years. All of Jane Austen's juvenilia known to survive have later been published: three notebooks full of tales and fragments which she herself collected and transcribed, calling them (with playful pretentiousness) *Volume the First*, *Second*, and *Third*.

Volume the First is made up of many small burlesque pieces, most of them introduced with the flourish of a mock dedication to one or another of Jane's family. Dr. Chapman shows how two of these dedications indicate dates before 1793, while 'June 3rd 1793' is written at the end of the collection. He goes on to say: "The handwriting, which in most of the book is large and not completely formed, becomes smaller and more mature towards the end, and in the concluding pages is not unlike the hand which wrote *The Watsons* not earlier than 1803." *Love and Friendship* (which may be called the second volume of this set of three) is made up of four parts; these are: two fairly ambitious tales told in letters—the hilarious burlesque (dated 13 June 1790) which has lent its name to the published collection, and the more ambiguous experiment Lesley Castle; there is a rowdy mock-history of the reigns of the kings of England from Henry IV to Charles I (dated Saturday, Nov. 26th, 1791); and there is a group of odds and ends.

It is not easy to date the earliest of her novels—*Northanger Abbey*, *Sense and Sensibility*, and *Pride and Prejudice*—since they existed in some forms when she was in her early twenties, but were not published until much later. All of them were much revised by their painstaking author, as is proved by the fact that *Sense and Sensibility*, at least, originally existed as a novel in letters. From 1796 onwards we have Jane's own letters to give us a direct impression (though at first very slight) of her life. It is vexatious that *Elinor and Marianne* should be lost, and that we must be content with what we are told about it: "that it was written before 1796; that it was cast in the form which Richardson had made popular—a fictitious correspondence—and was to be recast in direct narrative as *Sense and Sensibility*" (*Life* 80). We know, too, that it was read aloud; and we can assume that, however much it pleased the family, Mr. Austen did not take it seriously enough to think of publication. It may have been about this time that

Lady Susan, too, was written, although it survives only in a fair copy made not earlier than 1805. Like *Elinor and Marianne*, it is a tale told in a series of letters; but, though it is carried through resolutely in a mood of straightforward comedy to the end of the last letter, the plot is wound up in a conclusion which allows the author to make fun of the very device she has been employing: "This Correspondence, by a meeting between some of the Parties and a separation between the others, could not, to the great detriment of the Post Office Revenue, be continued longer" (*Lady Susan* 160). It is not impossible that the series of letters was written at Steventon and left incomplete—there is a great deal of winding up to be done in the Conclusion—and that this Conclusion was added at some time nearer to the date of the fair copy, when Jane Austen had lost patience with the device of the novel-in-letters. This is, of course, mere guess-work; but she certainly never used the device again (Lascelles 13-14).

At this point, Cassandra's Memorandum of dates begins to help. *First Impressions*, she records, was begun in October 1796, and finished in August 1797. Cassandra had heard and Anna overheard it read aloud, but the writing of it was a secret from the rest, perhaps because it was a more serious, ambitious venture than any that had gone before. Soon after it was finished, however, Mr. Austen must have shared the secret, for in the following November, he was offering it to the London publisher, Cadell. He describes it as being 'about the length of Miss Burney's *Evelina*', and asks whether Cadell will choose to be concerned, in it, what will be the expense of publishing it at the author's risk. The Austens, however, continued to think well of *First Impressions*; there are references to readings and re-readings of it in Jane's letters, and in its later form it remained a favourite among them. She was particularly attached to it herself, and seems to have recovered her confidence in it without waiting for encouragement.

In 1798 and 1799 she had, also, a new undertaking on her hands: she was at work, according to Cassandra's memorandum, on the first version of the story which (though originally called *Susan*) was eventually to be published as

Northanger Abbey—a version which probably differed a good deal from *Northanger Abbey* as we know it. The last two and a half years at Steventon seem to have yielded nothing; they were interrupted by several visits, and, towards the end, by the prospect of change. Mr. and Mrs. Austen had, in 1800, resolved to retire to Bath. Jane is said to have been distressed at leaving Steventon, and certainly she was not to find her life in Bath satisfying; but by January of 1801 she was already writing cheerfully of the plan, hoping that they would be freer than before to travel. This hoped—for travel took the form of 'rambles', the family—that is, the parents and daughters—visiting Sidmouth in 1801, Dawlish in 1802, Ramsgate in 1803, and Lyme Regis in the winter of 1803-04 (*Life* 172-76). One of these may have led to unhappiness. It was in Devonshire—so Caroline gathered, after Jane's death, from Cassandra—that Jane became acquainted with a gentleman who loved her and to whose love she responded; he died soon afterwards. Bath was meanwhile the settled home of the family, and to Bath, as a home, Jane Austen never became reconciled; the years spent there were unprosperous, and it must afterwards have been associated in her memory with some vexations, as well as real sorrows. In 1803, she revised her draft of *Northanger Abbey*.

The fragment which we know as *The Watsons* was begun not earlier than 1803; it was, however, to be left unfinished. It may be that the setting she had chosen for it failed to satisfy her. Mary Lascelles observes in *Jane Austen and Her Art*: "There was enough in the circumstances of her life to account for the silence which began when she had settled Emma Watson in her 'low' situation, and which lasted until 1809. She had to suffer two grievous losses in the death of her friend, Mrs. Lefroy in December of 1804, and of her father in the following month. She may, moreover, have felt the loss of his encouragement; certainly, with *First Impressions* refused unread and *Susan* buried, she wanted the encouragement of recognition outside her own family" (19).

Accord within herself was made more difficult after her father's death by circumstances: there was a change and demand for adaptation; the change (in particular) from a family party to the household of a widow and spinsters. Martha Lloyd, left alone when her mother died, joined Mrs. Austen and her daughters in 1805, and these four found themselves settled in a little world peopled by ladies in like circumstances. In October of 1808 Edward's wife died, leaving him with eleven children and Cassandra and Jane found themselves not only welcome, but necessary, to these nephews and nieces. On 25 April 1811, Jane tells Cassandra that she is at work on the proofs of *Sense and Sensibility*; and we are left to guess what has brought her to this point, and why *this* should be the manuscript chosen. Her reason for passing over *Northanger Abbey* is easily guessed at; the right to publish it would have cost her £10, and Crosby's treatment of it had not been encouraging: if he had thought its chances poor in 1803, what would they be now that *Udolpho* was eight years older? Besides, she may not yet have recovered her pleasure in burlesque. It is harder to understand her passing over *Pride and Prejudice*; but, in its first form, it had met with a rebuff, and she was not in a confident mood: she "laid by a sum...to meet the expected loss" (*Life* 255) on this her new enterprise—which would, if it had proved unsuccessful, probably have been her last. Compared with the other novels, *Sense and Sensibility* has the air of a mere venture: Cassandra knew of it, of course, when it was in the press, and very likely earlier, and both were concerned about its success; but, for some while after publication, its authorship was kept a secret even from Anna (*Life* 241). It was never to count for as much, to the author or her family, as the later novels: she would 'if asked'—tell them what became of Miss Steele, but her own imagination did not linger in the world of *Sense and Sensibility* as it was to do in that of *Pride and Prejudice*.

Jane Austen must have set about the revision of *Pride and Prejudice* out of sheer delight in the exercise of her own rediscovered gift, for it was already far advanced before the success of *Sense and Sensibility* could come to reassure her.

There was another unlucky silence after June, 1811, and when the letters began again in January 1813 *Pride and Prejudice* was already on the point of publication. Therefore we have no direct evidence as to the degree of revision that it underwent, beyond this reference in a letter of 29 January 1813: "I have lop't and crop't so successfully...that I imagine it must be rather shorter than *S. & S.* altogether" (*Letters* 298); but of circumstantial evidence there is enough. It is so clearly an advance upon *Sense and Sensibility* that it must, almost certainly, be an advance upon its own first draft—which had been written before *Sense and Sensibility* was cast in 'its present form'. Moreover Dr. Chapman shows how particular examination confirms this general impression, his principal argument being this: if *Pride and Prejudice* was written, as certainly appears, with an almanac of 1811 at hand, "we must infer", he says, "that the book as we know it was substantially rewritten in 1812; for it is certain that so intricate a chronological scheme cannot have been patched on to an existing work without extensive revision". One more small argument suggests itself: on 29 January 1813 Jane told Cassandra that the first copy of *Pride and Prejudice* had arrived: "I have got my own darling child from London": eleven days later she wrote to her: "I am exceedingly pleased that you can say what you do, after having gone thro' the whole work" (*Letters* 302-03). Cassandra, then, had not 'gone thro' the whole' of *Pride and Prejudice* before its publication; but Jane had teased her about her frequent re-readings of *First Impressions*. This seems to imply a real difference between them.

It may have been about this time that Jane Austen began, in her recovered confidence, to write more freely about her own work. The reticence that was a part of her would of course remain, but she was ready to speak of those artistic problems that would interest this or that one of her family, and of her own novels—at least so soon as they were in print. While Cassandra was reading the newly published *Pride and Prejudice*, Jane interposed with the mocking suggestion that it would have been improved by "an essay on writing, a critique on Walter Scott, or the history of Bonaparte" worked into it (*Letters* 300). And she entered gaily into the pretence that her imagined world, of Longbourn or Pemberly, was one with which they were all familiar. *Pride and Prejudice* lent itself admirably to this fiction; it had lived in its author's imagination for so long that she had developed a peculiar relation to its characters, and could say of her own Elizabeth Bennet "I must confess that I think her as delightful a creature as ever appeared in print, and how I shall be able to tolerate those who do not like *her* at least I do not know" (*Letters* 297). And, in another letter: "We have been both to the Exhibition and Sir J. Reynolds,—and I am disappointed, for there was nothing like Mrs. D. at either. I can only imagine that Mr. D. prizes any Picture of her too much to like it should be exposed to the public eye.—I can imagine he w'd have that sort of feeling—that mixture of Love, Pride and Delicacy" (*Letters* 312). This letter is a message to Fanny Knight; for the younger generation entered into the pretence with spirit, giving it fresh impetus. "She would, if asked, tell us many little particulars about the subsequent career of some of her people" (*Memoir* 157). At Chawton Jane Austen's work seems to recover that character of family entertainment to which it owes several of its charms, and on fault. The conditions under which she worked, and the way in which she adapted herself to them, may have strengthened this characteristic. Her nephew remembered that most of her writing "must have been done in the general sitting room, subject to all kinds of casual interruptions"; that, not wishing any one outside her own family to know what she was doing, she wrote on small sheets of paper and put them away when a creaking, door warned her of one of these interruptions. That was at Chawton, in comparative security; even when paying a visit, however—and many were paid within these years—she would contrive to go on with her work. One of Edward's younger daughters, speaking of her aunt's visits to Godmersham, recalled how she "would sit quietly working beside the fire in the library, saying nothing for a good while, and then would suddenly burst out laughing, jump up and run across the room to a table where pens and paper were lying, write something down, and then come back to the fire and go on quietly working as before". She must have developed to a remarkable degree her faculty for living (when she chose) apart in her imagined world—and, further, for keeping the regions of that world distinct in her imagination. To be engaged at once on *Pride and Prejudice* and *Mansfield Park*—and that while still correcting the proofs of *Sense and Sensibility*—and to preserve entire the peculiar atmosphere of each—this is an achievement which shows that she could project her imagination into one or another of these fragile bubble worlds, and let it dwell there.

"Jane Austen's way of life at Chawton seems to have been little disturbed, or animated, by contact with the human world outside her own family: Mrs. Austen, now growing old, gave up visiting her daughters, who chose to consider themselves middle-aged, may have lost the habit of adventurous social intercourse, and certainly could not afford to go far in search of it. But when Jane visited her brothers—particularly Edward and Henry—her range of acquaintance extended itself" (Lascelles 33). In London, there would be intercourse with Eliza's French friends, and visits to public places of entertainment, where "my preference for Men and Women, always inclines me to attend more to the company than the sight". After Eliza's death in April 1813 Henry came to depend more on his sisters, and their visits became more important, Jane's giving her opportunity to see her work through the press under his direction. On one score she objected to this widening of her social world: all her work was published anonymously, but Henry would not be persuaded to keep her secret. "...In the warmth of his Brotherly vanity and Love", she tells Francis, he has disclosed the authorship of *Pride and Prejudice*. "A thing once set going in that way—one knows how it spreads!—and he, dear Creature, has set it going so much more than once. I know it is all done from affection and partiality—but at the same time, let me here again express to you and Mary my sense of the *superior* kindness which you have shewn on the occasion, in doing what I wished" (*Letters* 340). She was always shy with strangers—"...though I like Miss H.M. as much as one can at my time of Life after a day's acquaintance, it is uphill work to be talking to those whom one knows so little" (*Letters* 419); and if they wished to meet her on account of her authorship she was even less bold and sanguine than usual. After all, the compensation for this effort was to be meagre; the tide of her fame flowed for so little a while that it only served to carry her as far as the Prince Regent's librarian.

This, however, is to look forward. *Mansfield Park*, 'begun about February 1811', had been finished 'soon after June 1813'. But it is not until March 1814 (when *Emma* is already on the stocks) that we hear of the manuscript of *Mansfield Park* being shown to Henry. This is significant; in his *Biographical Notice* Henry implies that this was always his sister's way: after referring to the novels which had been 'the gradual performance of her previous life,' he explains that "though in composition she was equally rapid and correct, yet an invincible distrust of her own judgment induced her to withhold her works from the public, till time and many perusals had satisfied her that the charm of recent composition was dissolved". And her treatment of the manuscript of *Persuasion* shows that this continued to be her practice until the end. "I suspect that the fortunes of the earlier novels had done much to form this habit; Jane Austen had found that she was able to return, cool and critical, to work that she had laid by, and to better it. In any case, it is clear that such a pause after the completion of any of the later novels signifies neither dissatisfaction nor want of confidence. The mood in which *Mansfield Park* was begun may well have been diffident and anxious; it was thirteen years since she had last drafted a novel which was to reach completion, and though she had meanwhile found that she could recast old work successfully this was another kind of undertaking. But by the time that she reached the end she can hardly have needed the successful publication of *Sense and Sensibility* and *Pride and Prejudice* to reassure her. She must have known that *Mansfield Park* excelled *Pride and Prejudice* in its subtler conception of human relations—by as much *Pride and Prejudice* had excelled *Sense and Sensibility* in its more subtly planned construction" (Lascelles 34-35).

Mansfield Park must have appeared soon after the announcement by the publisher (Egerton) in May. Meanwhile, on the 21st of January, *Emma* had been begun; either rising confidence or easier circumstances may have quickened its growth, for it was finished on the 29th of March 1815 (though it probably did not appear until early in 1816). Henry was probably a little impatient of the maturing process. And so far as his sister's practice was the outcome of diffidence, he could urge against it her steadily growing success: *Mansfield Park* had been favourably received; *Emma* was noticed in the *Quarterly*. There was a sting, for her, in some of its criticisms, but the review was, as a whole, complimentary, and it was a mark of attention; and, if she had known who was the writer, she could not but have been flattered, for it was Scott himself. Henry bought back the copyright of *Northanger Abbey* for her, and she was now free to prepare one of its manuscripts, if she chose, for publication. Clearly, she had this in mind in 1816, for she wrote in that year the note which was to stand as "Advertisement by the authoress to *Northanger Abbey*" in the first printed version; she may even have given it yet another polishing—her apology in the 'Advertisement' for "those parts of the work which thirteen years have made comparatively obsolete" need refer to no more than time's action on what had been of topical interest when Crosby bought the manuscript; and 'we are not bound to believe,' Dr. Chapman says, "that nothing was altered after 1803" (R.W.C. Introduction to *Northanger Abbey*, xiii). Therefore one should be cautious in drawing a line between the so-called earlier and later novels, and in asserting that "Jane Austen could write at twenty as well, or better, or very nearly as well, as at forty": we cannot be quite sure of knowing how she wrote at twenty.

She had a bigger undertaking on her hands at this time than any revision. *Persuasion* had been begun before she went to stay with Henry in London, in October 1815. It was not to be written in such leisure or comfort as *Emma*. During much of October, November, and December Jane was nursing Henry through a severe illness. The spring brought another anxiety: Henry's business was failing, and in March of 1816 he was declared a bankrupt. By May, Jane's own health and spirits were beginning to decline—so her friends thought, on looking back. But she went steadily on with *Persuasion*, and, on 18 July 1816, brought the story to a close. The tenth chapter of the second volume, however, did not satisfy her. She cancelled the greater part of it, and used the rest in a new draft, of two chapters, now the tenth and eleventh, the original eleventh chapter now standing twelfth (in the second volume). The arrangement of her first draft now obliged her to make a fair copy of this last chapter. Thus, she was in possession of a rough copy of two chapters, and, very fortunately, this manuscript survives to give us a little insight into her mode of revision. With that amendment, *Persuasion* achieved (so far as we know) its final form; but so long afterwards as 13 March 1817 she seems anxious that it should still rest in her possession, for she writes to Fanny: "I have a something ready for publication, which may perhaps appear about a twelve month hence"; and, in a letter of ten days later, implies that she had been anxious to keep its existence a secret from Henry: "Do not be surprised at finding Uncle Henry acquainted with my having another ready for publication. I could not say No when he asked me..." (*Letters* 487). This may well signify no more than a mood of despondency and self-distrust; even *Northanger Abbey*, which had been prepared for publication the year before, was now dejectedly laid aside: "Miss Catherine is put upon the Shelve for the present," Jane told Fanny in the earlier of these two letters, "and I do not know that she will ever come out." "She was by now very ill; it was only three days later that she relinquished her last work. On the other hand, these references to *Persuasion* may witness only her resolve to follow her usual practice; she will keep the manuscript by her, not because she has seen faults in it—those she has discovered she has already remedied—but in order to find out what faults yet lurk there. The proposed period of probation, longer than *Emma's*, may perhaps signify a distrust of Henry's affectionate impetuosity—or else a consciousness of the less favourable conditions in which *Persuasion* has been written" (Lascelles 58).

"The last work (which came to be known among her family as *Sanditon*) is a very surprising outcome of those last six months of her life (it had been begun on 27 January 1817): it is a hilarious comedy of invalidism, and (what was even less to be expected) a bold venture in a new way of telling a story. While each of the earlier novels had been, in some respect, an advance beyond its predecessors, none of them would, if broken off short at the eleventh chapter, have left us in such uncertainty as to the way in which it was going to develop: and her other pieces of unfinished work, *The Watsons*, seems, by comparison, almost to foreshadow its own fulfillment" (Lascelles 39). At the end of the manuscript of *Sanditon* stands the date 'March 18' (R.W.C. Introduction to *Sanditon*). It was in that month, Caroline remembered, that she first realized how ill her aunt was. In May Jane, with Cassandra, settled in lodgings at Winchester, where she might be attended by the best reputed surgeon of that neighborhood, Charles Lyford—who from the first seems to have had little hope of what his attentions could do (*Memoir* 172). Jane was still writing gay, mocking letters, describing herself as "a very genteel, portable sort of an Invalid", and proposing, "if Mr. Lyford should fail to cure her, to ask the Dean and Chapter for redress" (*Letters* 494), so late as the end of that month. The last letter of hers that survives has this characteristic passage: "You will find Captain—a very respectable, well-meaning man, without much manner, his wife and sister all good humour and obligingness, and I hope (since the fashion allows it) with rather longer petticoats than last year" (*Letters* 498). In June, James's wife, Mary, came to help Cassandra in nursing. On 18 July, Jane Austen died.

W.A. Craik writes in *Jane Austen in Her Time*, "Jane Austen's novels, like charity, begin at home. The centre of all her novels is a family or families, consisting usually of only two generations: parents, and children whose growing-up constitutes the novel's progress. The novels' happy conclusions all dismiss the heroines, not simply to ideal husbands, but to homes and families of their own. Though the stories may look like romances, in that they concern the adventures of their heroines which lead them to marriage, it is not these adventures for their own sake which Jane Austen cares about, but the way in which what happens prepares the heroine for the life that lies ahead of her, and enables her to choose the right life for herself" (Craik 3-4). There is a tendency in criticism to divide the novels into two groups of three—the one group (*Sense and Sensibility*, *Pride and Prejudice* and *Northanger Abbey*) lighter, the other (*Mansfield Park*, *Emma* and *Persuasion*) more psychologically complex—and to ignore or marginalise those writings which remained incomplete and in some cases did not see print until the twentieth century. We know Jane Austen made little money from her novels, and did not have a large public. She was, however, admired by men as distinguished as Sir Walter Scott, had her last books brought out by John Murray, the friend and publisher of Lord Byron, and dedicated *Emma*, at his own request, to the Prince Regent. Working with materials extremely limited in themselves, she developed themes of the broadest significance; the novels go beyond social record, beneath the didactic, to moral concern, perplexity, and commitment.

2 *Pride and Prejudice*: Composition and Publication

Jane Austen's plots, and her novels in general, were put together very 'deliberately and calculatedly'. But her interest in 'composition' is not something to be put over against her interest in life; nor does she offer an 'aesthetic' value that is separable from moral significance. The principle of organization, and the principle of development, in her work is an intense moral interest of her own in life that is in the first place a preoccupation with certain problems that life compels on her as personal ones. She is intelligent and serious enough to be able to impersonalize her moral tensions as she strives, in her art, to become more fully conscious of them, and to learn what, in the interests of her life, she ought to do with them. Virginia Woolf in "The Woman Writer" writes: "If a woman wrote, she would have to write in the common sitting room. And, as Miss Nightingale was so vehemently to complain—'women never have an half hour...that they can call their own'—she was always interrupted. Still it would be easier to write prose and fiction there than to write poetry or a play. Less concentration is required. Jane Austen wrote like that to the end of her days" (Littlewood I: 453). "How she was able to effect all this," her nephew writes in his *Memoir*, "is surprising, for she had no separate study to repair to, and most of the work must have been done in the general sitting-room, subject to all kinds of casual interruptions. She was careful that her occupation should not be suspected by servants or visitors or any persons beyond her own family party" (*Memoir of Jane*

Austen, James Edward Austen-Leigh). Jane Austen hid her manuscripts or covered them with a piece of blotting-paper. Then, again, all the literary training that a woman had in the early nineteenth century was training in the observation of character, in the analysis of emotion. Her sensibility had been educated for centuries by the influences of the common sitting-room. People's feelings were impressed on her; personal relations were always before her eyes. Virginia Woolf in "The Woman Writer" writes, "Therefore, when the middle-class woman took to writing, she naturally wrote novels,...Emily Bronte should have written poetic plays; the overflow of George Eliot's capacious mind should have spread itself when the creative was spent upon history or biography; one may even go further, I said, taking *Pride and Prejudice* from the shelf, and say that they wrote good novels" (Littlewood I: 453). Without boasting or giving pain to the opposite sex, one may say that *Pride and Prejudice* is a good book. At any rate, one would not have been ashamed to have been caught in the act of writing *Pride and Prejudice*. Yet Jane Austen was glad that a hinge creaked, so that she might hide her manuscript before anyone came in.

According to Cassandra's Memorandum, *Pride and Prejudice* (then called *First Impressions*) was begun in October 1796 and finished in August 1797. It was later published with 'alteration and contractions.' The first, and least successful attempt at negotiation to publish it was made by their father, the Reverend George Austen. Jan Fergus writes in "Biography" in Janet Todd's *Jane Austen in Context*: "The possibility of earning money from writing must have become increasingly important to Austen in the 1790s as the threat of loss of her home loomed, more so once it actually occurred in 1801. Her father spearheaded her first unsuccessful attempt at publication in 1797, writing to the publisher to offer 'First Impressions,' the early version of *Pride and Prejudice*. It was still conventional for male relatives of a woman writer to negotiate with publishers, though later on Austen would do so herself, attempting to increase her profits through an association with John Murray" (Todd 8). George Austen wrote, on 1 November

1797, to Thomas Cadell, a well-established London publisher, offering him:

> A manuscript novel, comprising 3 vols., about the length of Miss Burney's *Evelina*. As I am well aware of what consequence it is that a work of this sort should make its first appearance under a respectable name, I apply to you. I shall be much obliged therefore if you will inform me whether you choose to be concerned in it, and what you will venture to advance for the property of it, if on perusal it is approved of. Should you give any encouragement, I will send you the work. (*Life* 96-98)

In this context, Jane Aiken Hodge writes in "Jane Austen and Her Publishers": "It is hardly surprising that this lukewarm letter failed to catch the imagination of a publisher who had doubtless been rejecting hopeful imitations of Miss Burney's *Evelina* for years. Cadell is reported to have rejected the offer by return of post, thus leaving it open for *First Impressions* to be developed into *Pride and Prejudice*" (Littlewood I: 199). The final version of *Pride and Prejudice* is actually quite a bit shorter than *Evelina*, pointing to a general revision prior to publication. On January 29, 1813 Jane Austen wrote to Cassandra: "I have lop't and crop't so successfully...that I imagine it must be rather shorter than *S. & S.* altogether." It is impossible to tell whether Jane Austen 'lop't and crop't' *First Impressions* or—as R.W. Chapman has suggested (*Works* 2: xiii)—an intermediate 1811 version; but in any case the late revisions were radical ones. R.W. Chapman and Sir Frank MacKinnon have demonstrated that Jane Austen used the calendar of 1811-12 in plotting the novel, and Chapman is surely right when he says that "so intricate a chronological scheme cannot have been patched on to an existing work without extensive revision."

Sense and Sensibility was published by Thomas Egerton of the Military Library, Whitehall. Egerton was not a major publisher, and he took no great risk over *Sense and Sensibility*. Jane Austen had ended by publishing on commission. This meant that she paid the expenses of printing the book and took the receipts, subject to a commission paid to the publisher for his handling of it. Jane Aiken Hodge in "Jane Austen and Her Publishers" writes, "It is good to know that she covered her costs and netted £140 with the first edition of about 1,000 copies at 15 shillings, which Egerton advertised at least three times in the autumn of 1811 and which received good but short notices in the *Critical Review* and the *British Critic* in the spring of 1812" (Littlewood I: 203). Hodge further writes, "Egerton was encouraged. He offered to buy the copyright of *Pride and Prejudice.* Jane Austen asked for £150—too modest a sum considering the £140 she had made from *Sense and Sensibility.* She then made the further mistake of letting Egerton beat her down to £110. Egerton got a good bargain. The first edition, probably of about 1,500 copies at 18 shillings, came out in January 1813 and was sold out by July" (Littlewood I: 203). "I would rather have had £150, but we could not both be pleased, and I am not at all surprised that he should not chuse to hazard so much" (*Letters* 29-30, November 1812). Once again there were good notices in the *British Critic* and the *Critical Review*, and Egerton printed a second edition in November, presumably without telling Jane Austen, who might have asked for more money and would certainly have corrected the errors she had pointed out in the text. The second edition of *Sense and Sensibility* came out in the same month, and it is undoubtedly to it that Jane Austen refers when she writes to Cassandra: "Since I wrote last, my second edition has stared me in the face.... I cannot help hoping that many will feel themselves obliged to buy it."

Kathryn Sutherland writes in "Chronology of Composition and Publication," "...the possibility of a completed version of *Pride and Prejudice* before Austen was twenty-two gives her novel-writing career a different trajectory. Things become more complicated when we realize that *Pride and Prejudice* in its 1797 version was probably further removed from the novel finally published under that title in 1813 than *Northanger Abbey* in 1803 from the version eventually published posthumously in 1818" (Todd 12). Woolf writes in "The Woman Writer," "To Jane Austen there was something discreditable in writing *Pride and Prejudice*. And, I wondered, would *Pride and Prejudice* have been a better novel if Jane Austen had not thought it necessary to hide her manuscript from visitors? I read a page or two to see; but I could not find any signs that her circumstances had harmed her work in the slightest. That, perhaps, was the chief miracle about it. Here was a woman about the year 1800 writing without hate, without bitterness, without fear, without protest, without preaching. That was how Shakespeare wrote, I thought, looking at *Antony and Cleopatra*; and when people compare Shakespeare and Jane Austen, they may mean that the minds of both had consumed all impediments; and for that reason we do not know Jane Austen and we do not know Shakespeare, and for that reason Jane Austen pervades every word that she wrote, and so does Shakespeare. If Jane Austen suffered in any way from her circumstances it was in the narrowness of life that was imposed upon her. It was impossible for a woman to go about alone. She never travelled; she never drove through London in an omnibus or had luncheon in a shop by herself. But perhaps it was the nature of Jane Austen not to want what she had not. Her gift and her circumstances matched each other completely. But I doubt whether that was true of Charlotte Bronte, I said, opening *Jane Eyre* and laying it beside *Pride and Prejudice*" (Littlewood I: 454). Hodge comments: "She did not want to be a lion. She published anonymously and was appalled when the secret of her authorship of *Pride and Prejudice* was revealed. When publicity offered itself in the shape of the Prince Regent and his egregious librarian, she backed away as best she could" (Littlewood I: 206-07).

3 Characters and Places

THE MALE CHARACTERS

Fitzwilliam Darcy: The son of Lady Anne Darcy and nephew of Lady Catherine de Bourgh, Fitzwilliam Darcy is the hero of the novel. A close friend of Mr Charles Bingley, Darcy, the 28 years old bachelor, is the owner of the Pemberley Estate with an annual income of £10,000. His 'pride' results in 'prejudice' of Elizabeth whom he finally marries.

Charles Bingley: A member of a respectable family in the north of England, Charles Bingley rents Netherfield House in the neighbourhood of the Bennet family. He falls in love with Jane Bennet and finally marries her.

William Collins: William Collins, aged 25, is a cousin of Mr Bennet whose estate is entailed, in default of a male heir, to him. He is the Rector of Hunsford Parsonage under the patronage of Lady Catherine de Bourgh. After having rejected by Elizabeth, he married Charlotte Lucas.

George Wickham: The son of the steward of Darcy's father, George Wickham is a profligate and villain of the novel. He gets into Colonel Forster's. He elopes with Lydia to London and is finally compelled to marry her.

Mr Bennet: Mr Bennet is the head of the Bennet family and father of Elizabeth and four sisters. Mr Bennet's favourite pastime is to poke fun at his wife.

Colonel Fitzwilliam: Colonel Fitzwilliam, aged about 30, is the younger son of an Earl who is the brother of Darcy's mother and Lady Catherine de Bourgh.

Sir William Lucas: Sir William Lucas is the head of the Lucas family living in the neighbourhood of the Bennet family at Longbourn. Sir Lucas was at first a businessman in the town of Meryton; but, after having been knighted, he left his business and his residence in Meryton. Collins marries his daughter, Charlotte Lucas.

Colonel Forster: Colonel Forster is the colonel of the regiment staying first at Meryton and then at Brighton. He plays an active role in the search for the runaway couple, Wickham and Lydia.

Mr Edward Gardiner: The brother of Mrs Bennet, Edward Gardiner has a major role in the reconciliation of Lydia and Wickham. He is living in London with his wife and is a respectable trader.

The Gouldings: The Gouldings are acquaintances of Mrs Bennet living at Haye-Park in the neighbourhood of the Bennets.

William Goulding: To show her honourable status Lydia contrives to make William Goulding see her wedding-ring while driving home from London.

Haggerston: Haggerston is engaged by Mr Gardiner for making proper settlement in favour of Lydia, as stipulated by Wickham for marrying her.

Mr Hurst: Mr Hurst is the husband of Louisa, the eldest of the two Bingley sisters.

John: John is a servant, recommended by Lady Catherine de Bourgh, to Mrs Collins for accompanying Maria Lucas and Elizabeth Bennet on their journey back to London from Hunsford.

Mr Jones: An apothecary of Meryton, Mr Jones attended to Jane Bennet while she was lying ill at Netherfield House.

Sir Lewis de Bourgh: Sir Lewis is the deceased husband of Lady Catherine de Bourgh.

Morris: Morris is the owner of Netherfield House hired by Mr Bingley.

Dawson: Dawson is the coachman of Lady Catherine de Bourgh.

Denny: Denny belongs to Colonel Forster's regiment. He is a close friend of Mr Wickham. He aids Wickham to get into that regiment and later informs Colonel Forster about Wickham's real intention in eloping with Lydia.

Philips: Philips, an attorney, is the husband of Mrs Bennet's sister. He visits all the officers of Colonel Forster's regiment.

Pratt: Pratt is an acquaintance of Lydia and the Forsters.

Richard: Richard is the servant of Philips.

Robinson: Robinson is a participant at Meryton Ball. Bingley tells him that he considers Jane the prettiest of girls.

Stone: Stone is the man to whom Mr Gardiner was called away upon business, just when he was about to start for St. Clement's for marrying Lydia and Wickham. He is probably Wickham's lawyer.

THE FEMALE CHARACTERS

Mrs Bennet: One of the well-known comic characters in English fiction, Mrs Bennet is the mother of the five Bennet sisters and sister of Mr gardiner and Mrs Philips.

Catheine Bennet (Kitty): Aged 17, Catheine Bennet is the fourth daughter of Mr and Mrs Bennet. Till the end of the novel she remains unmarried.

Elizabeth Bennet (Lizzy): Aged 20, Elizabeth Bennet, the second daughter of the Bennet family, is the heroine of the novel. She loves Darcy but keeps away from him out of her 'prejudice' for his 'pride' and is ultimately united with him.

Jane Bennet: Aged 22, Jane Bennet is the eldest of the Bennet sisters. She loves Bingley and is finally married to him.

Lydia Bennet: Aged 15, Lydia Bennet, the youngest and tallest of the Bennet sisters, loves a gay life. She elopes with Wickham and is ultimately married to him by the earnest effort of Darcy.

Mary Bennet: The third daughter of Mr and Mrs Bennet, Mary Bennet works hard for knowledge and accomplishment. Mary is a half-pathetic and half-comic figure in the fiction.

Miss Caroline Bingley: The unmarried sister of Charles Bingley, Caroline Bingley becomes instrumental in separating her brother, Charles Bingley, from Jane so that her brother may marry Darcy's sister, Georgiana, and she, Darcy.

Lady Catherine de Bourgh: A very proud and arrogant kind of woman, Lady Catherine de Bourgh is the widow of Sir Lewis de Bourgh. She is the sister of Darcy's mother and Colonel Fitzwilliam's father. She is the owner of Rosings and patron of Collins.

Georgiana Darcy: A graceful and accomplished girl of 16, Georgiana Darcy is the sister of Darcy. With a fortune of 30,000 she is under the joint guardianship of Darcy and Colonel Fitzwilliam's father.

Miss Anne de Bourgh: The only child of Lady Catherine de Bourgh and Sir Lewis de Bourgh, Miss Anne is the heiress of Rosings.

Mrs Gardiner: Mrs Gardiner is the wife of Mr Edward Gardiner, the brother of Mrs Bennet. A well-wisher of the Bennet family, Mrs Gardiner has a great affection for all her nieces, particularly for Elizabeth.

Charlotte Lucas: The eldest of the Lucas daughters, Charlotte Lucas is a friend of Elizabeth Bennet. After being rejected by Elizabeth, Collins proposes to her and she at once accepts the proposal and marries him for security.

Lady Lucas: Lady Lucas is the wife of Sir William Lucas and a friend of Mrs Bennet. She is described as a good kind of woman.

Maria Lucas: The second daughter of the Lucas family and sister of Charlotte Lucas, Maria Lucas accompanies Elizabeth Bennet to Hunsford Parsonage when Elizabeth goes there to meet her friend Charlotte Lucas after Charlotte's marriage with Collins.

Mrs Annesley: Living with Miss Darcy in London, Mrs Annesley helps to ease the situation tactfully at Pemberley House of Darcy, where Elizabeth and others are invited to dinner.

Mrs Harriet Forster: Lydia claims her to be her close friend to whom she leaves a note on the eve of her elopement with Wickham mentioning their intended marriage at Gretne Green on the border of South Scotland.

Mrs Reynolds: The housekeeper of Mr Darcy's Pemberley House, Mrs Reynolds shows Elizabeth and her aunt round the house when they come to visit the house on invitation.

Mrs Hill: Mrs Hill is the cook of the Bennets.

Mrs Louisa Hurst: Mrs Louisa Hurst is the wife of Mr Hurst and elder sister of Caroline Bingley.

Mrs Jenkinson: Mrs Jenkinson is the governess of Miss de Bourgh, daughter of Lady Catherine de Bourgh.

Miss King: Miss King is a participant in the Meryton ball and object of interest of Wickham because of her fortune of 10,000.

The Misses Webb: Lady Catherine de Bourgh often cites the example of the Misses Webb while speaking of playing and singing.

Mrs Younge: A wicked woman living in London with Miss Darcy, Mrs Younge arranges the intended elopement of Miss Darcy with Wickham from Ramsgate. Later, being bribed, she reveals to Darcy the address of Wickham and Lydia after the two have eloped.

Mrs Long: Mrs Long is a neighbour of Mrs Bennet.

Mrs Nicholls: The wife of the cook at Netherfield House, Mrs Nicholls gives Mrs Philips, sister of Mrs Bennet, the news that Mr Bingley is expected to arrive at Netherfield House for the second time.

Pen: Pen is a female acquaintance of Lydia and the Forsters.

Mrs Philips: Mrs Philips is the wife of Mr Philips and sister of Mrs Bennet and Mr Gardiner. She is as talkative as Mrs Bennet.

Miss Pope: Miss Pope is in the employ of Lady Metcalfe on the recommendation of Lady Catherine de Bourgh.

Sally: Sally is a domestic of Mr Forster.

Sarah: Sarah is a domestic of the Bennets.

Miss Watson: Miss Watson is the lady whom Colonel Forster and Captain Carter often visit at Meryton.

THE PLACES—THEIR LOCATIONS

Hertfordshire: Hertfordshire is a county of England on the north of London.

Hunsford: Hunsford is a parish near Westerham in kent. The valuable rectory of this parish is gifted to Collins by Lady Catherine. Mr Darcy first proposes marriage to Elizabeth at Hunsford.

Hunsford Lane: Hunsford Lane is a passage that leads to Hunsford Parsonage separating its garden from Rosings Park.

Hunsford Parsonage: A house adjoining Rosings Park, Hunsford Parsonage is occupied by Collins.

Longbourn: A mile away from Meryton, three miles from Netherfield House and twenty-four miles away from London, Longbourn is a Village in Hertfordshire where the Bennets live.

Longbourn House: Longbourn House is the residence of the Bennets with a small park.

Lucas Lodge: A house with a park, situated about a mile from Meryton, Lucas Lodge was occupied by the Lucases.

Matlock: A beautiful spot in Derbyshire, Matlock is a watering place.

Meryton: Meryton is a market town one mile away from Longbourn House on the way to Netherfield Park.

Netherfield House: Three miles away from Longbourn House on the way to Meryton, Netherfield House was a grand house with its park and it was rented by Mr Bingley.

Netherfield Park: Netherfield Park is situated at a distance of three miles from Longbourn where the Bennet family resides.

Pemberley: Pemberley is in Derbyshire, to the north of Hertfordshire. It is about thirty-six hours' journey from Longbourn by post-chaise. It is Darcy's estate with Pemberley House and the woods.

Pemberley House: Pemberley House is the house owned by Darcy in the Pemberley estate. The palatial house is situated close to the town of Lambton.

Pemberley Woods: A beautiful wood in the Pemberley estate, Pemberley Woods is ten miles in circumference.

Clapham: Clapham is a town situated in the south of the Thames in central London. It was a village in Jane Austen's day.

The George: The George is an inn in a town in Hertfordshire, from where Mr Bennet's carriage takes Elizabeth's visit to Rosings.

Gracechurch Street: Gracechurch Street is a street near Cheapside in London, where the Gardiners live. There, in the house of the Gardiners, the two sisters, Jane and Elizabeth, and their friend Maria Lucas stayed for a few days on their way to Longbourn from Rosings.

Gretna Green: Gretna Green is a place on the border of England in Dumfriesshire in South Scotland. Here runaway couples from England could marry with impunity.

Grosvenor Street: Grosvenor Street is a street in London, where Mr Hurst, husband of Louisa, the eldest of the Bingley sisters, has a house. It is a very fashionable area in London.

Haye-Park: Haye-Park is a place in the neighbourhood of Longbourn where the Gouldings lived. Mrs Bennet thought of renting the house there for Lydia after her marriage with Wickham.

Hatfield: Hatfield is a place on the way to Hertfordshire from Brighton through Epsom and Clapham.

Clarke's Library: Clarke's Library is situated in Meryton.

Edward Street: Edward Street is in London, where Mrs Younge has taken a large house which she intends to use for letting purposes.

Epsom: A health resort in Jane Austen's time, Epsom is a town in Surrey in the south of London.

Purvis Lodge: Purvis Lodge is a house in the neighbourhood of Longbourn House.

Ramsgate: Ramsgate is a coastal town in the south-east of London.

Rosings: Rosings is the residence of Lady Catherine de Bourgh in Kent, near Hunsford Parsonage.

Rosings Park: Rosings Park is a park of Rosings adjoining Hunsford Lane and Hunsford Parsonage.

Scarborough: Scarborough is a sea-side town on the east coast of Yorkshire and north-east of Derbyshire.

St. Clements: St. Clements is a church in the city of London, where Wickham and Lydia are married.

Stoke: Stoke is a place near the Longbourn House, where there is a great house which Mrs Bennet is thinking of renting for Lydia after her marriage.

Warwick: A county town on the river Avon, Warwick is eight miles south-west of Coventry in England.

Ashworth: Ashworth is a place ten miles away from Longbourn House of the Bennets.

Barnet: Barnet is a place on the way to Hertfordshire from Brighton through Epsom and Clapham.

Jones's Shop: Jones's Shop is situated at Meryton.

Kenilworth: Four miles south-west of Coventry, Kenilworth is a market town in Warwick.

The Lakes: The Lakes refer to the lakes in Westmoreland, Cumberland and Lancashire in England. The area is known as the Lake District and is still a popular spot for tours.

Lambton: Five miles away from Pemberley, Lambton is a small market-town in Derbyshire.

The Little Theatre: The Little Theatre is in London near the lodgings of Wickham.

Birmingham: Birmingham is an important place on the way to Derbyshire from Longbourn.

Blenheim: Blenheim is an important place on the route from Longbourn to Derbyshire.

Brighton: Brighton is a well-known coastal town in Sussex, south of London.

Bromley: Bromley is a place on the way to London from Hunsford.

Chatsworth: Chatsworth is a famous aristocratic mansion in Derbyshire.

Cheapside: A part of London where generally the people of lower classes live, Cheapside is a place of business.

Newcastle: Newcastle is a well-known sea-coast town in Northumberland in the north of England.

Oakham Mount: Oakham Mount is in the neighbourhood of Longbourn House.

The Peak: The Peak is a beautiful spot in Derbyshire.

4 The Story Outline

The Bennet family, comprising Mr and Mrs Bennet and their five daughters, Jane, Elizabeth, Mary, Kitty and Lydia live on an estate which is entailed upon their nearest male relative, the foolish clergyman Mr Collins. The daughters have no fortunes, a silly mother, some vulgar relations, and, except for Jane and Elizabeth, not much sense. Mrs Bennet's hopes are all of good marriages for them. When the young and unattached Mr Bingley rents Netherfield nearby, she marks him down for the family beauty, Jane, with what looks like a good chance of success, for the two to fall in love. However, Bingley's sister Caroline and his proud and wealthy friend Mr Darcy (whom Caroline would like to marry herself) disapprove of Jane's lack of fortune and connections, persuade Mr Bingley that Jane is indifferent, and bear him away to London. Mr Darcy, however, has found himself susceptible to the lively and unconventional Elizabeth, with whom he has been thrown together when she has stayed briefly at Netherfield, to take care of Jane, who fell ill while visiting there. Elizabeth, who dislikes Darcy for finding her not handsome enough to dance with at their first meeting, suspects nothing. In the meantime a handsome stranger, Wickham, has arrived, who claims to have been deprived by Mr Darcy of a living which Darcy's father had promised him. All the girls, including Elizabeth, find Wickham fascinating. He becomes an officer in the local regiment of the militia.

The heir to the Longbourn estate, Mr Collins, pays a visit, and hopes to find a wife. He is warned off Jane by Mrs Bennet, and settles upon Elizabeth 'equally next to Jane in birth and beauty.' When he proposes and she refuses him he, in chagrin and pique, promptly proposes to Elizabeth's closest friend Charlotte Lucas who, plain and no longer young, accepts him out of a 'disinterested desire for an establishment.' They are soon married, and return to Mr Collins's parsonage at Hunsford. His patron is Lady Catherine de Bourgh, Mr Darcy's aunt, far prouder than he, and an infinitely greater snob. Elizabeth in due course pays a visit to her friend Charlotte, now Mrs Collins, and with her is invited to various social engagements at Lady Catherine's house Rosings, where she re-encounters Mr Darcy. After several meetings Mr Darcy proposes to her. Remembering how unhappy he has made Jane, and how he has, supposedly, ill-treated Wickham, she rejects him angrily and tells him why. He is surprised, hurt, and angry in his turn. Next day he gives her a letter explaining his conduct: that he did not think Jane in love with Bingley; and that Wickham has pursued an irresponsible and extravagant career, ending with an attempt to elope with Darcy's sister Georgiana, so as to get his hands on her fortune.

Elizabeth goes home confused and unhappy, to find that Jane also is not happy, having been slighted in London by Bingley's sisters and not having seen Bingley at all, and that her sisters, silly as ever, are lamenting the departure of the soldiers stationed at Meryton. Wickham has been trying to court a girl for her money, so Elizabeth is glad that she has taken the advice of her sensible aunt Mrs Gardiner, and not allowed herself to become attached to him. She begins to believe the truth of Mr Darcy's letter, and think she has misjudged him. She looks forward to her coming holiday travelling in Derbyshire and the Lakes with her aunt and uncle Gardiner. Her youngest sister Lydia then receives an invitation to accompany the militia Colonel Forster and his young wife to Brighton. Mr Bennet, despite Elizabeth's doubts, agrees. Lydia is in ecstasies. Elizabeth's own holiday is curtailed to cover Derbyshire only, and eventually takes her, unwillingly, to Mr Darcy's house at Pemberley. Here she unexpectedly meets him, and despite their mutual confusion, allows him to resume the acquaintance and introduce her and the Gardiners to his sister Georgiana. Their relationship ripens fast, but is suddenly cut off when Elizabeth receives letters from Jane to say that Lydia has runaway from Brighton with Wickham—purportedly to get married at Gretna, but apparently getting no further than London. Elizabeth cannot help telling Darcy, and makes instant arrangements to return home.

Eventually the runaways are found. Wickham is bribed and persuaded, and marries Lydia quietly in London. They pay a brief visit to Longbourn on their way to Newcastle, where Wickham is to join the regular army. Lydia lets fall that Mr Darcy was present at her wedding. Elizabeth, astonished, writes to her aunt for information and learns that he has been the one who found Wickham in hiding in London, who persuaded him to marry Lydia, and who is thus the one to whom her family should be most grateful. Then Bingley unexpectedly returns to Netherfield, raising Mrs Bennet's hopes that he will after all propose to Jane, as he very soon does. Mr Darcy is with him, but relations between him and Elizabeth are uncomfortable and constrained. He leaves for a few days during which Elizabeth receives an unexpected call from Lady Catherine, who tries to make her promise not to marry Mr Darcy. Elizabeth, much surprised, refuses, and Lady Catherine, enraged, departs. Mr Darcy returns, Elizabeth thanks him for his generosity to Lydia, he proposes for the second time, and is at last made happy.

5 A Chapter-wise Critical Summary

CHAPTER–1

When Mr Bingley, a handsome bachelor with an income of four or five thousand pounds a year settles in Netherfield Park from a place in North England, Mrs Bennet of the neighbouring Longbourn with five marriageable daughters urges her husband to visit the newcomer. She worries that Sir William Lucas and Lady Lucas, who also have daughters to be married, may establish contact before the Bennet family. Mr Bennet teases his wife by pretending his reluctance, although he really wishes to make the visit. Mr Bennet says that if Mr Bingley chooses one of his daughters, it would give him (Mr Bennet) much pleasure if Elizabeth is chosen. On the contrary, Mrs Bennet hopes that Mr Bingley would choose either Jane or Lydia.

The theme and tone of the novel are set by the famous opening sentence: "It is a truth universally acknowledged, that a single man in possession of a good fortune, must be in want of a wife". In a way characteristic of a stylist of ironic nuances, the mock philosophical solemnity of the first clause is immediately deflated by a notion of marriage appropriate to high comedy. Further, while that opening sentence applies directly to the subject of the first chapter, the arrival in the neighbourhood of a very eligible bachelor, this novel, like all the others, starts from a more comprehensive and more valid truth, that every young woman, with or without a fortune, is in want of a husband. Thus, the initial generality is completely reversed by the second sentence, which affirms that a new arrival is considered by alert mothers "as the rightful property of some one or other of their daughters." Then, through the talk of one ill-mated couple, the goal is set up for their progeny. At the same time, we are made aware of the genteel, gossipy families, which make up local society and the competitive marriage market. The short chapter ends with a short paragraph which crisply defines the characters and minds of Mr and Mrs Bennet; it underlines what dialogue had already revealed.

CHAPTER–2

Although Mr Bennet had rebuffed his wife's suggestion that he should call upon Mr Bingley, he is one of Mr Bingley's earliest callers; but he keeps his wife in suspense about the visit and enjoys her apprehension that some other neighbouring woman may capture Mr Bingley. Mrs Bennet tells Elizabeth that Mrs Long (a friend) cannot be trusted to introduce them to Bingley because she has two nieces of her own. Then as he reveals the pleasing fact of his visit to Mr Bingley, Mrs Bennet becomes enthusiastic in her praise of her husband, and to avoid her effusive gratitude Mr Bennet leaves the room. The mother and the daughters now engage themselves in discussing about Mr Bingley. Mrs Bennet hopes that at a ball which is going to be held soon, Mr Bingley would dance with Lydia.

The relationship among the members of the Bennet family is flashed a lot in this chapter. From the social viewpoint the chapter throws light on the atmosphere of upper middle-class life. Mr Bennet has an ironical bent of mind for all that his wife says or does. He appears to be intellectually superior to his wife and most of his daughters. He is rather cold and, sometimes, unpleasant. Some of the social codes and conventions prevalent at the time are revealed: for example, the time that should be allowed to pass before inviting a new acquaintance to dinner.

CHAPTER–3

Mr Bennet refuses to tell the family about Bingley. So it is from Lady Lucas that Mrs Bennet learns that Bingley is not only rich, but handsome, gracious, and fond of dancing. Mrs Bennet even now looks forward to having one of her daughters "happily settled at Netherfield." The Bennet family come to learn that Sir William Lucas had also paid a visit to Mr Bingley, and Lady Lucas informs Mrs Bennet that Sir William had felt delighted with Mr Bingley. After a few days, Mr Bingley pays a short return visit to the Bennets but declines an offer for dinner because he is, as he says, going to London for a few days. After a few days, Mr Bingley comes back to Netherfield Park with six guests. He, however, attends a ball at Meryton, within a fortnight, where he comes with his two sisters, one brother-in-law and a friend, Mr Darcy. Mrs Bennet attends this ball with all her daughters. Mr Bingley takes a particular fancy to Jane and dances with her twice. Darcy, who is more handsome and richer than Bingley, fails to impress the assembly for his pride and vanity. He declines to dance with any of the Bennet girls because he thinks that none of the girls suits him as a partner. He does not mix with Meryton society. He dances only with Miss Bingley. When Bingley suggests that Darcy should dance with Elizabeth, Darcy comments that she is 'not handsome enough to tempt me.' This talk between Mr Bingley and Mr Darcy is overheard by Elizabeth and this fills the mind of Elizabeth with a deep prejudice against Darcy. Elizabeth, though offended, enjoys recounting the incident to her friends. Mr Bennet, of course, preferred to stay at home with a book and hears the story of the beautiful Jane's success from Mrs Bennet. She concludes her accounts by saying how much she detests the proud Darcy for his behaviour at the ball.

While in the other Austen novels the heroine (even Emma, though unaware of her feeling) is in love from the start, in *Pride and Prejudice* dramatic tension is much heightened because romance begins with cool disdain on both sides—disdain which soon gives unwitting evidence of mutual fascination. At a ball we are reminded of Lord Osborne's aloofness in *The Watsons* by Darcy's supercilious refusal to dance with anyone except Bingley's sisters; we are reminded also of Evelina's first encounter with her future husband, Lord Orville (*Evelina*, Letter xii), by Darcy's disparaging remark about Elizabeth, a remark audible to her. If this seems a doubtfully credible lapse in manners, even on the part of a proud, shy man who is out of his element, it is an early preparation for what is to offend Elizabeth in his proposal. Now, she has "no very cordial feelings towards him," though she tells the story for fun among her friends. Almost all the major characters have been introduced in this chapter. We see that from the very first meeting of Darcy and Elizabeth their pride and prejudice are established. This chapter lays the foundation of the conflict presented in the novel. Austen shows how prejudice can form an erring view of a person. Elizabeth does not appear as a romantic heroine here. She feels insulted by Darcy's remarks, although at first seems to be amused by it; and her prejudice is the offshoot of her wounded pride because of Darcy's remarks. If Darcy feels proud of his social status and prejudiced against people of lower rank, Elizabeth is proud of her superior intellect and becomes prejudiced against Darcy who fails to recognise her quality.

CHAPTER–4

When Jane and Elizabeth are alone, they talk about the ball at Meryton. Jane confides to Elizabeth how much she likes Bingley. She is delighted also with Bingley's sisters. Jane being incapable of seeing ill in anyone, Elizabeth does not give much importance to her opinion, although she admits the merits of Bingley and considers his sisters not much agreeable. Mr Bingley, with a property of about a hundred thousand pounds, is free, frank and accommodating. Mr Darcy is proud, haughty, reserved and aristocratic. Yet, the two are very good friends. They talk a lot about the Meryton assembly. While Bingley is charmed with the whole assembly and particularly with Jane, Darcy does not make much of it, although he makes a qualified approval of Jane. The Bingley sisters, however, admire Jane as a sweet girl.

Two pairs of contrasting characters who are to perform major roles in the novel are introduced, and they are Jane and Elizabeth, on the one hand, and Bingley and Darcy, on the other. The discrepancy of class and status is meticulously established in the attitudes of Darcy and Elizabeth to each other. Dialogues reveal characters. To Jane the whole world appears as simple and decent as she herself is. Darcy is almost like Elizabeth in his intelligence, candour and clear-sightedness. Some positive aspects of Darcy's character are revealed in this chapter, although they are not developed till much later. Elizabeth's critical approach to life and people has been artfully contrasted with the uncritical credulity and easy manners of Jane. The plot receives a slight push forward by the Bingley sisters' favourable opinion of Jane, on which some subsequent incidents are constructed.

CHAPTER–5

Sir William Lucas formerly was "in trade" in Meryton, but he had been knighted when, as mayor, he made an address to the King. Like the Bingley girls, he is ashamed of having been in business. The Lucases and the Bennets meet to discuss the ball. In the village of Longbourn, Sir William Lucas lives with his family and the Bennets are very intimate with them. Having made enough money for his purposes, he had left his business and also the house in Meryton. Sir William and Lady Lucas have several children, and their eldest child is Charlotte who is aged about twenty-seven. Mrs Bennet is upset that Bingley chose Charlotte as his first dance partner although he danced later twice with Jane. Darcy's comment about Elizabeth is then mentioned and while Mrs Bennet condemns him outright as a proud insolent person, Charlotte defends him on the ground of his wealth and position, supported also by her brother.

In this chapter, pride and prejudice, the key themes of the novel, are juxtaposed explicitly for the first time. This chapter adds to the climate of near desperation among marriageable women. Darcy's pride is seriously discussed and condemned without any knowledge of his true character, and this is only because a general social prejudice is against him. Elizabeth's prejudice has its root in her pride and it is manifest in her remark, 'I could easily forgive his pride, if he had not mortified mine'. Through Charlotte and her brother Austen seems to warn the reader against forming any hasty opinion about Darcy.

CHAPTER–6

The Bennet and the Bingley sisters exchange visits and soon Jane and Mr Bingley become fonder of each other. Jane being reserved will not disclose the feelings of her heart and so Elizabeth feels happy that the good name of their family will not be stained if Jane's love does not culminate in marriage. Elizabeth and Charlotte Lucas (her intimate friend) have a discussion about marriage. Elizabeth mentions that she is happy that Jane is not forward in showing her feelings. Charlotte believes that if a woman is to get a man, she must let him know her feelings for him. The important thing is to catch him before someone else does, even though one may not be sure that she is in love with him. Elizabeth replies that one must be sure of one's own affection and of the nature of the other person first. Charlotte says that the important thing is to get married; happiness in marriage is just a matter of chance and, therefore, "love" is not so important. Elizabeth replies that she knows Charlotte would never act in the way she says. Meanwhile, Darcy has developed his interest in Elizabeth. On the occasion of a party at Sir Lucas's house, Charlotte makes Elizabeth play on the piano and Elizabeth's performance is pleasing enough. After Elizabeth, Mary plays several tunes at the piano. Darcy does not feel interested in the musical entertainment. But at the Lucases' party he watches Elizabeth closely and notices her big eyes and easy playfulness. When Sir William asks Elizabeth that he should dance with Elizabeth, he is ready to dance with her, but Elizabeth, remembering the unhappy Meryton episode, refuses to dance with him. This strong-mindedness of Elizabeth attracts Darcy even more. Miss Caroline Bingley, who cherishes hopes to marry Darcy, becomes jealous of Elizabeth.

That marriage as a social as well as financial contract has been presented for the first time in this chapter. It is, however, ironic that eventually both Charlotte and Elizabeth make financially sound marriages. Charlotte's attitude towards marriage is an emblem of her own uncertainty and a preparation for choosing a husband. Darcy's prejudice against Elizabeth changes in this chapter while Elizabeth's prejudice will take some more time to dissolve. Her intellect and her independent personality attract Darcy very much. The behaviour of Caroline Bingley, a shallow selfish woman, helps Darcy, in a way, to realise the true merit of Elizabeth.

CHAPTER–7

Mr Bennet's estate of Longbourn with an annual income of two thousand pounds is entailed, in default of a male heir, on a distant relation. Mrs Bennet, the daughter of an attorney at Meryton, has a sister, Mrs Philips, whom Catherine and Lydia visit after being motivated by the arrival of a regiment in the town. Mr Bennet is disgusted by his daughters' fondness for the army officers and calls them the silliest girls on earth. Jane receives an invitation to dine and spend a day with the Bingley sisters. Mrs Bennet, anticipating rain, advises Jane to go there on horseback, thinking that the rain and the absence of a carriage will detain her at Netherfield giving her an opportunity to improve her relations with Mr Bingley. As has been expected, Jane arrives at Netherfield wet, and falls ill. Mrs Bennet is delighted that Jane has to remain at Netherfield longer as she has caught cold. On hearing about Jane's illness Elizabeth becomes very worried and thinks it necessary to go and keep company with Jane. Elizabeth walks about three miles to visit her sister. Catherine and Lydia accompany her as far as Meryton, and thereafter Elizabeth has to go alone. When she arrives at Netherfield Park, all the inmates of the house feel surprised that a young girl has walked three miles so early in the day and in such foul weather. A physician, Mr Jones, is called to examine Jane, and he says that Jane has caught a violent cold, and he suggests her complete rest. Despite Miss Bingley's antagonism, Elizabeth is invited to stay on and look after Jane.

The chapter exposes the silliness of the two youngest Bennet sisters and their mother's wanting in good sense. The beginning of this chapter reveals the harsh economic realities of the contemporary society. At that time the typical English woman had no economic or legal standing in society. The characters of Mr and Mrs Bennet are revealed more in this chapter. Mrs Bennet's shallow values and coarseness are exposed in approving the flirtations of her daughters. This chapter shows Elizabeth's real concern for Jane. Her walk to Netherfield reveals her impetuosity, and the reactions of Caroline Bingley and Darcy to her arrival show their characters quite well.

CHAPTER–8

Elizabeth stays in attendance on her sister Jane as her condition has not improved. At dinner that evening, Elizabeth notices Bingley's genuine concern for Jane's welfare, but sees that his sisters' interest is superficial. In her absence the Bingley sisters criticise her as a low and uncultivated person. Mrs Hurst appreciates Jane as a sweet girl but speaks of her low connections. As Jane falls asleep in the evening, Elizabeth goes downstairs to find the party busy playing cards. Elizabeth decides to read rather than play cards. Mr Hurst feels surprised that Elizabeth should prefer reading to playing cards. Caroline taunts her for this and makes a remark like this: "She is a great reader and has no pleasure in anything else." Elizabeth feels somewhat upset, and protests against such type of opinion. Caroline then turns the talk to Darcy's fine library at Pemberley. She now continues her talk with Mr Darcy on the matter of a lady's real accomplishment. The sisters praise Darcy's magnificent home and Darcy's young sister Georgiana. Darcy criticises the contemporary idea that music and needlework alone are sufficient accomplishments and lays emphasis on the improvement of mind by extensive reading. Throughout the conversation, Bingley's sisters cater to Darcy. After Elizabeth retires, Caroline Bingley says that she artfully tries to win the attention of men, but Darcy replies ambiguously that all women try cunningly to win attention, implying thereby that he is aware of and disapproves of Miss Bingley's pursuit of him. Because Elizabeth says that Jane is worse, they decide to send for the apothecary, Mr Jones.

This chapter is crucial for character revelation. The romance of Jane and Bingley develops and Darcy and Elizabeth get to know each other. Elizabeth's vivacity and candour kindle an interest which Darcy comes to recognise as dangerous bewitchment, and he deliberately sheers off.

Caroline's narrowness and jealousy and Bingley's kind and gentle nature are also revealed in this chapter. Darcy, by his distaste for Miss Bingley's flattery and sarcasm, and by a tacit appreciation of Elizabeth, foreshadows the future development of the plot. Elizabeth shows another facet of her character by her love for her sister Jane and concern for her illness.

CHAPTER–9

Elizabeth sends home a note requesting that her mother come and visit Jane. Mrs Bennet arrives with Lydia and, not wishing Jane to leave Bingley's company, declares that Jane seems worse than ever. In conversation, Mrs Bennet, seeking to raise Jane's status, tries to impress about her family. Darcy suggests that one finds more variety of character in town than in the country, but Mrs Bennet loudly objects. Everyone is surprised. Elizabeth is mortified and tries her best to fill the awkward silence. Lydia jumps in to remind Bingley of his promise to give a ball at Netherfield. Bingley says he hasn't forgotten but will wait until Jane recovers.

In this chapter Darcy and the Bingleys come into their closest contact with the Bennets, and Darcy's feeling of superiority causes further problems. This chapter shows Mrs Bennet with all her stupidity, vulgarity and shallowness in the affairs of the world. Elizabeth's comments show her interest in people, although her judgment of the characters of Bingley and Darcy is not altogether correct. Lydia's request to Bingley leads to the crucial Netherfield ball.

CHAPTER–10

Jane feels a little better by evening, so Elizabeth again joins the party in the drawing-room. Darcy is trying to write a letter to his sister, but Miss Bingley repeatedly interrupts him by calling out messages from her to include in his letter to his sister. When Darcy finally finishes the letter, he turns his attention to the conversation in the room. He notices that Elizabeth talks animatedly on every subject and is impressed by her sharp observations and succinct way of wording ideas. Darcy is also magnetically drawn towards Elizabeth's fine eyes. Elizabeth notices that he frequently stares at her.

Caroline Bingley who is intent on marrying Darcy becomes jealous of Elizabeth as she is receiving more notice of Darcy. Miss Bingley appears more detestable by her crude effort to capture Darcy. Darcy and Elizabeth learn more about each other. Elizabeth's emotion and Darcy's logic are finely contrasted in their conversation about Bingley. Darcy, however, seems to be bewitched by Elizabeth's coolness and reticence. But as Elizabeth is perhaps unaware of his feelings, her prejudice still continues to work on her.

CHAPTER–11

After dinner Jane comes downstairs for the first time and is received with great pleasure by everybody. Mr Bingley sits together with Jane and talks throughout the evening. Darcy takes up a book and Miss Bingley, having failed to distract Darcy from his book, attempts to read a book, to impress him, but without success. Mr Bingley tells Elizabeth that he wants to give a ball at his residence. Miss Bingley advises her brother not to have a ball at Netherfield because there may be some persons who are not much interested in dancing and therefore a ball would be rather a punishment than pleasure. Mr Bingley catches the reference that his sister means Darcy, and he makes it clear that he is surely going to give a ball at his house. Then to catch the attention of Darcy, Miss Bingley starts pacing the room and finally, in desperation, asks Elizabeth to walk with her. Darcy notices the ladies but declines the invitation to walk with them. Miss Bingley seems to be offended. Elizabeth suggests that Miss Bingley should laugh at Darcy. Then there is an exchange of ideas between Darcy and Elizabeth regarding the importance of laughter and jokes in life. Elizabeth says that others' follies make her laugh and refers to Darcy's vanity and pride. Darcy admits that he has a hardness of temper. Miss Bingley, finding herself completely overlooked, comes forward with some music, and Darcy, fearing that he is too attentive to Elizabeth, turns to it.

Austen's keen observation and use of gentle irony make the chapter very interesting. The romance of Jane and Bingley developing well. The conversation between Darcy and Elizabeth shows that both the characters are revealing their pride and prejudice. Elizabeth ridicules what is wise and good by mocking Darcy and is thus guilty of poor judgment based on prejudice. Darcy seems to be confident that his own pride is controlled, and so is Elizabeth, while both are wrong.

CHAPTER–12

Jane is recovered from her illness. So, Elizabeth writes to her mother to send the carriage for their return home at Longbourn. Mrs Bennet wants them to remain there as long as possible so that Jane's matrimonial prospect with Mr Bingley becomes brighter. Mrs Bennet answers that she will not send the carriage now. Elizabeth then gets Jane to borrow Mr Bingley's carriage and it is agreed that they will leave the next morning. Mr Bingley is really sad that Jane should depart so soon. Darcy, who feels that Elizabeth's appeal has grown very strong, wants to be rid of her presence and welcomes the news that two sisters would be leaving on the following day. On Sunday, after the morning prayers, Jane and Elizabeth get ready to depart. Miss Bingley becomes extra polite to Elizabeth as she is happy that Elizabeth is leaving and it would cost her nothing to show this politeness to her. When the girls arrive home, Mrs Bennet feels disappointed as she has not expected them back home so soon, while Mr Bennet is happy to welcome his two sensible daughters back.

The episode of the stay of Jane and Elizabeth at Netherfield ends in this chapter and with it ends one small cycle of the movement of the plot. The chapter again shows Darcy's pride and his misunderstanding of Elizabeth's character, in spite of his supposed love for her. Darcy here appears as no romantic or passionate lover, but a rational one. He deliberately detaches himself from Elizabeth in order that he should think deeply of the nature of his attachment to her. Miss Bingley is glad for the departure of Elizabeth but shows her courteous veneer by asking her to stay with them for a few more days.

CHAPTER–13

At breakfast, on the following day, Mr Bennet announces the visit of a stranger, a cousin, Mr Collins who, as

Mr Bennet's nearest male relation, is heir to his property by entail. Mr Bennet then reads out the letter from Mr Collins. Mr Collins, the Rector of Hunsford Parsonage under the patronage of Lady Catherine de Bourgh, regrets the differences that existed between his late father and Mr Bennet. In his letter written from Hunsford in Kent, he writes that it is his duty, as a clergyman, to promote and establish peace and harmony in all the families within the reach of his influence. In the pompous letter, he expresses his willingness to visit the Bennets. Mrs Bennet is not at all pleased at the prospect of entertaining a guest who will deprive her daughters of their father's property. But after listening to Collins's letter she is softened by hopes of a possible husband for one of her daughters. Mr Bennet and Elizabeth guess from the tone of the letter that Mr Collins is somewhat ridiculous and when he actually arrives he proves himself to be just that, a mixture of conceit, servility and exaggerated compliments. He incurs the displeasure of Mrs Bennet at the dinner table by asking which of the cousins has cooked the food, as Mrs Bennet informs him that they have the services of a good cook. Collins profusely apologises for his mistake.

The advent of Mr Collins in this chapter begins a new plot line as Collins's addresses of Elizabeth and Charlotte Lucas is one of the important events of the chapters that follow. In this chapter, we first have information of Lady Catherine de Bourgh. Austen has finely revealed the character of Mr Collins by his pompous letter. Collins's compliments to the Bennet girls also insinuate at his real purpose of visiting the Bennets.

CHAPTER–14

After dinner Mr Bennet talks with Mr Collins about his patroness Lady Catherine de Bourgh. Mr Collins becomes eloquent in her praise. He tells of Lady Catherine's sickly daughter, Miss de Bourgh, and of his own adept flattery. It was she who had appointed him the rector of his parish. He says that although Lady Catherine is generally regarded as a proud woman, he has never seen any signs of pride in her. He further says that her only daughter is the sole heiress of her very extensive estate. He says that in his opinion Lady Catherine's daughter was born to be a Duchess. Then when Mr Bennet takes him to the drawing room for tea, where being invited to read to the ladies, he reads out from Fordyce's sermons, which bored the young ladies. As Lydia interrupts him and talks to her mother on some insignificant topic, Collins feels insulted, stops reading and offers to play backgammon with Mr Bennet.

This chapter shows that the character of Collins is both ridiculous and conceited, hypocritical and pretentious. His continual reference to Lady Catherine is to improve his own standing. In this chapter, we also gain an indirect view of Lady Catherine who appears to be an unpleasant personality. Mr Bennet's humorous nature and Lydia's silliness are once again proved.

CHAPTER–15

Collins's poor upbringing has not made him a sensible man in spite of his training at college. On the other hand, his unexpected prosperity makes him conceited while his veneration for his patroness turns him into a servile creature. Under the advice of his patroness he has come to marry one of the Bennet girls. He starts with Jane, but on learning that she is going to be engaged, he turns to Elizabeth, being the second in line. He accompanies the Bennet girls, with the exception of Mary, to their aunt's house at Meryton being advised by Mr Bennet who thus wants to get rid of him. On the way, they meet an army officer Mr Denny and his friend Mr Wickham, an attractive young man, who is also a commissioned officer in the army. Meanwhile, Darcy and Bingley ride down the street and stop to talk to the girls. Elizabeth notices how Darcy and Wickham are visibly surprised, shocked, and embarrassed to see each other. She is curious about the reason for this. Mr Denny and Wickham accompany the girls to their aunt's house. They are all received cordially by the aunt, Mrs Philips, who arranges for an evening party the following day. Mrs Philips proposes to invite a few militia officers also to the dinner party. Mr Collins is also invited and he greatly appreciates the invitation.

The character of Collins is further developed here. His practical attitude to marriage is revealed by his instant change of direction from Jane to Elizabeth. Wickham is first introduced in this chapter and his strained relation with Darcy is at once hinted at.

CHAPTER–16

The next evening when the Bennet sisters accompanied by Collins reach Meryton at the Philipses' party, they learn that Mr Wickham has already arrived. Mr Wickham appears to be the most pleasant personality and an interesting talker. So, while Collins is engaged in talking with Mrs Philips about furniture and other trifles, Elizabeth seeks opportunity to talk to Mr Wickham, particularly with a view to knowing his relation with Darcy. Soon Elizabeth gets the opportunity. He says Darcy's father had been his godfather, and out of gratitude and friendship for Wickham's father, he had informally bequeathed a very fine parish to Wickham who was to enter the church. Darcy, however, out of pride and jealousy, disregarded his father's wishes and thus it is that Wickham has come to enter on a military life. Wickham also informs Elizabeth that Miss Darcy also is very proud and that Darcy will marry the daughter of Lady Catherine who is dictatorial and insolent. He also hints at Darcy's hypocritical nature saying that Darcy is a past master in making friends. Elizabeth believes all this and her prejudice against Darcy is not only confirmed but increased, although she thinks that Darcy is not so bad as this.

Elizabeth's acquaintance with Wickham provides fuel for strong aversion. Much attracted by Wickham's elegant looks and manners, and curious about his relations with Darcy, she fails—as the reader should not fail—to see the impropriety of a new acquaintance's volunteering a self-pitying autobiography. She swallows without question his story of Darcy's thwarting his career in callous disregard of his father's intentions (Wickham's father had been the steward of Darcy's father's estate). Wickham speaks also of Darcy's unbending pride, a quality shared by his sister, and of his being expected to marry his cousin, Lady Catherine's daughter. Elizabeth's complete trust in Wickham is perhaps understandable in the circumstances, but it is the one case in which her discernment is blinded by prejudice; even the mild Jane Bennet, while not disposed to question Wickham's veracity, is much less sure than Elizabeth that they have the whole truth.

CHAPTER–17

The next day Elizabeth tells Jane of Wickham's accusations of Darcy. Jane, who is too good to think ill of anybody, does not wish to believe ill of either Darcy or Wickham. The Bingleys now arrive with the invitation to the promised ball at Netherfield next Tuesday. The Bingley sisters ignore all the members of the family except Jane while inviting and leave as soon as possible. Everyone is excited about the ball and while Jane thinks of dancing with Mr Bingley, Elizabeth is elated at the thought of getting an opportunity to dance with Wickham. Catherine and Lydia are also excited because a ball is for them always a pleasurable occasion. Mr Collins says that he would have the opportunity to dance with each of the Bennet girls. Elizabeth, however, is upset when Collins requests her to promise to dance with him the first two dances. Her worry is increased when her mother hints that Collins is about to propose marriage. To avoid any unpleasantness Elizabeth remains silent about any such proposal and agrees to dance with Collins. Her sisters also eagerly wait for the ball.

Austen seems to emphasise the point that appearance is sometimes not the reality. There is a subtle indication that Elizabeth has developed a romantic attachment to Wickham. As a contrast to this romantic relationship there is the materialistic proposal of Collins supported by the materialistic Mrs Bennet. The unmannerly behaviour of Bingley sisters towards the Bennets reveals their mental structure. Elizabeth's chief impetus is due to Wickham; but there is hardly a character in the story who contributes no momentum to it, nor any pressure from without to which she does not respond characteristically.

CHAPTER–18

Upon arriving at the Netherfield ball, Elizabeth realises that Wickham would likely not to attend because of Darcy. Mr Denny relays that he had to go to town on business instead. Elizabeth is mortified in the first two dances by Mr Collins being "awkward and solemn, apologising instead of attending, and often moving wrong without being aware of it." Darcy once again asks for her hand to dance and she relents this time, offering him the next two dances. To throw him off, she breaches conversation during the dance and quickly turns to the topic of Wickham, hoping to disrupt him. He only states that Wickham is very good at socialising and making friends, but has problems with keeping those friends. Sir William drops nearby and hints at future congratulations for Bingley and Jane. The night continues and Elizabeth is duly embarrassed by her family as her mother uncouthly reminds everyone of Jane and Bingley's budding relationship and her sister Mary does a poor job of singing. The last to leave, the Bennets are not missed by Bingley's sisters.

Darcy's pride and prejudice in his attitude to the Bennets and Collins is revealed in this chapter. Elizabeth's prejudice is manifest in rejecting the information imparted to her by Caroline and Jane about Wickham and Darcy. Jane's romantic relationship with Bingley is having its own course and a kind of subterranean love is growing in the hearts of Darcy and Elizabeth. The embarrassment of Elizabeth by her family's behaviour paves the way for her acceptance of Darcy's criticism in his letter. Mr Collins's lack of social discretion and Mrs Bennet's total ignorance of such matters are highlighted in this chapter. Darcy suddenly becomes conscious that Bingley's marriage with Jane is nothing but a plot by the social-climbers and he thinks of thwarting this plot. Bingley's plan to go to London is a hint of the cooling of his affair with Jane.

CHAPTER–19

The day after the ball, Mr Collins proposes to Elizabeth, who wastes no time in declining the offer. Mr Collins, undeterred by Elizabeth's rejection, replies that it is usual for young ladies to initially turn down a proposal for marriage. He believes that Elizabeth really wants to accept and intends to do so in the end; as a result, he repeats his proposal. Elizabeth declines again, refuting his arguments. Mr Collins, however, is blinded by conceit and does not realise that the lady is truly not interested in him. Elizabeth decides she will seek her father's help if this vulgar suitor continues to believe her repeated refusals to be really "flattering encouragement."

A lot about Collins's character is revealed in this chapter. Collins is a mocking figure. He sees Elizabeth as the right woman for all the wrong reasons. He offers marriage as a financially and socially sound contract. He thinks his offer attractive as it promises a comfortable life not only for Elizabeth but also for her family. Hence, Elizabeth's rejection of this offer is an act of courage and firmness for the principle she believes in. Elizabeth is courteous and honest despite her bitter feelings against Collins. That marriage is the union of two souls and not a mere assurance of financial security is the view of Jane Austen, suggested by Elizabeth's declining the proposal of Collins.

CHAPTER–20

Soon after Elizabeth leaves the room, Mrs Bennet enters and congratulates Collins on the most happy prospect of his becoming her son-in-law. Mr Collins accepts her good wishes and gives her the particulars of what has happened with Elizabeth. He explains his belief that Elizabeth's refusal stems from her "bashful modesty and the genuine delicacy of her character". Mrs Bennet, who knows her outspoken daughter very well, does believe that her denial is meant as shy encouragement. She explains to Mr Collins that Elizabeth is headstrong and foolish, but assures him that her daughter will be brought to reason. When Collins hears Mrs Bennet's assessment of Elizabeth's personality, he doubts whether he has chosen the correct daughter and voices his concern. A flustered Mrs Bennet, who sees a marriage opportunity slipping away, contradicts her prior statements about Elizabeth. She then hurries to tell her husband, asking him to advise Elizabeth to accept Mr Collins' proposal. Mr Bennet tells Elizabeth that her mother will never see her face again if she does not marry

Collins, but at the same time, he will not see her face again if she does marry Collins. Mr Collins' pride is finally hurt by Elizabeth's refusal. He has truly wanted to find an amiable companion among the Bennet daughters and convinced himself that a marriage to one of them would be an advantage to all the Bennet family. He says he is sorry that he is misunderstood and apologises if he has been rude in any way.

Mr Bennet supports Elizabeth's refusal of Collins' proposal. This leaves the way clear for Charlotte Lucas's relationship with Collins to develop. Charlotte Lucas has also been brought to this scene at the right moment. As Collins has withdrawn his proposal, he is open for matrimonial relationship with any other woman. Mrs Bennet's selfish and emotional outburst in front of Elizabeth reveals her nagging concern with the financial aspect of marriage. It is noteworthy to observe Elizabeth's confident handling of the emotional pressure and remaining victorious.

CHAPTER–21

After Elizabeth's refusal of Collins's proposal the atmosphere in the Bennet family is heavy with gloom. Collins, however, sticks to his old programme and does not leave Longbourn early. To escape from the morose atmosphere of the house the Bennet sisters decide to go to Meryton. At Meryton Elizabeth enjoys meeting Wickham, discusses the ball at Netherfield and when he walks back to Longbourn with the Bennet girls, Elizabeth introduces him to her parents. A letter arrives for Jane from Miss Bingley, which informs her that Mr Bingley, who has gone to London, is not likely to return and that he is likely to marry Darcy's sister, Georgiana. Elizabeth interprets the letter to mean that Miss Bingley is following her brother to London in order to keep him from coming back and marrying Jane. This letter from Miss Bingley shocks Jane and Elizabeth very much as they had been hoping that Mr Bingley would soon propose marriage to her. Elizabeth assures Jane that it is merely a part of Miss Bingley's scheme to marry Darcy, and that Bingley will not be influenced by her to part from Jane, and he will surely return to Jane during winter. The ever gentle Jane refuses to think that her friend,

Miss Bingley, is playing such a dirty game. The two sisters, however, agree not to worry their mother with this news.

We notice that there is a subtle indication about Collins's interest in Charlotte, paving the way for their engagement. Elizabeth introduces Wickham to the Bennets, and it is a step for furthering the romantic relationship between Elizabeth and Wickham. Miss Bingley's letter complicates the plot further by apparently making an end of Bingley's first courtship of Jane. This chapter shows Collins's pretentious nature. It highlights contrast between Elizabeth and Jane further. Although Elizabeth is intelligent and perceptive, her perception of Mr Bingley and his sister is not quite correct.

CHAPTER–22

The Bennet family have been invited to dinner by the Lucases. As Mr Collins is staying with the Bennets, he will naturally join them for dinner. But as Elizabeth is trying to avoid Collins's company, she seeks Charlotte's help to keep him busy and Charlotte takes upon herself the duty of keeping Mr Collins engaged. Charlotte remains busy attracting the attention of Collins towards her, with the ulterior motive to win him for herself. For, she is already twenty-seven and needs a husband at the earliest. Early next morning Collins pays a secret visit to Charlotte, proposes her and is accepted with the consent of her parents. Charlotte asks Collins not to disclose the news to the Bennet sisters. So Collins, expressing his desire to visit the Bennets once more, takes his leave. Charlotte breaks the news to her friend, Elizabeth, who is shocked that her friend has consented to be the wife of such a fool. Charlotte is sure she will be happy and Elizabeth, for politeness's sake, agrees with her.

Here Austen presents the panorama of a society which looks upon marriage of any kind as its ultimate goal. An unmarried girl like Charlotte has a wretched existence. Either she has to work as a poorly paid governess to wealthy children or she has to work as a companion to a richer person or even a rich relative, for her living. Such a girl often has to become a burden on her brother. Against this background we can understand Charlotte's efforts to get Collins as her husband. Elizabeth who is, unlike her friend Charlotte, romantic and idealistic in matters of marriage, cannot justify Charlotte's decision to marry Collins. The Lucas family feels happy to have a guarantee for Charlotte's economic security even at the cost of sacrificing her to a fool like Collins.

CHAPTER–23

Sir William Lucas arrives at Longbourn with news of the engagement between Charlotte and Collins and is met with total disbelief by Mrs Bennet and her younger daughters. Mrs Bennet is more upset than ever to think that her best friend's daughter Charlotte has not only gained a husband but will inherit Longbourn as the wife of Collins. She goes on scolding Elizabeth for a whole week and does not speak well to Mr and Mrs Lucas for a month. Mr Bennet, however, is pleased to discover that Charlotte is as foolish as his wife and more foolish than Elizabeth. To add to the distress of Mrs Bennet there is no information about the whereabouts of Mr Bingley, and Elizabeth, too, begins to doubt Bingley's faith. Collins informs in a letter to Mr Bennet about his engagement with Charlotte, which, he writes, is approved by Lady Catherine. Mr Collins writes to thank Mr Bennet for his hospitality and to express his desire to return in a couple of weeks. He expresses his desire to finalise the matter with Charlotte. His arrival only further adds to the distress of Mrs Bennet who ruefully thinks of losing Longbourn to Collins.

The chapter carries the narrative forward by indicating the passage of time and also through the analysis of the different characters. In this chapter, the rivalry between the two families, the Bennets and the Lucases, is clearly welled out. It is worthwhile to observe here that the first volume of the novel, as originally published, comes to a conclusion in this chapter. We have, by this time, a fairly clear idea of all the major characters of the novel. The story seems to have reached a very twisted situation here. Charlotte's marriage to Collins is a proof of the irresistible power of the economic forces channeling human lives. Bingley is taken away from Jane, and

Elizabeth blames Miss Bingley and Darcy for this estrangement, thus, strengthening her prejudice against Darcy. Besides, Mrs Bennet's imprudent behaviour contributes much to the disturbing situation.

CHAPTER–24

A letter from Miss Bingley gives the news that they will spend the winter in London and that Mr Bingley has become more intimate with Miss Darcy. At first Elizabeth, unable to believe in Mr Bingley's attachment to Miss Darcy, thinks it to be a dirty scheme of Miss Bingley. But later, thinking of Charlotte's behaviour in accepting as her husband a fool like Collins, she develops misgivings about Bingley's nature. Jane, however, does not find anything wrong with Charlotte and she says that as Charlotte belongs to a large family and as she has no fortune, she could not have missed the opportunity of settling down in life. Jane does not blame Bingley but resigns herself to fate. Yet she believes that if Mr Bingley really loves her no influence can part them. Mrs Bennet is distressed at Bingley's departure, but she hopes that he will surely return the visit in the next summer. Mr Bennet finds the matter amusing and suggests that all women benefit from being jilted and says in a mood of jest that Elizabeth should be the next to be jilted by Wickham. Meanwhile the story of ill-treatment of Wickham at the hands of Darcy is spread everywhere and Darcy is hated by everybody.

Miss Bingley's letter gives a new twist to the plot by falsely representing Bingley's love for Miss Darcy and this results in Elizabeth's intensification of prejudice against Darcy resulting in her drawing close to Wickham. The chapter shows the difference in the characters of Jane and Elizabeth and their views on relationships. If Jane accepts the view that strong emotion is no guarantee of love, Elizabeth believes in the strength of emotions and, perhaps, can more easily accept rejection. Elizabeth is against financial-based marriages whereas Jane is more practical and conventional. Mr Bennet's cynical remarks about rejection by lovers seem to have some truth in them.

CHAPTER–25

After courting Charlotte a week and finally settling the date of marriage Collins returns to his parish on Saturday. The following Monday Mrs Bennet's brother, Mr Gardiner, arrives at Longbourn with his family. Mrs Bennet tells Mrs Gardiner the whole episode relating to Bingley, Elizabeth and Collins. Mrs Gardiner, who is an intelligent, amiable and elegant woman, later tells Elizabeth that all that has happened to Jane regarding Bingley is quite natural as young men fall in and out of love easily. She suggests a visit to London to soothe Jane's feelings. Elizabeth feels hopeful to think that Jane might meet Bingley there despite Darcy's obstruction, and renew her love. During the Gardiners' stay at Longbourn Wickham is an occasional visitor. Mrs Gardiner had lived in Derbyshire and enjoys hearing news of it from Wickham, who with other officers is a frequent guest at the Bennet home. She knows Pemberley, Darcy's estate, and knew of his father. Mrs Gardiner watches Elizabeth closely and is worried by her obvious attachment to Wickham and warns Elizabeth not to be too intimate with him. Later, however, Elizabeth becomes a bit close to Wickham and, as she has little knowledge about Darcy, she seems to believe what Wickham says about Darcy's pride and ingratitude.

The Gardiners are introduced and that Mrs Gardiner has a real concern for the Bennet girls is revealed here. Mrs Gardiner's words and demeanour prove her intelligence. The practical comments she makes about the affairs of Jane and Elizabeth are quite worthwhile. Her suggestion to take Jane to London makes the plot move.

CHAPTER–26

Mrs Gardiner tactfully advises Elizabeth not to encourage Wickham, for, as neither has any fortune, the relationship will be impossible. At first Elizabeth argues in favour of Wickham as the most agreeable man she has ever seen, but finally she assures Mrs Gardiner that she will try to avoid Mr Wickham. Charlotte and Collins marry and leave for Hunsford Parsonage. Charlotte, happy with everything, is eager to renew the friendship with Elizabeth who, despite her misgivings, agrees to visit them in March along with Charlotte's father and younger sister. Jane goes to London with the Gardiners. Hearing nothing from Caroline, she visits her and receives a polite but cold welcome. Miss Bingley's return visit to Jane is equally brief and resentful. Jane realises that her relationship with Bingley is at an end, particularly, as Caroline has hinted that Mr Bingley knows that Jane is in London and yet he has not come to see her. All this Jane informs Elizabeth through her letters. Meanwhile, Mrs Gardiner reminds Elizabeth of her warning about Wickham. Her niece replies that Wickham no longer pays her any attention. A certain Miss King has just acquired 10,000 pounds which has suddenly given her remarkable charm in Wickham's eyes, so he transfers his affections to her. Elizabeth writes that she is still well-disposed to Wickham and that she thinks that his action was only sensible. She considers her lack of anger as proof that she could not have been in love. As for Mr Wickham, he is interested in marrying a girl by the name of Miss King who has a fortune of ten thousand pounds.

In this chapter Charlotte and Collins make a happy pair by marriage. Jane gives up all hopes of Bingley, and Wickham rejects Elizabeth for a rich heiress. The theme of marriage for money is brought out here by Mrs Gardiner's advice and Wickham's courtship of an heiress. Caroline here separates Bingley and Jane further by not informing her brother about the presence of Jane in London and telling a blatant lie to Jane that her brother is not willing to meet Jane in spite of his having known that Jane is there. We also notice in this chapter Mrs Gardiner's tactful good sense, Jane's tacit acceptance of her lot and Elizabeth's prejudicial judgment of Bingley.

CHAPTER–27

In March Elizabeth goes to Hunsford to visit Charlotte with Sir William and his second daughter, Maria Lucas. Elizabeth now looks forward to this visit with some pleasure as it will give her an opportunity to see her sister in London on the way. Her only regret is that she must leave her father. Wickham and she part as friends. The party stops in London. Elizabeth is pleased to find Jane in a happy mood, but

Mrs Gardiner says that Jane is often depressed. Mrs Gardiner again warns Elizabeth against Wickham referring to his mercenary attachment to Miss King, although Elizabeth tries to defend Wickham. Now, to Elizabeth's great delight Mrs Gardiner invites her on a tour of the Lakes that summer.

This chapter draws an end to Elizabeth's first period at Longbourn. She starts visiting Hunsford. It also marks the end of her innocent, uncritical opinion of Wickham, although affection for him bids her defend Wickham against the charge brought by Mrs Gardiner. The theme of the role of money in marriage is here again emphasised. Wickham, being without fortune, abandons Elizabeth and turns to the rich heiress, Miss King. Elizabeth seems to understand this necessity and so she is quite resigned to her lot. Her visit to Hunsford leads to some significant development of the plot. Austen has portrayed Elizabeth's state of mind in this chapter with her deep acumen and subtle artistry. Being jilted by Wickham, and her relationship with Darcy being not happy, Elizabeth is now without any emotional support around her. Charlotte has overthrown all the values they once agreed on, by marrying Collins. The parents of Elizabeth show no sympathy in her sorrow. Elizabeth also feels sad for Jane for her separation from Bingley. And now she is going to the house of Collins where she may meet Lady Catherine, both of whom she hates.

CHAPTER–28

Elizabeth and the Lucases arrive at Hunsford and are received warmly by Charlotte and Collins waiting for the party. Elizabeth finds Mr Collins ridiculous as ever, as he pretentiously guides them around his home and the neighbourhood, discoursing on the beauty of Rosings (Lady Catherine's estate) and the importance and generosity of his patron. He boasts that they dine at Rosings twice each week. Elizabeth is, however, impressed by the neatness of the arrangements inside, made by Charlotte. At dinner Collins suggests that his guests will have the honour of getting an invitation to dine at Rosings with Lady Catherine. About the middle of the next day Lady Catherine's daughter comes with Mrs Jenkinson with such an invitation. Elizabeth slyly remarks that the sickly and cross Miss de Bourgh will be the perfect wife for Darcy.

Charlotte seems to be happy by wisely remaining deaf to the foolishness of her husband. Elizabeth's coming to Hunsford and the invitation to Rosings are indeed significant for the development of the main plot. Austen thus prepares the readers for Elizabeth's meeting with Lady Catherine and later with Darcy.

CHAPTER–29

Despite too much fuss by Collins about the greatness and grandeur of his patroness, Lady Catherine de Bourgh, Elizabeth remains quiet and confident during her visit to the Rosings. The house and grounds of Lady Catherine are impressive, the Lady herself is formidable and her daughter appears insignificant. As the party enters the room Lady Catherine rises to receive them. Sir Lucas and his daughter Maria are overwhelmed with awe at the opulence. Every dish at dinner is praised lavishly by Collins and Sir William Lucas. After dinner the ladies are taken to the drawing-room where they listen to the opinions, queries and advice of Lady Catherine. Lady Catherine questions Elizabeth impertinently about her accomplishments, education and age. She expresses her disapproval at discovering that the Bennets had no governess. Elizabeth, who resents Lady Catherine's impertinence and condescension, shows her independence and annoys her Ladyship by lightheartedly refusing to give her age. The evening ends after various games are played and Collins drives the party home with all praise for his patroness.

The offensive, loud, foolish and tyrannical Lady Catherine de Bourgh, the patroness of Collins, appears in this chapter. Collins's sycophancy towards this lady makes him also a comic character. The behaviour of the Lucases shows the power and influence riches have in Austen's society. Elizabeth's personality as presented at Rosings elevates her from her circle to be looked upon with respect later by Darcy.

CHAPTER–30

After a week Sir William returns to Meryton satisfied that his daughter is most comfortably settled. Maria and Elizabeth stay on with Mr and Mrs Collins. Her next meetings with Darcy (after the Netherfield dance) take place at Hunsford, when she is visiting Mr and Mrs Collins and, Darcy and a Colonel Fitzwilliam are visiting their aunt, Lady Catherine. Fitzwilliam is a charming young man of about thirty. Fitzwilliam is quite agreeable in manners while Darcy is still reserved but courteous enough to inquire of Elizabeth after the health of her family. Elizabeth provokes Darcy by asking whether he has seen Jane while in London, to which Darcy answers in the negative with some confusion giving out that he may have some role in keeping Bingley away from Jane.

In Lady Catherine's house—where Darcy has as much reason to be ashamed of her ill-breeding as Elizabeth had of her mother's—Darcy, in smiling mood, converses amiably with Elizabeth, who, as usual, holds her own in liveliness. In this chapter, Elizabeth is once again brought into contact with Darcy. Elizabeth's feeling against Darcy is strongly intensified by what she suspects to be his responsibility for the Bingleys sudden migration to London and the blighting of her sister's happiness. This meeting of Elizabeth and Darcy once again shows Jane Austen's use of coincidence in her novel. Colonel Fitzwilliam is introduced here as another admirer for Elizabeth. We notice that Darcy's behaviour towards Elizabeth has changed as Darcy is no longer haughty and rude as he had been before. In this way Jane Austen gradually brings these two close together.

CHAPTER–31

On Easter Day the Collinses and their guests are invited to Rosings by Lady Catherine. As Lady Catherine's attention is directed to Darcy, Mr Fitzwilliam attends to the guests and he particularly busies himself with Elizabeth whom he admires. After coffee Elizabeth plays some tune at the request of Fitzwilliam and Darcy watches both curiously. Now there is an exchange of witty, humorous and clever banter between Elizabeth and Darcy. In the course of conversation, she playfully tells Colonel Fitzwilliam of Darcy's reluctance to dance at the first ball in Meryton. Darcy claims that he is uncomfortable in unfamiliar company. But Elizabeth indicates that his excuse is unacceptable. Darcy, however, compliments Elizabeth as a truly accomplished woman. Lady Catherine intervenes in the conversation and remarks that though Elizabeth has sung fairly well, yet she is no match to her own daughter, Anne. She goes on offering her remarks about Elizabeth's performance, which Elizabeth bears patiently and the visit ends.

As Darcy gets closer to Elizabeth in this chapter, it reveals how much he admires her. Colonel Fitzwilliam's interest in Elizabeth also highlights Elizabeth's qualities and faculties. Lady Catherine embarrasses everybody by her self-important and foolish talks. The exchange of wit between Darcy and Elizabeth shows Jane Austen's skill in employing witty dialogues.

CHAPTER–32

The next morning, Elizabeth is surprised by a visit from Darcy. Conversation is awkward, and they struggle to avoid awkward silences. Elizabeth asks Darcy about Bingley's suddenly departing Netherfield. Darcy suggests that Bingley is not likely to return there because of his connections in London. After Darcy leaves, Charlotte tells Elizabeth that the only explanation for Darcy's odd behaviour in calling on her is that he must be in love with her. Elizabeth finds this idea hard to believe. Darcy and Colonel Fitzwilliam continue their visits, but Darcy is unreadable and Charlotte comes to think that maybe it's Fitzwilliam who loves Elizabeth.

In this chapter, the stage is set for Darcy's proposal to Elizabeth. We feel that Darcy loves Elizabeth and is ready to take her to Pemberley with him thinking that she is too good for Longbourn. Elizabeth professes publicly her approval of the practical marriage of Charlotte and Collins. Charlotte here appears to guess clearly about the romantic situation developing between Darcy and Elizabeth.

CHAPTER–33

Darcy makes frequent calls at the parsonage and apparently seeks to meet her when she walks in the park, although he has little to say; she only laughs at Charlotte's notion that he is falling in love. One day in particular she comes across Fitzwilliam while walking and they walk for a while, eventually talking about Miss Darcy. He announces that he has joined Darcy in caring for her and she guesses correctly that Miss Darcy is a difficult lady to handle. She asks about Bingley and Darcy and learns that Bingley is in Darcy's debt for his helping to get him out of an unwanted marriage to an undesirable suitor. Elizabeth assumes this to mean the marriage to Jane and is upset as to how Darcy has so much control over other men. The "very strong objections against the lady" assumes that Bingley was talked out of the suit. She later refrains herself from joining the others for a visit to Lady de Bourgh's that evening.

Elizabeth's hostility is greatly strengthened by Colonel Fitzwilliam's unwitting corroboration of her suspicion about Darcy's having separated Bingley and Jane. When alone, she is overcome by thoughts of such heartless conduct. She believes that Darcy is totally motivated by pride, and so, becoming biased, she does not reason through the possible alternatives or rational arguments in Darcy's favour. What Colonel Fitzwilliam says serves to remind Elizabeth of the importance of fortune in marriage and to inform her of Darcy's role in separating Bingley from Jane. This may be considered a coincidence in the Hardyan sense, as when Darcy is about to move close to Elizabeth, Fitzwilliam unwittingly drives him away from her.

CHAPTER–34

Declining to go with the others to have tea at Lady Catherine's, Elizabeth sits down to reread Jane's letters from London, "as if intending to exasperate herself as much as possible against Mr Darcy". Elizabeth has been reading the letters of Jane written to her since her arrival at Kent. The letters betray her sister's lack of cheerfulness. Elizabeth is, however, comforted by the thought that Darcy, who is the cause of Jane's suffering, is not going to trouble her any more by his visit, as he is leaving Rosings soon. At this moment, so artfully and naturally .contrived, Darcy comes in, asks about her health, sits still, walks about the room, and after more silence approaches her "in an agitated manner" and says:

> In vain have I struggled. It will not do. My feelings will not be repressed. You must allow me to tell you how ardently I admire and love you.

Elizabeth is too completely astonished to speak. Then gratification over "the compliment of such a man's affection" gives place to anger as his eloquent tenderness gives place to equally warm recognition of her family's defects—all this with no apparent doubt of his being accepted. He in turn is astonished and angry when she cites his offensive acknowledgement that he has forced himself to stoop, his ruining her sister's happiness, his cruel treatment of Wickham. She saw him start at this, but he said nothing, and she continued, "You could not have made me the offer of your hand in any possible way that would have tempted me to accept it." Again his astonishment was obvious; and he looked at her with an expression of mingled incredulity and mortification. She went on. Darcy makes no attempt to answer her accusations and retreats quickly. After Darcy's departure Elizabeth feels great agony and weeps for a while and composes herself when she hears the sound of Lady Catherine's carriage.

Jane Austen's readers discover in time that almost the only proposal she stages in full are those that are rejected; these—including Mr Collins' comic effort in an earlier chapter (xix)—have more dramatic possibilities than happy acceptances, which, summarily handled, run no risk of banality. Darcy's proposal gives us a pleasant shock of surprise in realizing Elizabeth's power over such a formidable man, though we knew he was bound to speak, since the growth of his interest has been steadily recorded. We are also given new evidence of Elizabeth's courage, family loyalty, and vigorous, unlady like candour not to mention what she never thinks of, the allurements of wealth and position. We are left, almost exactly in the middle of the book, wondering if and how the chasm just created can be bridged; of course we know, but the story never grows stale.

CHAPTER–35

When Darcy the next day puts into her hand his long letter of self-defense, her first reaction, that it is "all pride and insolence," gives way, as she reads and rereads it, to exoneration on the two main charges. He explains that he had been unaware that a marriage between Bingley and Jane was in the offing until Sir William Lucas hinted at it at the ball at Netherfield. Since he could observe no sign that Jane had any special regard for Bingley, he felt free to try to dissuade his friend from imprudently pursuing her. It was not especially the low connections to which he objected, but rather to the "total want of propriety" so often displayed by her mother, her three younger sisters, and occasionally, even by her father. He admits that the conduct of Jane and Elizabeth was beyond reproach. He, therefore, conspired with Bingley's sisters to prevent his return from London and endeavoured to persuade his friend of Jane's indifference to him. This last is what made Bingley yield. Darcy further admits (with some guilt) to having concealed from Bingley the fact that Jane had come to London. He regrets having unknowingly hurt Jane's feelings, but he does not think it necessary to apologize for his motives. Regarding Wickham, Darcy refers to his weak and dissolute nature. Darcy's father, who loved Wickham, recommended him, at his death, to the best living falling vacant in the Pemberley estate. But as Wickham preferred to enter the law rather than the church, Darcy gave him three thousand pounds and Wickham soon squandered that amount and later applied for the vacant living in the Pemberley estate. As Darcy refused to grant him the post, he revenged himself by planning an elopement with Georgiana, which was, however, prevented at the last moment. Since then Wickham maligned the character of Darcy everywhere. Finally, Darcy suggests that Elizabeth can verify all this with Colonel Fitzwilliam. As for Darcy's strictures on her family, and the family's share in wrecking

Jane's prospects, Elizabeth feels "depressed beyond any thing she had ever known before."

Some critics have doubted the possibility of a proud, reserved man's volunteering "so much, and such, information...unless under pressure from his author, anxious to get on with the story," since Elizabeth's whole impression must be revised before the visit to Pemberley. But we may remember that the letter was written "in a dreadful bitterness of spirit" (lviii), when Darcy was greatly upset. It would be far less plausible and effective if he gave the necessary information *viva voce* and Elizabeth had no time to reflect on it. And surely high comedy is not traditionally bound by the strictest realism in every particular. Finally, the letter may be said to establish its credibility because at earlier stages in the novel most of its points had been lodged in our minds by casual evidence or strong hints.

CHAPTER–36

Elizabeth reads Darcy's letter with a strong prejudice, unwilling to believe his account of the Bingley and Jane episode, and as for Wickham's story she very much wishes it to be false. But she is very much stirred by the letter and reads it again and again. She remembers that Darcy's story of the planned elopement is supported by Colonel Fitzwilliam's reaction to her comment about Georgiana. Besides Wickham's attention to Mary King after being close to Elizabeth shows his unscrupulous and mercenary nature. Darcy may be proud, but he never has acted wrongly. It is true that Jane's habitual composure might have convinced the most acute observer that she was not seriously in love. Elizabeth now seems to realize that she has been blinded by prejudice and her judgments about Darcy and Wickham have been totally wrong. She feels greatly disturbed in mind and returns to the Parsonage from her walk to be informed that Colonel Fitzwilliam has been waiting for about an hour to whom Darcy has joined a few minutes ago, to take leave of her.

In Elizabeth's mind Darcy, with good reason, is pretty well cleared of blame. She feels "absolutely ashamed of herself."

She who had been so proud of her discernment, "had been blind, partial, prejudiced, absurd." But this correcting of a mistaken judgment is given a larger dimension which belongs to the essence of Jane Austen. Elizabeth, since she cannot look to either parent or get much light from the gentle and uncritical Jane, must throughout the novel depend on her own experience, instincts, and judgment; and for the most part these had hitherto been or seemed reliable guides.

CHAPTER–37

The next morning Darcy and Fitzwilliam left Rosings and the Hunsford party is again invited to dinner by Lady Catherine. Seeing Elizabeth in low spirits Lady Catherine asks her to stay longer at Hunsford, but Elizabeth sticks to her previous plan of going back home. Her Ladyship then instructs the girls on the necessity of having a servant with them when they travel because it is improper for young women to be alone. Elizabeth replies that her uncle is sending a servant for her. Elizabeth is relieved of her sad thoughts of regret and pain at the dinner at Rosings—regret on the behaviour of her mother and sisters leading Darcy to detach Bingley from Jane and pain for the fact of Jane's losing Bingley as her husband and also because of her wrong estimate of Wickham's character. After this she visits Rosings almost frequently and at parting Lady Catherine wishes her and Maria a good journey and extends invitation to them to come to Hunsford again next year.

In regard to Darcy, Elizabeth has at this point moved from strong hostility to benevolent neutrality: she is grateful for his attachment and respects his general character, "but she could not approve him; nor could she for a moment repent her refusal, or feel the slightest inclination ever to see him again." Although Darcy's comments about her family makes Elizabeth feel upset, she realizes that those are painfully true. We can imagine Jane Austen planning the best conditions for the next meeting between the two: it should be involuntary, the result of circumstances; Elizabeth should first see Pemberley, as a fresh image or reflection of its owner, and should hear testimony on his character from a trustworthy witness; she should encounter Darcy there, on his own ground, and find him quite altered in manner; and he should see her in the company of thoroughly presentable relations.

CHAPTER–38

On Saturday morning after breakfast Elizabeth leaves Hunsford with Maria, sincerely thanking Collins for the visit although she does not join Collins in his praise of Lady Catherine. Collins speaks of Charlotte as an ideal partner and Elizabeth agrees to it. The party leaves for London where they will stay with the Gardiners for a few days before returning to Longbourn with Jane. Elizabeth does not tell Jane of Darcy's proposal and his letter immediately, as she thinks it to be prudent to keep these secret till they reach home.

This is a transitional chapter taking us from Hunsford to London. Elizabeth endorses Charlotte's marriage with Collins and she has no regret for refusing Collins.

CHAPTER–39

In the second week of May Elizabeth, Maria and Jane set out homewards from London. Kitty and Lydia meet them on the way to take them in the carriage sent by Mr Bennet. The girls have their dinner at an inn and Lydia goes on talking about the bonnet she has purchased, about the military officers stationed there and about Wickham's marrying Miss King not coming off. On reaching Longbourn the girls are welcomed by Mr and Mrs Bennet. A large party gathers at the dinner table where all the Lucases are present. In the afternoon Lydia proposes to walk to Meryton, which Elizabeth opposes for fear of seeing Wickham there. Soon Elizabeth finds that her parents are discussing the proposal of going to Brighton.

Lydia's talking at length in this chapter shifts light on her real character, that she is immature, self-centred, impractical and interested only in flirtation and marriage. Lydia gives the information that Wickham is not going to marry Miss King. After having the information, Elizabeth has reason to feel worried.

CHAPTER–40

The next morning Elizabeth relates to Jane about Darcy's proposal and her refusal. Jane is surprised to hear this, but sympathises with Darcy at his disappointment on Elizabeth's rejection of his proposal. When Elizabeth tells her of the wickedness of Wickham, Jane finds it hard to believe. But as Wickham is leaving the neighbourhood soon, Jane advises Elizabeth not to reveal Wickham's true nature to the Longbourn society. Elizabeth, however, conceals from Jane Darcy's part in Bingley's absence, as it might hurt Jane. Observing Jane's tender feeling for Bingley existing still, Elizabeth feels sad. Mrs Bennet mentions Jane's unhappiness and thinks that Bingley has betrayed Jane. She resentfully talks about Charlotte and Collins and bitterly thinks that Collins must always be talking about their estate which he will occupy, after Mr Bennet's death, by entail.

Elizabeth feels that she has been mistaken in taking Wickham by his appearance. She also realizes her failure to judge Darcy's goodness and she admits her faults to Jane. Her love and consideration for Jane checks her from exposing to her Darcy's role in separating Bingley from Jane. Elizabeth realizes later that it was indiscretion of her not to reveal Wickham's true character, which contributes to Lydia's elopement.

CHAPTER–41

The regiment is leaving Meryton and all the young ladies in the neighbourhood except Jane and Elizabeth feel sad. But Kitty and Lydia are particularly dejected. Witnessing the unseemly behaviour of Lydia and Kitty and her idiotic mother's encouragement of them, Elizabeth feels with shame the justice of what Darcy had said about her family. Lydia's depression is soon over as she is invited by Mrs Forster, the wife of the colonel of the regiment, to accompany them to Brighton. Both Elizabeth and Jane try to dissuade Lydia from accepting the invitation. But Mr Bennet thinks that Lydia needs to go in order to learn the realities of life and her own insignificance. Meanwhile, Elizabeth meets Wickham several times. On the last day of his stay at Meryton Wickham dines with other officers at Longbourn. His affair with Miss King being over, Wickham now turns to court Elizabeth again, to her utter annoyance. Elizabeth gives him the clear hint that she knows the truth about him from Darcy. Wickham is embarrassed. The two part with mutual civility. Lydia leaves for Meryton with Mrs Forster. The next morning they will leave for Brighton. The gloom that pervades Hertfordshire over the regiment's departure is a comment on the nature of life in small, English country towns. The regiment has brought a breath of fresh air to their boring small-town existence; their departure implies the return to boredom and a narrow cycle of routine life. Mrs Bennet identifies with the beautiful, brainless, and flirtatious Lydia; one can only assume she was exactly like Lydia in her youth. Like Lydia, she grows sad when the regiment prepares to leave; she does not want to return to boredom. She easily grants permission for Lydia to go to Brighton for summer vacation and even suggests that Mr Bennet take the rest of the family there for a while. Mr Bennet has no intention of going to Brighton; neither does he try to stop Lydia from going, in spite of Elizabeth's warnings. Caught between an over-indulgent mother and an uninvolved father, the Bennet girls are in a sad plight.

Elizabeth deliberately brings up Darcy in her conversation with Wickham; his discomfiture confirms to Elizabeth the veracity of Darcy's account. She is now beginning to understand the real Darcy, accepting him as good rather than being prejudiced against him as evil. When Wickham questions her about her change of heart, she remarks that Darcy "improves on acquaintance."

CHAPTER–42

The Bennets are not a happy couple. Elizabeth's father had apparently married the simple-minded Mrs Bennet for her good looks. Very early in their marriage he began to lose interest in her. Mr Bennet has no respect for his wife and he delights in mocking her. Elizabeth, because of Darcy's comments on her family, is also aware of the disadvantages of her family background. As the regiment has left Meryton, life there has become very dull and boring. Although glad that

Wickham has left, Elizabeth is distressed at the thought of Lydia among the officers at Brighton, a resort town on the English Channel. Elizabeth, however, is excited by the prospect of a tour to the Lake District with the Gardiners. But the plans are changed and the holiday is cut short because of Mr Gardiner's heavy engagement. Instead of the Lake Districts they will visit Derbyshire a fortnight later. Elizabeth is disappointed by the change in the programme and also for excluding Jane from the tour. Four weeks later, in mid-July the Gardiners come and set off the next morning with Elizabeth. After visiting many places in Derbyshire the party reaches Lambton and Mrs Gardiner suggests visiting Pemberley which is not far away. Being informed that Darcy's family is not there, Elizabeth agrees to visit Pemberley.

This chapter further presents the marital situation of the Bennets, which is a mismatched relationship between a man of some intelligence and a simple and obnoxious woman; leading totally separate lives, there is little affection or communication between them. Mrs Bennet rules the household, and her husband stands by as a spectator. Elizabeth now notices everything that is wrong with and between her mother and father. She promises herself never to marry until she finds the right husband. At first Elizabeth is disappointed that the Gardiners will not be taking her to the north, beyond Derbyshire. She soon, however, accepts the idea and eagerly begins the journey. Her visit to Lambton with the Gardiners is vital because it takes her to Pemberley, where she will see Darcy in a more favourable light.

CHAPTER–43

Ascending for half a mile the party finds the Pemberley House, a magnificent stone building at a distance. Elizabeth receives a visual impression of the owner's taste. She has the feelings "that to be mistress of Pemberley might be something!" The interior of the house reflects the same fine taste and renews the exciting fancy, a fancy immediately saved "from something like regret" by the recollection that she would not have been allowed to invite her uncle and aunt there. She has, of course, no reason to think that a proud suitor, angrily rejected, would be disposed to try again; nor have we reason to think that, at this stage, she would be ready to accept him. The tour of the rooms with the housekeeper, Mrs Reynolds, has much quite ironic drama, since the Gardiners believe Elizabeth has some attachment to Wickham and complete antipathy for Darcy. But the housekeeper, after mentioning Wickham's generous upbringing and later wildness, pays warm tributes to the exemplary goodness and kindness Darcy has always shown as son, brother, landlord, and employer; She has known him since he was four and has never had a cross word. As Elizabeth looked at his portrait, "she thought of his regard with a deeper sentiment of gratitude than it had ever raised before." The party next walks outside in the garden. Suddenly Darcy appears. Elizabeth is horribly embarrassed at being found there, and Darcy though quite civil, even gentle, in his inquires about her family, is himself too confused to linger. "She longed to know" what he was thinking, and whether, in defiance of every thing, she was still dear to him. Encouragement soon comes. Darcy, having collected his wits, puts himself in their way again while they are admiring the grounds. He asks to be introduced to Elizabeth's friends (whom he would be taking for "people of fashion") and she rejoices in "every sentence of her uncle, which marked his intelligence, his taste, or his good manners." Darcy, to Mr Gardiner's surprise, cordially invites him to fish whenever he likes and Elizabeth, recognizing the compliment to herself, wonders too. She explains that the housekeeper had said he would not return until the next day. Darcy says that he had changed his plans and the next day the Bingleys will be arriving with his sister, whom he wishes to introduce to her. When they leave, the Gardiners are impressed but still suspicious, and on one point, Darcy's supposed ill treatment of Wickham, Elizabeth enlightens them.

Elizabeth's visit to Pemberley is contrived by the author for several purposes. First, it creates a sense of wonder in Elizabeth for Darcy. She finds everything about Pemberley—the architecture, the grounds, the furnishings, to be lovely; she realizes that the home is a clear expression of Darcy's taste and wealth. She is also struck by Pemberley's grandeur. Elizabeth is becoming less prejudiced. Secondly, at Pemberley, Elizabeth hears all kinds of good things about Darcy, which begin to color her thinking. The housekeeper reveals that he is a kind and generous landlord, a devoted brother, and a promising and unselfish young man. Elizabeth realizes that this is a very different picture of the arrogant man that she has rejected. Thirdly, Elizabeth's visit puts her into direct contact with Darcy again. The accidental encounter embarrasses Elizabeth because she is aware of the "impropriety of her being found there". But, Darcy puts her at ease and is very cordial with the Gardiners. Elizabeth is wonder-struck at his kind and gentlemanly behaviour. She is further impressed when her aunt and uncle, people of good sense, reveal that they really like Darcy.

CHAPTER–44

It had been agreed that Mr Darcy would bring his sister to meet Elizabeth the day after her arrival at Pemberley, but Darcy and she come to the inn where Elizabeth is staying the very day of their arrival. Elizabeth is flattered by this prompt visit. Soon Bingley comes and joins them. Elizabeth finds Miss Darcy not proud as she has heard about her, but exceedingly shy and gentle. It is pretty clear to Elizabeth that Bingley is not in love with Miss Darcy but is still in love with Jane. Darcy himself wears "an expression of general complaisance," with no trace of hauteur; he seems anxious only to please. The Gardiners feel that Mr Darcy is in love with their niece. The travellers hear that Wickham is known in town to have left many debts behind him, which Mr Darcy paid. During the evening and part of the night Elizabeth, recalling her angry and unjust response to his proposal, can account for the miraculous changes only on the conviction that he is still ardently in love, and her gratitude swells. In the evening she and her aunt decide to return the compliment to Miss Darcy by visiting Pemberley the next day.

Since Jane Austen's stronger heroines are not passive Elizabeth "only wanted to know…how far it would be for the happiness of both that she should employ the power, which her fancy told her she still possessed, of bringing on the renewal of his address." It proves Darcy's real trust in Elizabeth. The appearance of Bingley is significant in the renewal of his romantic relationship with Jane. Darcy's love for Elizabeth is judged by the Gardiners as genuine and their judgment is to be trusted. The change in Darcy's behaviour works a change in the mind of Elizabeth who begins to think of marrying Darcy a real possibility. Jane Austen tactfully brings the situations in favour of the protagonists. But a happy ending must not come too easily, there must be suspense and a closer, surer bond established, and the next seven chapters raise a new and presumably fatal obstacle.

CHAPTER–45

At Pemberley Elizabeth and Mrs Gardiner are politely received by Miss Darcy. The Bingley sisters also are present there. Miss Bingley, who has been watching Elizabeth closely, does not speak for about a quarter of an hour. Later, when Darcy enters the room she sarcastically asks Elizabeth whether the regiment's departure has not been a great loss to her family, in order to discredit Elizabeth in the eyes of Darcy. Darcy perceives the malicious suggestion in the question and restrains his indignation with some difficulty. Elizabeth and her aunt depart soon afterwards. After they leave, Miss Bingley criticizes Elizabeth's looks, manner and self-sufficiency and reminds Darcy of his poor opinion of Elizabeth. Darcy, though annoyed, tells her that he considers Elizabeth one of the handsomest women of his acquaintance. After returning to Lambton, Elizabeth and Mrs Gardiner discuss about everything and everybody they have seen at Pemberley, except Darcy.

Miss Bingley's behaviour with Elizabeth betrays her jealous and uncivilised nature. She is defeated by Elizabeth's dignified behaviour and Darcy's calm reactions to her attack against Elizabeth. Darcy and Elizabeth now seem to have discovered their love only after establishing it firmly on a foundation of experience and mutual understanding, belying the notion of love at first sight or romantic love as a proper guide for marriage. Darcy's pride and Elizabeth's prejudice are gone and Jane Austen thus paves the way for their union at the end.

CHAPTER–46

To cause Elizabeth's great displeasure, two letters from Jane arrive. One says that Lydia has eloped from Brighton with Wickham, that no one knows where they are, and that they are probably not married. The second letter reveals that Wickham does not intend to marry Lydia at all and has not gone to Gretna Green. It is believed instead that Wickham and Lydia have gone to London. Mr Bennet is going to London with Colonel Forster to try to find his daughter. Jane asks Elizabeth to return to Longbourn immediately. As the Gardiners have gone out for a walk, Elizabeth is just about to rush out to find her uncle, when Darcy comes. Elizabeth is so concerned that she discloses the contents of the letters to Darcy. She blames herself for not revealing Wickham's true character. Darcy is shocked and deeply concerned and assures her of his help in this matter in all possible ways. Having promised to convey to his sister Elizabeth's apologies for not dining at Pemberley as arranged and also to conceal the unhappy secret from her and others Darcy departs. Mr and Mrs Gardiner arrive soon after and are distressed to hear the news and arrangements for going to Longbourn are immediately made.

Lydia's elopement with Wickham is a relatively violent incident that Jane Austen commonly uses to start the wheels rolling toward the denouement. Both Elizabeth and Darcy blame themselves for the catastrophe since they have not spoken out and revealed the truth about Wickham. As Darcy tries to comfort Elizabeth over the catastrophe, it is the first time the two of them are understanding and intimate with each other. Trusting Darcy as never before, Elizabeth opens up and talks about her family's disgrace. Sophisticated readers may laugh at Elizabeth's declaration that, since Lydia has nothing to tempt Wickham to marriage, "she is lost for ever," but perhaps there is still enough support for the institution to make her bourgeois feelings comprehensible. With Darcy at hand, walking up and down, "his brow contracted, his air gloomy," Elizabeth cannot help thinking that this crowning family disgrace must extinguish his love. And the thought brings understanding—less than full understanding—of her actual state of mind: "never had she so honestly felt that she could have loved him, as now, when all love must be vain." The author here puts in a brief defense of Elizabeth's present feeling for Darcy as founded on "gratitude and esteem" (a topic lightly touched in the second-last chapter of *Northanger Abbey*), although such an idea may offend believers in the common romantic doctrine of first impressions, love at first sight—which she had given "somewhat of a trial...—in her partiality for Wickham." She is not unemotional, but she is unsentimental, or antisentimental, and always honest.

CHAPTER–47

On their way to Longbourn Elizabeth and the Gardiners speculate on whether Wickham will marry Lydia. While Mr Gardiner is hopeful of Wickham's marrying Lydia, Elizabeth is not inclined to agree with him as she knows the true nature of Wickham. Elizabeth hints to her aunt and uncle that she has other reasons that she cannot reveal for suspecting the worst of Wickham. She mentions his having deceived Elizabeth into believing that Georgiana was proud and disagreeable. Elizabeth confesses that she and Jane decided not to make their knowledge of Wickham's character and past public. She had no reason to think that there might be an attachment between Lydia and Wickham. Throughout the journey home, Elizabeth blames herself for not having revealed what she knew about Wickham. On reaching home Elizabeth and Jane comfort each other. Elizabeth learns from Jane that their father is in London and that he will not write again unless he has any news of Lydia. Jane then reads the note Lydia left to Colonel Forster's wife. Lydia lightheartedly informs Harriet Forster that she will soon be signing her name "Lydia Wickham." Mrs Bennet foolishly fears that Mr Bennet will fight a duel with Mr Wickham, get killed and leave all of them paupers. Mr Gardiner comforts her by saying that he will bring Mr Bennet back from London and then the two together will make plans to trace the eloped couple. Mrs Bennet becomes cheerful at the prospect of Lydia's marriage. The Bennet sisters engage themselves in discussing about the eloped couple and the steps their father might take to find them out.

In this chapter, Elizabeth makes a bold analysis of her family and even does not spare herself for hiding Wickham's real nature. She blames herself for not warning Lydia about Wickham before her trip to Brighton. Mrs Bennet by her talks proves as silly as before. Mary with her dry and useless platitudes appears to be as removed from the realities of life as ever. Lydia has no idea of the effect of her action on the family or herself. Her letter to Harriet exposes her at once as an irresponsible, foolish young girl. Austen shows her insight into different types of characters by presenting them through different styles of expression they use.

CHAPTER–48

Mr Gardiner sets off for London the next morning as no communication from Mr Bennet arrives. At London he finds Mr Bennet who plans to inquire at all the chief hotels of London for the fugitives. Mr Gardiner writes to Mr Forster to inform him of any friends and acquaintances of Wickham with whom he might possibly stay. Elizabeth has never heard of any relations of Wickham and thinks that his companions in the regiment might give some information. Meanwhile a letter from Collins addressed to Mr Bennet arrives and it contains only pompous condolences and a quite unchristian condemnation of Lydia, advising Mr Bennet to cast off his unworthy daughter and leave her to reap the fruit of her own offence. Collins also expresses satisfaction at having escaped from entering into relationship with such a family. Mr Gardiner's next letter informs that Wickham has incurred heavy gambling debts. Mr Bennet is persuaded to return home. Mrs Gardiner also leaves for London with her children. Mr Bennet arrives the following day as calm and philosophical as usual and makes himself responsible for all that has happened. He recalls that last May she advised him not to permit Lydia's going to Brighton. When kitty says that she would behave better should she go to Brighton, Mr Bennet answers that he has learned his lesson, that no officer shall set foot in this house again.

Action is little in this chapter. Collins's letter shows his hypocrisy and lack of Christian charity. There is an awakening in Mr Bennet of his duties as a father, which he has so far neglected. Wickham's insolvent nature is exposed and it adds more stain to his character. Mr Gardiner's earnestness to trace the runaway pair shows his genuine concern for the Bennet family. This chapter also marks the passage of time since the elopement.

CHAPTER–49

Two days after Mr Bennet's return he receives a letter from Mr Gardiner informing him that the eloped couple have been found and that they are going to marry soon. Wickham has agreed to marry Lydia on condition that Lydia should be promised an equal share of five thousand pounds in her mother's property and that Mr Bennet should pay him an annuity of one hundred pounds till Mr Bennet is alive. Mr Gardiner believes that after paying off his creditors Wickham will still have some money left and so he has agreed to the condition of Wickham and asks Mr Bennet to give his consent. The news is a great relief to Jane and Elizabeth. Mr Bennet, however, suspects that Wickham has been given money by Mr Gardiner to make him agree to marry Lydia. He retires to the library to write the letter of consent. Jane and Elizabeth go away to give the good news to everybody. Mrs Bennet's joy knows no bounds when she hears the news and is ready to make arrangements for the marriage. While Jane thinks Wickham has a true love for Lydia, Elizabeth is doubtful about Lydia's being happy with the husband she has found.

The marriage of Wickham and Lydia is, in fact, a loveless marriage based on financial considerations. In fact, Wickham has been bribed to marry Lydia. Mr Bennet agrees to pay Wickham's blackmail amount so that his other daughters' honour is saved. Even Mr Gardiner arranges Lydia's settlement with Wickham, lest any stigma spreads to his branch of the family. Elizabeth's independent thinking and sensitivity is obvious as she questions a society preferring a loveless marriage for the sake of reputation, to no marriage at all.

Mrs Bennet's reactions to the marriage shows that she has no real awareness of the moral problems of Wickham's real character.

CHAPTER–50

When the Bennets married they had at first been confident that they would bear a son to inherit their estate and so Mr Bennet had not saved anything from his annual income. By the time their five daughters had been born, it was too late to start saving. Without any savings it is now difficult for Mr Bennet to repay Mr Gardiner whatever he might have personally spent on Lydia. Still he is determined to find out the extent of Mr Gardiner's assistance and free himself from the obligations as soon as possible. Of course, there is no difficulty in agreeing to Wickham's conditions as Lydia can easily have an equal share of her mother's fortune of five thousand pounds and regarding the annuity of one hundred pounds, Mr Bennet has already been spending that amount annually on Lydia. Elizabeth meanwhile regrets that she ever told Darcy about the elopement, for, now there seems to be no need for anyone to know about the scandalous event. She knows that Darcy cannot be expected to marry into a disgraced family. But what she has learnt and seen of Darcy has convinced her that Darcy and she are in fact perfectly suited. She is now anxious to gain Darcy's esteem. News of the wedding spreads. Mr Bennet's declaration is that he will never receive his daughter and son-in-law into his house and that he will not give Lydia any money to buy clothes. Mr Gardiner writes to Mr Bennet not to mention again what has been spent for Lydia and Wickham. He says that Wickham is quitting the militia and obtaining a commission in the regular army in a regiment now quartered in the North of England. His creditors in Brighton have been promised satisfaction and those in Meryton will receive the same speedy payment. He says that Lydia would like to visit her family before going on to Newcastle. Eventually Mr Bennet allows the couple to visit Longbourn after the wedding when Jane and Elizabeth request him to do so. Wickham is to join a northern regiment after his marriage.

Like some other chapters, this chapter also shows the importance of the financial side of marriage. Like that in the Lydia-Wickham episode, the Bennets' relationship had been based on physical attraction and so it has been an unhappy and financially unstable marriage. Elizabeth now seems to realize how much she values Darcy as her future husband. She now learns that the right relationship is the one that meets, answers and complements and not the one that merely flatters and agrees. The extent of Mr Gardiner's financial help to make Wickham agree to marry is kept vague in this chapter.

CHAPTER–51

After much negotiation, Wickham and Lydia are married. Lydia and Wickham marry in London and on the very day of their marriage come to Longbourn to stay for ten days. Mrs Bennet warmly welcomes the couple, while Mr Bennet is reserved. The couple seem unembarrassed. While Lydia talks on in her flippant, irresponsible manner about her elopement, her ring and her married status, Wickham also is his usual self, talking and smiling. Lydia asks if everyone in the vicinity knows that she was married that day. Later she says she is sure that all her sisters envy her. They must all go to Brighton: "that is the place to get husbands." She promises to get husbands for her sisters before the winter is over. Disgusted, Elizabeth replies that she does not like Lydia's way of getting husbands. Lydia, while describing her wedding to Elizabeth and Jane lets slip the fact that Darcy had attended her wedding. Elizabeth is amazed and rather than questioning Lydia, writes to Mrs Gardiner to ascertain the details about Darcy's part in the marriage.

This chapter shows in detail Lydia's irresponsible and self-centred nature. Wickham is shameless and talks as if nothing untoward has happened. We can think that it is merely because of the force of Lydia's love for romance that led to her elopement with Wickham and the other developments. Elizabeth learns that Darcy was at the wedding of the two people whom he must have detested, and her attempt to discover the truth will later unravel to her Darcy's honest generosity.

CHAPTER–52

Wickham and Lydia are married, and Elizabeth is enabled to extract from Mrs Gardiner the information that Darcy had managed the whole business. Mrs Gardiner replies to Elizabeth's letter informing her of the details of Darcy's part in Lydia's marriage. With the help of Mrs Younge, Wickham's confidante, Darcy traced the runaway couple. He first tried to persuade Lydia to go back to her parents, but as she was adamant, he with great difficulty made Wickham agree to marry Lydia. Darcy explained that he felt that it was because of him that Wickham's worthlessness had not been made known. His mistaken pride had made him reluctant to have his own affairs known. After doing so much Darcy had met Mr Gardiner, told him everything, got his consent and exacted a promise from him to keep his share in the affair a secret. He told Mr Gardiner that he had done all this as he thought himself responsible for Lydia's ignorance of the true nature of Wickham. By promising to pay his debts (well more than a thousand pounds), by giving him another thousand, and by purchasing for him a commission in the regular army, Darcy was able to persuade Wickham to agree to the marriage. But Mrs Gardiner suggests in her letter that perhaps it is out of love for Elizabeth that Darcy has done all this. She ends her letter by hinting that it would be a good thing if Elizabeth were to marry Darcy. Elizabeth is overcome by all that Darcy has done. She begins to think very high of Darcy. Wickham interrupts as she is reading the letter. Elizabeth manages the conversation with great skill and without being unnecessarily rude lets him know that she has heard the truth about old Darcy's will and Wickham's renouncing the opportunity to enter the church. Wickham feels embarrassed and Elizabeth suggests that they should forget the past and live in future like brother and sister.

Elizabeth is cheered by the knowledge of Darcy's undergoing so much trouble, mortification, and expense (the expense of bribing Wickham). Darcy has overcome his pride and prejudice to do the right thing. Elizabeth's feelings towards him are even more positive as she has now the clear approval of her aunt, Mrs Gardiner, whose advice she values, for a matrimonial relationship with Darcy. Yet she cannot expect to have Darcy whom she has once refused and who certainly will not like to be the brother-in-law of Wickham, by marrying her. Once again the theme of family pride and honour is reinforced. Elizabeth here completely frees herself from the charm of Wickham who, though exposed, does not admit his lies.

CHAPTER–53

Lydia and Wickham leave for Newcastle after ten days. Mrs Bennet is depressed, but her gloom is over at the news that Mr Bingley is to visit Netherfield in a few days. She requests her husband to invite Mr Bingley to Longbourn on his arrival, but Mr Bennet curtly refuses to do so. Annoyed by her mother's talk about ensnaring Bingley, Jane tells Elizabeth that no one can know "how much I suffer from what she says." But to Mrs Bennet's great surprise Bingley comes to Longbourn with Darcy of his own accord on the third morning after his arrival. Although Jane and Elizabeth are greatly delighted to have their favourites, they sit through the visit without much visible embarrassment. But, Mrs Bennet invites them to dine at their place after a few days.

Elizabeth feels that Darcy's arrival at Longbourn is an indication that his positive feeling for her has not been ruined by Lydia's elopement with Wickham. Mrs Bennet's bitterness towards Darcy, an example of uninformed prejudice, makes Elizabeth feel more insecure about him. Darcy is now seen to reassess Jane's and Bingley's relationship and also the feelings of Elizabeth towards him. Austen has deftly brought Mr Bingley and Jane together again so that their love may develop and ultimately find culmination in marriage.

CHAPTER–54

Darcy's silent, grave and indifferent behaviour during his visit makes Elizabeth ponder about the cause. Jane now comes and tells Elizabeth that she will treat Mr Bingley as her friend and nothing more, which Elizabeth refuses to believe. On Tuesday, Darcy and Bingley come to the Bennets for the dinner. It is a big party. Bingley sits next to Jane at the table, but

Darcy takes his seat by the side of Mrs Bennet, far away from Elizabeth. Even at the cards table Elizabeth is disappointed when she does not get Darcy as her partner. Disturbed at Darcy's avoiding her all evening, she concludes that since she had once refused him, he will never suffer the indignity of making another proposal. Mrs Bennet is, however, satisfied on seeing Bingley's behaviour with Jane although Jane refuses to admit her love for Bingley.

In this chapter, the suspense goes up. Elizabeth feels unhappy at not being able to be close to Darcy. She now admits his right not to be humiliated by rejection and regrets having rejected him. She now recognizes in Darcy the basic decency and gentlemanliness of him. Meanwhile Jane's and Bingley's romance develops easily and quickly, although Jane refuses to admit it. Elizabeth's change of heart has been convincingly brought about, but it must be made known to Darcy and he must be given an occasion to renew his proposal.

CHAPTER–55

Darcy leaves for London on an urgent business. Bingley calls at Longbourn and is warmly welcomed. He begins to visit the Bennets very often. On one such visit he proposes Jane and is accepted. Jane confides this secret to Elizabeth. Soon the whole family is in a jovial mood. Mr Bennet congratulates Jane on having been engaged to Bingley and Mrs Bennet is delighted to have yet another daughter engaged. Jane learns from Bingley that he did not know that she was in London during the spring and realizes that Miss Bingley is responsible for this. She now finds that people are not necessarily as good as she would like to think them to be. Jane also finds out that when Bingley left Netherfield for London last November, he really loved her; but because he thought that she was indifferent, he did not return. Jane wishes that Elizabeth could be as happy as she is. Lizzy replies that she may be lucky enough to meet another Mr Collins in time. Mrs Bennet proudly announces the news to her sister, Mrs Philips, who spreads the word all over Meryton. Jane's good fortune makes the townspeople forget Lydia's disgrace.

In this chapter, Jane and Bingley get united. Jane accepts the dashing hero as the happiest creature in the world. Their relationship is quite unrealistic. This is a significant chapter as the sub-plot concerning Jane and Bingley is concluded. Elizabeth realizes that she will never have Jane's happiness as she will never be the perfect romantic heroine. She is however happy that Bingley has not betrayed his friend Darcy by telling Jane about Darcy's role in separating him from Jane.

CHAPTER–56

About a week after Jane's engagement, the Bennets are amazed to see Lady Catherine de Bourgh at their door. Despite the fact that Mrs Bennet is much impressed at her high importance, Lady Catnerine is "more than usually ungracious." She abruptly asks Elizabeth to walk out with her alone on the lawn. Speaking to her rudely and in angry tones, Lady Catherine tells Elizabeth that she has heard that she is to marry her nephew, Mr Darcy. Although she claims to disbelieve this report, Lady Catherine demands that Elizabeth tell her that it is not true. Offended by her abusive remarks, Elizabeth answers her sharply and ambiguously. When Lady Catherine asks if her nephew has made her an offer of marriage, Elizabeth says, "Your Ladyship has declared it to be impossible". When Lady Catherine says that she is entitled to know all Darcy's concerns, Elizabeth retorts that she is not entitled to know *hers*. When Lady Catherine announces that Darcy is engaged to her daughter, Elizabeth comments that she has no reason, then, to fear that he will make an offer to her. Lady Catherine explains that Darcy has made no proposal; rather, her daughter and he are "intended" for each other. Their marriage will not be prevented by a "young woman of inferior birth, of no importance in the world". Elizabeth defiantly replies that she is a gentleman's daughter. But Lady Catherine rebuts her with objections to her mother's side of the family (Lizzy's uncles and aunts in trade). Elizabeth says that Lady Catherine de Bourgh's intentions for her daughter do not interest her. Lady Catherine then accuses Elizabeth of being ungrateful for her attentions last spring. As Elizabeth says that she is not engaged to Darcy, Lady Catherine demands an assurance from her that she will never accept any such proposal from Darcy. Elizabeth curtly refuses to give such an assurance and Lady Catherine returns to her carriage in high temper threatening Elizabeth all the way and drives away.

The confrontation, in which Elizabeth stands up to the dragoness, Lady Catherine, with such forceful dignity, is one of Jane Austen's stirring scenes—and very different from the overwrought rhetoric of Fanny Burney's Mrs Delvile and the meek Cecilia (*Cecilia*, 4, bk. Vii, c. 8). Lady Catherine who stands for the traditional view of the rigid class structure fails to realize that the love between Darcy and Elizabeth is not the result of an impulsive infatuation, nor a reflection of Elizabeth's social ambitions to rise above her class by marrying Darcy, but rather the union of two sensible people. Her officious and stubborn nature presents her as an epitome of false pride and prejudice. Elizabeth's victory over Lady Catherine lies in the fact that she stands up for herself as a person, shows courage, argues rationally and boldly and loves Darcy enough to fight for him.

CHAPTER–57

After the departure of Lady Catherine, Elizabeth feels uneasy. She wonders how the false report about her engagement to Darcy has spread. She suspects the Lucases as the originator of the rumour. She fears that Lady Catherine might advise Darcy not to propose to her, and if Darcy fails to return to Netherfield on the appointed day it may be taken as a sign of his acceptance of his aunt's advice. A letter from Collins reaches Mr Bennet congratulating him on Jane's engagement but warning that acceptance of Darcy's proposal to Elizabeth will incur the wrath of Lady Catherine. Mr Bennet has knowledge of Elizabeth's dislike for Darcy and not of her changed attitude. So, to amuse her he conveys the news to her and she pretends to take it very lightly.

In this chapter Elizabeth faces her final trial. In her suspended state of confusion, even now she is not confident about Darcy. Yet she seems to be hurt by the fact that even her father can ridicule the idea of Darcy's ever loving her. Collins, out of his peculiar notion of Christian forgiveness advises Mr Bennet to forgive Lydia and Wickham, as a Christian, but never to admit them in his sight nor allow their names to be heard.

CHAPTER–58

A few days after Lady Catherine's visit Darcy returns to Netherfield and visits Longbourn with Bingley. Jane, Elizabeth and Kitty accompany the gentlemen on a walk outside. Bingley and Jane wanting to be alone walk in advance and Kitty goes to the Lucases to meet Maria. Elizabeth and Darcy are now together. Having Darcy alone, Elizabeth says that she must thank him for what her family does not know of, the "unexampled kindness" and "generous compassion" he had shown in regard to Lydia; this of course leads at once to a proposal, Elizabeth's somewhat embarrassed acceptance, and Darcy's "heart-felt delight." Elizabeth now explains how much her feelings have changed and Darcy, too, tells her of his love in a way that shows how genuine it is. Now both Darcy and Elizabeth discuss their faults. Elizabeth admits how ashamed she is of her previous dealings with Darcy and how Darcy's letter has removed her former prejudices. Darcy also confesses how he took to heart Elizabeth's accusations of his ungentlemanly behaviour and makes his father responsible for developing his own haughty mien. He explains that what he has learnt about Elizabeth's reaction to Lady Catherine makes him realize how much she cares for him. He also tells Elizabeth that it is he who has advised Bingley to propose to Jane when he realizes how much the two love each other.

The story of the novel is very near its denouement in this chapter. R.A. Brower, after skilfully analyzing the ironic ambiguities of dialogue between Elizabeth and Darcy, regrets the virtual disappearance of that double or multiple vision in the last third of the novel (after Lydia's elopement), in which the "events seem to belong to a simpler world where outright judgments of good and bad or of happy and unhappy are in place" ("Light and Bright and Sparkling: Irony and Fiction in *Pride and Prejudice*". *The Fields of Light.* New York: Oxford University Press, 1951). The characters, especially Darcy, fall automatically into the grooves prepared for them by hundreds of novels of sentiment and sensibility. But surely this romantic-realistic story had reached a point where—as when Beatrice says to Benedick, "Kill Claudio"—the hero and heroine must be seen, under stress, as their essential selves, above the ironic ambiguities of comedy, firmly joined in their judgment of good and bad.

CHAPTER–59

At night Elizabeth tells everything to Jane who takes some time to believe it and some more time to assure herself that her sister really loves Darcy. Elizabeth tells Jane that since the previous April her feelings towards Darcy have undergone a radical change. Next morning Bingley and Darcy again visit Longbourn. To allow Jane and Bingley all by themselves Mrs Bennet proposes that Darcy and Elizabeth should go to Oakham Mount. During the walk it is decided that Darcy will apply for Mr Bennet's consent in the evening while Elizabeth should seek her mother's consent to their marriage. Accordingly Darcy meets Mr Bennet and gets his approval. But Mr Bennet, doubtful of Elizabeth's love for Darcy, calls her to him and Elizabeth assures her father of her changed attitude and tells him of Darcy's goodness and nobility and discloses to him the help Darcy has rendered secretly in Lydia's affairs. Mr Bennet is happy and Mrs Bennet's joy also knows no bounds when she learns the news.

Elizabeth of course dominates the conclusion as she had dominated throughout. But Jane Austen compels our belief in genuine love (witness Elizabeth's talk with her father) while rounding out a conclusion in the vein of comedy. When trying to convince the incredulous Jane that she has fallen in love, Elizabeth jocosely dates it from her first sight of Pemberley—an idea which, on the plane of material possession, Sir walter Scott, that great admirer of Jane Austen, and some other hasty readers have taken seriously. One peak of comedy is reached in the dithyrambic ecstasies of Mrs Bennet who, in the awesome presence of her prospective son-in-law, is fortunately cowed into self-restraint.

CHAPTER–60

Elizabeth now becomes familiar with Darcy. One day she playfully asks him when he actually started loving her. As Darcy is unable to give her any information about it, Elizabeth helps him with clever guesswork. Darcy, however, comments that her spirit and kindness to Jane first attracted him to her. Elizabeth argues that he loved her as she did not seek his approval or flatter him like other women. The same day Darcy writes to Lady Catherine informing her of his engagement with Elizabeth, Elizabeth writes to Mrs Gardiner giving her the happy news and inviting her to Pemberley at Christmas, and Mr Bennet writes to Collins in reply to the latter's letter of warning, asking him in his usual caustic manner to console Lady Catherine in her disappointment. Collins, instead of replying to the letter of Mr Bennet, comes with his wife to the Lucas Lodge, to be out of the way of the wrath of Lady Catherine. Darcy bears well with Elizabeth's family, but Elizabeth now realizes the difference in quality between them.

This chapter draws us very near the resolution of the novel. The readers learn the reasons for Darcy's attraction for Elizabeth from both Darcy and Elizabeth. Elizabeth now prepares herself—both physically and mentally—for her transition to Pemberley. In Jane Austen's world there is very little display of passion. Darcy and Elizabeth seem to be happy to talk, analyse and reason over their love rather than to exchange words of passion and emotion.

CHAPTER–61

Mrs Bennet is ecstatic on the marriage day of her daughters, Jane and Elizabeth, referring to them as Mrs Bingley and Mrs Darcy. Mr Bennet is often in Pemberley to visit his daughter, and Jane and Bingley soon buy an estate much nearer to Pemberley. Kitty spends a lot of time with Jane and Elizabeth as well and is disallowed from visiting Lydia in The North. Wickham and Lydia for their part are often in need of money and constantly ask Elizabeth and Darcy for some, which they will often provide. Mary is left alone at home with her mother where she is rather forced to stop reading and spend time with her mother. Miss Bingley tries to be nice to

Elizabeth, despite her anger over the match, so she can still visit Pemberley. Miss Darcy, now permanently settled at Pemberley, becomes close to Elizabeth immediately. Lady de Bourgh's anger is immense, but after a while she decides she cannot bear the curiosity and visits Pemberley to see how Elizabeth handles herself. The Gardiners visit often and are favorites of the Darcy's for bringing the two together.

The last chapter provides a satisfactory conclusion to the novel. Here Jane Austen emphasizes more the social than the personal happiness resulting from marriage. Instead of showing the love relations between Elizabeth and Darcy, the protagonists of the novel, their continuing relations with other people have been referred to. One may remember the opening sentence of the novel and find that Darcy, a man in possession of a good fortune, at last gets his wife, although it is not his 'fortune' by which he wins her. Andrew H. Wright writes in *Jane Austen's Novels: A Study in Structure*: "Against clarity, in *Pride and Prejudice,* involvement is set: both are desirable, but each, ironically, works against the other and the reader cannot believe that the marriage of Darcy and Elizabeth, however happy or beneficial, will ever quite close the breach between these two opposites" (117-18).

6 Issues

(I) TITLE

In the novel *Pride and Prejudice*, Austen's title-words prove slippery in the trial of character. While the word "Pride" evokes the prime deadly sin, in eighteenth-century social registers and philosophy, it might denote a sense of rational self-worth, or (alternatively) smugness primed for "mortification." "Prejudice" might seem kin to dubious "first impressions"; but it might signify sound "latent wisdom"—the phrase Edmund Burke used with positive English pride in his conservative *Reflections on the Revolution in France*: "Prejudice renders a man's virtue his habit...part of his nature" (2nd edn, 1790: 130). Susan J. Wolfson writes in "Re: Reading *Pride and Prejudice*": "No less a question is Austen's assignment of these attitudes: whose *pride*? whose *prejudice*? No character will have exclusive claim. Austen involves her readers in the question, using 'free indirect discourse,' a pulse of feelings, thoughts, and self-examination, to convey a voice of consciousness, at once personal and inflected by a shared social grammar" (*A Companion to Jane Austen* 115).

The original title, *First Impressions*, had in sentimental fiction carried the special connotation of immediate surrender to sensibility, love at first sight—the kind of experience enjoyed in *Love and Friendship*. The opposed view, that sensibility needed rational restraint, was enunciated by the exemplary Miss Byron early in one of the novels Jane Austen knew well, *Sir Charles Grandison*: "O sir Rowland, I thought you were too wise to be swayed by first impressions: None but the *giddy*, you know, love at first sight." The first title was discarded probably because it was used for a book published in 1800. Both it, in a general and ironical sense, and the final title would apply to both heroine and hero, Elizabeth and Darcy in the novel. Both were mistaken in their first impressions of each other, as Elizabeth was also in regard to Wickham and Darcy in regard to Jane Bennet. And Elizabeth, as she later admitted to herself, was guilty of prejudice based on pride in her own discernment, Darcy—as he also came to admit—of prejudice born of his chief fault, personal and social pride. The phrase "pride and prejudice" has been observed in a dozen or more books, mostly of the later eighteenth century, where Jane Austen might have seen it. The most likely and significant source would be Fanny Burney's *Cecilia* (1782), where the phrase is used three times, in capitals, in a paragraph of the last chapter: Dr Lyster is summarizing the moral of the work, the havoc wrought in young lives by their elders' fanatical pride in an aristocratic name and lineage. Jane Austen set up a partly similar conflict between Darcy and Elizabeth and related conflicts within each of them. It requires experience and self-examination on the part of the heroine and hero, the "intricate" characters who are capable of such reflection, to recognize their failings and correct their view of themselves and others.

Gilbert Ryle in "Jane Austen and the Moralists" included in Southam's *Critical Essays on Jane Austen* comments, "*Pride and Prejudice* really is about pride and about the misjudgments that stem from baseless pride, excessive pride, deficient pride, pride in trivial objects, and so on" (Southam 107). In *Pride and Prejudice* almost every character exhibits too much or too little pride, pride of a bad or silly sort or pride of a good sort, sham pride or genuine pride and so forth. Elizabeth Bennet combines a dangerous cocksureness in her assessments of people with a proper sense of her own worth. Jane is quite uncocksure. She is too diffident. She does not resent beings put upon or even realize that she is being put upon. There is no proper pride, and so no fight in her. Their mother is so stupid and vulgar that she has no sense of dignity at all, only silly vanities about her dishes and her daughters' conquests. Mr Bennet has genuine pride. He does despise the despicable. But it is inert, unexecutive pride. He voices his just contempt in witty words, but he does nothing to prevent or repair what he condemns. It is the pride of a mere don, though a good don. Bingley has no special pride, and so, though a nice man, spinelessly lets himself be managed by others where he should not. His sisters are proud in the sense of being vain and snobbish. Darcy is, to start with, haughty and snobbish, a true nephew of Lady Catherine de Bourgh. His early love for Elizabeth is vitiated by condescension. He reforms into a man with pride of the right sort. He is proud to be able to help Elizabeth and her socially embarrassing family. He now knows what is due from him as well as what is due to him. As to the character of Mr Collins, Gilbert Ryle in "Jane Austen and the Moralists" comments: "Mr Collins is the incarnation of vacuous complacency. He glories in what are mere reflections from the rank of his titled patroness and from his own status as a clergyman. He is a soap bubble with nothing at all inside him and only bulging refractions from other things on his rotund surface" (Southam 109).

Gilbert Ryle observes that Austen had a true interest in 'theoretical problems about human nature' even if her approach to them was from a sunnier aspect than the philosopher's. Though Bernard Mandeville won notoriety for his claim that pride was the human quality most beneficial to society, he also warned that it could blind understanding, and this point, much developed by the Scottish schools, is illustrated by Austen when Darcy boasts that "where there is a real superiority of mind, pride will be always under good regulation" (*PP* 1:11). David Hume had argued in *A Treatise of Human Nature* (Ed. David Fate Norton. Oxford: Oxford University Press, 2002. 381-83) that a natural propensity to over-value the self-made pride offensive unless it was kept 'well-regulated'; to which Adam Smith added that the high self-esteem of others, even when well founded, 'mortifies our own,' a caveat turned by Elizabeth into epigram when she says of Darcy, "I could easily forgive *his* pride, if he had not mortified *mine*" (*PP* 5). Control of the virtuous vice is thus partly a matter of social skill, and Bingely (unlike Darcy) shows himself to be an adept in this department when he calls attention to the speed and careless rapture of his letter writing, his 'humility' on the occasion masking a proud show of what he rates as a flattering trait.

Adam Smith argues that self-love nourishes virtue because of the way it excites the desire to be approved to be seen to excel. Though Smith balks at the word 'pride' in this context, reserving it for an inflated sense of self, David Hume is only too ready to point that the deadliest sin is the most fertile of many ambivalent energies that yield a harvest for the good (Hume, *Enquiry Concerning Principles of Morals*. Ed. Tom L. Beauchamp, Oxford: Clarendon Press, 1998. 147). Peter Knox-Shaw observes in "Philosophy" in Jenet Todd's *Jane Austen in Context:* "...the line drawn by Hume between different grounds of self-esteem in his popular second *Enquiry* finds a parallel in *Pride and Prejudice* when Darcy, convicted first by Elizabeth of the 'worst kind of pride' (2:10), is at last declared free of all 'improper' varieties. Hume insists that 'character' is a truer object of approbation than 'rent-rolls,' however much store the world sets by riches and power; and he proceeds to note that in aristocratic societies—as opposed to commercial ones whose vice it is to foster greed—a premium is placed on birth with the result that 'spiritless minds remain in haughty indolence, and dream of nothing but pedigrees and genealogies' (*Enquiry*, Section VI)" (Todd 352). *Pride and Prejudice* surveys the no man's land between these warring societies, Lady Catherine de Bourgh's estate providing a comic epitome of a backward-looking absolutism shored up, intriguingly, by 'reason' and 'humility.' Darcy, who has been taught from childhood to care for no one beyond his own family circle, and who inherits some of his aunt's horror of bad connections, renounces his pride of rank when he tracks down the disgraced Lydia in Eastcheap with the help of the city-based Mr. Gardiner, who duly reports his motive—'His character was to speak for itself.' Speak to Elizabeth it does, and while she is happy to suppose Darcy doubly inspired by compassion and honour, his rescue of Lydia strikes the reader as no worse for being prompted by romantic attachment also—like so many other worthy deeds in Austen's work. Sympathy and pride are again twinned as joint goads to right action when Jane exclaims of the supposed evil fathered on Wickham by Darcy, "No man of common humanity, no man who had any value for his character, could be capable of it" (*PP* 17); and in the same context Elizabeth underlines the value of pride when she exclaims that she would at least have expected justice and honesty of Darcy from 'no better motive' (*PP* 16).

Hume complained that there was no proper word for the admirable 'sentiment of conscious worth' that he identified as pride, but this is precisely the quality that Elizabeth and Darcy so attractively embody, and which accounts for the more lived-in level of the novel's two-storied moral scheme. As the various characters are united in a common plot and by an analogy of action, so do most of them exhibit variations of the same moral feelings and confer justifiability to the title of Austen's *Pride and Prejudice.*

(II) PLOT

Ernest A. Baker writes in *The History of the English Novel,* "A novel is not a play, and should never pretend to be a play. Literature always simplifies, and drama carries the process to the farthest lengths, making an abstraction from reality. Fiction, however, is no mere abstract, it is a representation of reality, a more or less full representation of a segment of life" (84). Jane Austen's plots, and her novels in general, were put together very 'deliberately and calculatedly.' But her interest in 'composition' is not something to be put over against her interest in life; nor does she offer an 'aesthetic' value that is separable from moral significance. Susan J. Wolfson in "Re: Reading *Pride and Prejudice*: What Think You of Books?" says in *A Companion to Jane Austen* that Austen's four lifetime novels, *Mansfield Park, Emma, Pride and Prejudice,* and *Sense and Sensibility* "carried a subtitle: *A Novel in Three Volumes.* 'Novel' was the new genre: of the eighteenth century, in full bloom in the 1790s, when Austen drafted the manuscript that would become *Pride and Prejudice.*

'In three Volumes' is a reader-friendly form, enabling sequential purchasing or borrowing, and family sharing. Austen cannily shapes each volume along a dramatic arc" (Ed. Claudia L. Johnson and Clara Tuite. 112-13). Volume I climaxes in crises: Elizabeth's refusal and Charlotte's acceptance of Mr Collins's proposal of marriage, Mrs Bennet's railing about the entailment of their estate to Mr Collins, and her husband's needling rejoinder: "I leave it to yourself to determine" (*PP* 130)—precisely what women can't do legally, with a hint of Mr Bennet's complicity in the arrangement (Irvine 2002:17-18). Volume II ends Elizabeth's angry rebuff of Mr Darcy's proposal, his long follow-up letter, then an impending tour with her unknowing aunt and uncle of Darcy's Pemberley, the "dreadful" prospect eased by assurance of his absence. The volume closes in a dramatic, one-sentence' paragraph, vibrating with expectation: "To Pemberley, therefore, they were to go" (*PP* 241). Volume III works an elaborate denouement. In *Pride and Prejudice,* at all events, "Jane Austen was necessarily most dramatic, even approximating to the stage in her preference to description and analysis of that which is infinitely more telling, that which goes on before our eyes and ears, the human drama in action. Just as the playwright drops at times into makeshift soliloquy, she may write out the whole of her heroine's meditations at a crucial juncture. But for the most part she lets the scene proceed without interference. And in the present case she was so dramatic that it is tempting to divide the narrative into the five acts of high comedy" (Baker 84).

That which may be taken as the first act opens briskly, and with the arresting first sentence introduces the Longbourn people, hitting off their leading traits, foibles, and prejudices with such dexterity that a closer acquaintance can only deepen the first impression. Elizabeth and Darcy meet, and affect each other so unfavourably that nothing seems more remote than the possibility of a warm attachment between such predestined foes. But presently it is evident that, if this is dislike, it is not indifference; so far from it that Darcy "feels the danger of paying Elizabeth too much attention," whilst she is puzzled by a gallantry which belies his former arrogance. Along with these hints of future developments, the sub-plot also begins to outline itself, in the mutual attraction of Darcy's friend Bingley and Elizabeth's sister Jane. Both affairs come to an apparent end with the departure of the two girls from Netherfield, and Bingley's silence. The heart-burnings are entirely on Jane's side, Elizabeth's disappointment is only for her sister. Such is the posture of affairs at the beginning of the second act, in which the plot stands almost still or dallies for a while with other matters, matters not so irrelevant as they seem. It is largely taken up with the absurd antics of Mr Collins, who is refused by Elizabeth and marries her less squeamish friend Charlotte Lucas. Elizabeth flirts with the handsome scapegrace Wickham, but remains heart-whole, though his airs of injured innocence and his mendacious revelations set her inflexibly against Darcy. That gentleman continues to be fascinated by Elizabeth, but is still more repelled by the follies of the Bennet family. A master-stroke of irony is preparing, however, throughout this act; for Mr Collins and Wickham are both to be instrumental in bringing about a most unexpected result, the complete reconciliation of Elizabeth and Darcy. That is still hid in the future; but there is another stroke, the irony of Darcy's interference between Jane and Bingley, since what he has deliberately done now will have to be deliberately undone later.

The turning point of the story which may be called the critical third act of *Pride and Prejudice* occurs as Elizabeth goes on a visit to the Collinses, and at Lady Catherine de Bourgh's meets Darcy and his friend Colonel Fitzwilliam. Darcy surprises her, and perhaps the reader, with a proposal of marriage, which she rejects, stigmatizing his pride and the alleged wrongs done to Wickham. His long letter of exculpation gives her food for thought, and may be regarded as of decisive moment in the plot structure of the novel. She sees that there is another side to the case put by Wickham; Colonel Fitzwilliam's talk about Darcy sinks in, and combined with other facts tends to open her eyes. Things begin to move decisively in the fourth act, of which the big event is the visit to

Pemberley. The Pemberley visit is to supplement this tevised impression of Darcy with evidence as to character: Mrs Reynolds is a useful piece of machinery. It is more to the purpose that here Darcy and Elizabeth see one another for the first time in favourable—even flattering—circumstances: he at his best on his own estate (a piece of nice observation), and she among congenial companions. Lydia's disgrace has still to come—to give him opportunity for proving that he has taken her strictures to heart, to show her how much she values those hopes of a better understanding which it seems bound to frustrate. Any Lady Catherine will involuntarily give the last turn to the plot by her interference.

The climax, the final act, comes with one surprise following fast upon another. Elizabeth's father and her excellent uncle Mr Gardiner are in quest of the run-a-ways, Lydia and Wickham, in London; and before long news arrives that the pair have been traced, and that pressure has been put upon Wickham and the wherewithal provided to induce him to make Lydia an honest woman. Mr Gardiner is supposed to have done all this; but the giddy Lydia coming home unabashed with her husband lets out that Darcy had been present at the wedding. Elizabeth writes off at once to inquire of her aunt, and learns by return of post that the person who had taken the chief part in rescuing her sister was no other than Darcy. He pretended to have done it because he held himself responsible for the mischief done by Wickham. Elizabeth cannot be sure whether there was a more powerful motive. The situation is still an enigma. It is not cleared up even by Darcy's reappearance at Longbourn, along with his friend Bingley. And even when the latter renews his addresses to Jane, and is accepted, Elizabeth's gladness on her sister's account is not yet enhanced by any ray of hope for herself. Of course, the reader had recognized the sterling nature of Darcy's character long before this becomes manifest to Elizabeth, and standing on one side has marked the dramatic change that has taken place within him. It is the spectator that sees most of the game. But as yet both parties are tormented with doubts and hesitations. Neither can forget that Darcy had once been rejected by Elizabeth. Only some happy accident can now break down the barriers and make plain speaking possible. The accident occurs. A visitor who came to intimidate changes to be the agent of Elizabeth's happiness. There is no more brilliant scene in fiction than the duel of wit and aristocratic insolence when Lady Catherine de Bourgh, in presuming to browbeat Elizabeth Bennet, manages to ensure the event which she is most anxious to avert. Darcy, who arrives shortly after, confesses that he had not allowed himself to hope till now. But till his arrival Elizabeth still did not permit herself to hope, and her father's ironical compliments on the receipt of a letter of remonstrance from Lady Catherine's today, Mr Collins, while it hurts her to be reminded of her former abuse of Darcy, renews her misgivings:

> Her father had most cruelly mortified her by what he said of Mr Darcy's indifference; and she could do nothing but wonder at such a want of penetration, or fear that, perhaps, instead of his seeing too *little,* she might have fancied too *much.*

But the lovers meet, and it does not take long for two such intelligent and sensitive persons to make sure that pride and prejudice are at length beaten. Baker writes in *The History of the English Novel,* "They have, however, not yet done with the irony that has dogged them from the beginning. They still have to explain themselves to their sceptical friends and relation. The reader has learned to look out for irony in every twist of the story, and particularly in the speeches, many of which have had to be unsaid by the speakers, or wished unsaid, not least by Elizabeth. It penetrates the whole structure of the novel" (87-88).

Mary Lascelles observes in *Jane Austen and Her Art*: "*Pride and Prejudice* is...deliberately shaped; its pattern shows...delight in the symmetry of correspondence and antithesis;... This pattern is formed by diverging and converging lines, by the movement of two people who are impelled apart until they reach a climax of mutual hostility, and thereafter bend their courses towards mutual understanding and amity. It is a pattern very common in fiction, but by no means easy to describe plausibly" (160). Austen has employed a complex plot in the novel. There are five stories evolving concurrently in the novel. The main plot concerns itself with the love of Elizabeth and Darcy, and, as a foil to the main plot, is the secondary plot involving Jane and Bingley. The next two sub-plots relate the stories of Lydia and Wickham, and Charlotte and Collins. The novelist provides a fifth pair and Mr and Mrs Bennet comprise the fifth pair. If the Elizabeth-Darcy episode is told with surface romanticism and if the Jane-Bingley story is purely romantic, the Wickham-Lydia and Charlotte-Collins episodes are romantically and realistically treated with rather grim or unhappy implications. The Bennets implicitly emphasize the consequence of indiscretion in choosing marriage partner. The resolution starts as Elizabeth and Darcy meet at the Pemberly house, with her changed attitude towards Darcy and Lydia's elopement with Wickham. The denouement is reached through the marriage of Lydia and Wickham as a result of Darcy's cordial endeavour, Elizabeth's affection for Darcy and acceptance of his proposal, and Jane's marriage with Bingley. The marriage of Elizabeth and Darcy is a possible solution of the plot. It is observable how skilfully Wickham's rascality is made the chief agency in the reconciliation of Elizabeth and Darcy, providing a signal occasion for Darcy's magnanimity to transpire. It is notable how the pompous stupidity of Mr Collins's proposal to Elizabeth, the crowning example in fiction of pertinacious and unacceptable addresses, softens by contrast the infatuated assurance of Darcy's, which speedily follows. Jane Austen herself pauses to count the nails which Miss Bingley hammers into her own coffin when she teases Elizabeth, in Darcy's presence, about the departure of the officers, including Wickham, little aware of the pain she is inflicting by reminding him of Wickham's nearly successful attempt to run off with his sister Georgiana. It is Darcy, his solemnity gone now that he is an accepted lover, who points out the irony of his aunt's intervention; "Lady Catherine has been of infinite use, which ought to make her happy, for she loves to be of use." Elizabeth, with her formidable wit, can hold her own with anyone; she can also be humorous about herself, as when she answers Jane's inquiry when she first found out that she loved Darcy, "It has been coming on so gradually, that I hardly know when it began; but"—and this is only half raillery—"I believe I must date it from my first seeing his beautiful grounds at Pemberley."

The structure of *Pride and Prejudice* is so clearly articulated and cleverly played against *conventional* expectations about love stories that at least two strange and original effects are taken in by any reader without the least difficulty: first, the dynamics of love is based on initial disconcertment, dislike and embarrassment instead of the commonplace melting moods, so that obstacles are psychological and internal, not a matter of external bars—bars, by the way, which are later parodied in the ineffectuality of the would-be tyranny of Lady Catherine de Bourgh. In this way, Jane Austen dramatises a deep insight *vis-a-vis* the genesis of passion by showing it as an emotional disturbance or a nagging disquiet which can first of all be interpreted by its subject as prickling hostility. We are likely to infer that Elizabeth probably loves Mr Darcy, so suitable really, from the start. Second, the relatively simple question of who loves whom is settled almost exactly two-thirds of the way through so that, the rest can be devoted to a comical dramatic analysis of notions of proper dignity; and a demonstration that the *justification* of rank may be through decent conduct—both of which are much more amusing and interesting. One can remember here what Somerset Maugham comments in his essay "Pride and Prejudice": "*Pride and Prejudice* seems to me a very well-constructed book. The incidents follow one another very naturally and one's sense of probability is nowhere outraged. It is, perhaps, odd that Elizabeth and Jane should be so well-bred and well-behaved, whereas their mother and three younger sisters should be so ordinary; but that this should be so was essential to the story Miss Austen had to tell" (Littlewood I: 463-64).

(III) THEME OF MONEY AND MARRIAGE

J.F.G. Gornall writes in "Marriage and Property in Jane Austen's Novels": "Jane Austen's novels describe the social life of the English landed gentry at the turn of the eighteenth century from the point of view of a number of young women in their late teens, or early twenties, who are trying to find a husband. Many of the problems they encounter arise from the fact that marriage, at that time and in that class, was not only a matter of mutual affection and social compatibility, but also an institution through which the landed gentry maintained and increased its financial position" (Littlewood II: 46). Gornall further writes: "The landed gentry and peerage in 1790 comprised about 25,000 families, whose livelihood depended chiefly on the ownership of land. The average yearly income of the great landowners (about 400 families) was £10,000. 4,000 to 5,000 families received £1,000 to £5,000 a year, and the remainder less. Jane Austen's families fall, on the whole, into the upper and middle income groups, but exclude the peerage and the wealthiest landed gentry" (Littlewood II: 46). The richest landowner whose precise income is given is Mr Rushworth in *Mansfield Park,* who had £12,000 a year, the poorest is Willoughby in *Sense and Sensibility,* with only £600 to £700. An idea of what was considered a reasonable income in the class Jane Austen wrote about can be gathered from Marianne's remarks in *Sense and Sensibility*:

> £2,000 a year is a very moderate income. A family cannot well be maintained on a smaller.... A proper establishment of servants, a carriage, perhaps two, and hunters, cannot be supported on less.

£2,000 to £4,000 a year is probably the average income of the principal landed families in the novels.

People with incomes from sources other than land are, of course, mentioned. Admiral Croft in *Persuasion* had made a fortune by the capture of prizes. In *Pride and Prejudice,* Mr Bingley's fortune of £4,000 to £5,000 a year had been made in trade, and lawyers and clergymen are also well represented. But the landed gentry are the focus of interest. It is their characteristics that set the stage. Trade, in which there was plenty of money to be made, was regarded by the upper and middle ranks of the landed gentry with the utmost horror. 'I am a gentleman's daughter...' says Elizabeth Bennet to Lady

Catherine de Bourgh. "True," is the reply, "You *are* a gentleman's daughter. But who was your mother? Who are your uncles and aunts? Do not imagine me ignorant of their condition." Elizabeth's mother was the daughter of a lawyer, and lawyers, unless members of the bar, were more or less in the same category as traders. One uncle had succeeded him in the business, and the other was in trade. Her father was a gentleman because he derived his income from the ownership of land. Many instances could be given from all the novels of this attitude towards trade, but there were, nevertheless, two connecting links between the landed gentry and the commercial interest. A wealthy trader could purchase an estate—as Mr Bingley's father had hoped to do—and his daughters might, and frequently did, marry into the landed interest; but the sons of the upper and middle ranks of the landed gentry rarely engaged in trade and the daughters would not normally marry into it. Gornall writes, "The establishment of younger sons, then, whether in the church or the other professions, necessitated a considerable financial outlay from the family estate. The amount of this outlay depended on the terms of the marriage settlement, which, in addition to prescribing the amount of the wife's jointure, also laid down what was to be provided for maintaining or at least launching, younger sons. This amount like the jointure depended, not only on the annual value of the husband's estate, but also on the amount of the portion contributed by the wife. Apart from this and such income as they could get from the limited employment considered open to them, younger sons could hardly improve their financial position except by marriage" (Littlewood II: 49). "Younger sons cannot marry where they like," says Colonel Fitzwilliam to Elizabeth Bennet. "...Our habits of expense make us too dependent."

Gornall writes, "The position of the daughters was governed by a third important convention—the marriage position. There was, of course, no question of their earning anything; but a portion was intended not so much to give financial independence as to enable them to make a suitable marriage. The novels contain a great deal of information about the size of the portion, which was usually fixed in the marriage settlement of the girl's parents" (Littlewood II: 49). The highest mentioned is that of Miss Gray in *Sense and Sensibility* who had £50,000. Some had much less than this; Mr Bennet's daughters had only £1,000 each. Gornall observes:

> It might be thought that a class of people who regarded marriage as a matter of arranging an equal alliance between families could not at the same time also see it as a romantic encounter between two individuals. This is not so. Jane Austen's novels are concerned quite as much with romance as with settlements. It is clear that both aspects of marriage had an equally strong grip on the mind, and often the result was conflict. (Littlewood II: 50)

Sometimes the conflict between the two aspects of marriage becomes explicit. Darcy, who knows that marriage with Elizabeth Bennet would be an unequal alliance from his point of view, takes a long time to make up his mind, but eventually comes down on the side of romance: "In vain have I struggled. It will not do. My feelings will not be repressed." Elizabeth's sister, who thinks she is marrying Darcy only for his money, says to her: "Oh, Lizzy, do anything rather than marry without affection. Are you quite sure that you feel what you ought to do?" Mr Bennet—parents were not necessarily always on the side of the settlements—is equally worried: "I know your disposition, Lizzy. I know that you could be neither happy nor respectable, unless you truly esteemed your husband.... My child, let me not have the grief of seeing you unable to respect your partner in life. You know not what you are about." Charlotte Lucas is a woman who has reached an age—twenty-seven—that has dimmed her marital chances. Charlotte Lucas, the daughter of Sir William and Lady Lucas, is seven years older than Elizabeth and they are good friends. Charlotte Lucas is sensible and intelligent and completely conscious of her modest fortune and plain appearance. She knows well about her getting old and also about her social and economic insecurity. She feels that happiness in marriage is 'entirely a matter of chance', and that however well husband

and wife know one another at the beginning they are bound to 'grow sufficiently unlike afterwards to have their share of vexation.' That being the case, it is "better to know as little as possible of defects of the person with whom you are to pass your life" (*PP* 23). Elizabeth Bennet's response is to say: "You make me laugh, Charlotte; but it is not sound. You know it is not sound, and that you would never act in this way yourself" (*PP* 23). But she acts exactly in that way. With such a view of marriage she is prepared—unflinchingly ready—for Mr Collins. The hard reality is that she is motivated by a "pure and disinterested desire of an establishment..." (*PP* 122). Gornall writes, "...by reading between the lines of Jane Austen's novels, it is possible to understand how the English landed gentry of the late eighteenth century managed to fit together the two components of marriage in their day—equal alliance and mutual affection. The sanctions were the need for parental consent and the threat of elopement; but freedom of selection and the secret engagement provided a method of compromise" (Littlewood II: 52).

The theme and tone of the novel are set by the famous opening sentence: "It is a truth universally acknowledged, that a single man in possession of a good fortune, must be in want of a wife." In a way characteristic of a stylist of ironic nuances, the mock philosophical solemnity of the first clause is immediately deflated by a notion of marriage appropriate to high comedy. Further, while that opening sentence applies directly to the subject of the first chapter, the arrival in the neighbourhood of a very eligible bachelor, this novel, like all the others, starts from a more comprehensive and more valid truth, that every young woman, with or without a fortune, is in want of a husband. Thus, the initial generality is completely reversed by the second sentence, which affirms that a new arrival is considered by alert mothers "as the rightful property of some one or other of their daughters." Then, through the talk of one ill-mated couple, the goal is set up for their progeny. At the same time, we are made aware of the genteel, gossipy families, which make up local society and the competitive marriage market. The short chapter ends with a short paragraph which crisply defines the characters and minds of Mr and Mrs Bennet; it underlines what dialogue had already revealed.

In the first three quarters of *Pride and Prejudice,* money is mentioned only twice, both in incidental ways: in the first, Lydia borrows money from Jane and Elizabeth to "treat her sisters to lunch at the Meryton inn" (*PP* 219); in the second, the Gardiners pay their bill at another inn when they are suddenly recalled to Longbourne *(PP* 281). As soon as the narrative reveals that Wickham has eloped with Lydia, however, the subject of money virtually explodes into the text, and references to it quickly amass the coherence of a full-fledged plot. Even after it makes its presence known, however, this money plot initially unfolds away from the narrative we read, for the events it includes all occur in places that Elizabeth does not occupy. Thus, because Lydia has been allowed to follow the militia to Brighton and Elizabeth is travelling with the Gardiners, Elizabeth first hears about her sister's elopement through a letter from Jane, who has stayed behind in London. This same letter also reveals that Colonel Forster fears that Wickham might have no intention of marrying Lydia (*PP* 273). Finally, when Elizabeth's father and Mr Gardiner go to London, they discover (and then report) that Wickham is deep in debt and that he now demands money to marry Lydia. Thus, the subject of money erupts into the domestic plot through a mode of narration that calls attention to its status as representation (the letters) but it does so because of a role it has long played in an unwarranted, but profoundly consequential, money plot: all the while that he was flirting with Elizabeth and Lydia, Wickham was incurring bills he could not pay.

Poovey writes: "What we are seeing here is a narrative that embeds its allusions to real situations in a complex system that simultaneously invokes these situations and manages their effects—both in the narrative and, as a consequence, for the reader. Thus, we have seen two of the forms this management takes: the foreclosure of reference, which is clearest in the military allusions; and direction of the reader's attention, which is achieved by controlling access to various plots and the information they contain. This last dynamic foregrounds the mediation that representation performs, both as a theme in the novel and, through the embedded letters, as a distinctive mode of narration. In *Pride and Prejudice*, the reader can experience the real threat that war and family debt might have posed for a young woman like Elizabeth only by—and through the buffer of—an imaginative engagement with the novel's domestic romance. As my description suggests, this narrative management operates within the textual system at the same time that it polices its borders" (*A Companion to Jane Austen* 253).

Thus, for the first three quarters of the novel, the narrative's focus on the domestic plot blocks the reader's access to the money plot; as it does, it implicitly discourages a literal reading of the novel's events and actively modulates the reader's response to the danger an actual lack of money would have posed. Over the course of the narrative, she gradually recasts or translates the money plot's primary terms into another set of terms that promise comfort instead of posing a threat. Thus, Austen transforms the fiscal jeopardy the Bennet girls face into a romantic threat, which, while potentially emotionally painful, can be solved within the domestic plot. Bringing the money plot out from under the romantic plot inaugurates this transformation, for only after events that are initially kept in the background of the narrative system become the primary strand of narration can Austen begin to rework their terms.

This reworking begins when it becomes obvious that Lydia poses a financial threat to her family. Initially, the amount Wickham demands seems like a sum the Bennets can manage: a settlement of the girl's share of the 5,000 pounds she is to receive upon her parents' death and 100 pounds a year for her father's lifetime (*PP* 302). But Mr Bennet immediately realizes that this cannot be correct, and, in a conversation between Mr Bennet and his oldest daughters, the magnitude of the danger suddenly becomes clear. "There are two things that I want very much to know," Mr Bennet tells Jane and Elizabeth in his characteristically laconic way: "one is, how much money your uncle has laid down, to bring it about; and the other, how I am ever to pay him" (*PP* 304). His daughters' shock forces their father to be more explicit. "'Money! my uncle!' cried Jane, 'What do you mean, Sir?'" When Mr Bennet speculates that 10,000 pounds is probably Wickham's real asking price, one of the girls bursts out again: "Ten thousand pounds! Heaven forbid! How is half such a sum to be repaid?" (*PP* 304). At this point, the narrative foregrounds the monetary issues that, within the narrative system, have always underwritten the domestic plot and also lays out the monetary arrangements that will dictate the future: the narrator informs us that Mr Bennet never saved any money; Mr Bennet says he will not advance money for Lydia's wedding clothes; Mr Gardiner uncovers exactly how much Wickham owes; and we find out that Wickham ran away with Lydia only because he was trying to evade his creditors.

The most important revelation about money, however, does not appear in these scenes, but in another letter, which begins to neutralize the twin threats of poverty and disgrace, the money plot introduces. In this letter, Mrs Gardiner informs Elizabeth that Darcy, not her uncle, paid off Wickham's debts. Instead of wondering how much money Darcy paid, Elizabeth's first response is to imagine that he has done this for her. Only after she has indulged this fantasy does she realize that the obligation the Bennets have thus incurred can never be repaid in kind. Soon, Mr Bennet makes it clear that if Mr Gardiner had paid Wickham, the "obligation" would have been financial and the "return" would have had to be cash. Since Darcy has paid the money, however, this particular obligation has been dissolved.

> And so, Darcy did every thing; made up the match, gave the money, paid the fellow's debts, and got him his commission! So much the better. It will save me a world of trouble and economy. Had it been your uncle's doing, I must and *would* have paid him; but these violent young lovers carry every thing their own way. I shall offer to pay him tomorrow; he will rant and storm

> about his love for you, and there will be an end of the matter. (*PP* 377)

As this passage makes clear, Darcy's actions neutralize the threat that a monetary obligation would have posed to the Bennets by translating debt into a gift of love. Even before Mr Bennet makes this explicit, in fact, Darcy has already alluded to this translation by rebuffing Elizabeth's attempt to thank him on behalf of her family. "Your *family* owe me nothing," he says to Elizabeth in the scene in which she expresses this gratitude. "Much as I respect them, I believe, I thought only of *you*" (*PP* 366). Once Elizabeth says she will marry Darcy, he completes this translation by saying that he "owes" her for the rebuke she has given his pride (*PP* 369). Thus, by marrying Darcy, Elizabeth is able to "repay" him—not in money, but in love. And by making the money plot first disrupt, then be absorbed by, the domestic plot, Austen translates a monetary debt into mutual love.

Poovey writes, "In the narrative system that is *Pride and Prejudice*, these translations—the transformation of a financial payment into the bestowal of a gift, then the conversion of the gift into love—address and symbolically resolve the threat that the money plot posed to its romance counterpart. This resolution culminates when the money plot is banished from the novel, as the romantic relationships the narrative has long followed conclude successfully in marriages. The event that initiates this resolution is actually not Darcy's decision to help Wickham but Elizabeth's change of heart about Darcy, for,... he acts in order to respond to or communicate with her. Elizabeth begins to change her mind because of a series of portraits of Darcy: the letter Darcy writes to explain his relationship with Wickham, then two images of the gentleman that Elizabeth encounters at Pemberley. The letter inaugurates the change, but it is not until she arrives at his family estate, hears the admiring servant's praise of Darcy, and then sees the portrait that hangs in Pemberley's gallery that Elizabeth realizes she has been wrong. At this point, Elizabeth knows that she would now accept Darcy if he were to offer again, and, for the first time, she imagines the fantastic scenario to which the narrative is leading: marriage with Darcy and herself as mistress of Pemberley" (*A Companion to Jane Austen* 255).

If Lilian Robinson writes in "Why Marry Mr Collins?" in *Sex, Class and Culture* that the "great subjects" of *Pride and Prejudice* are "class, love, money and marriage" (179), the producer of the successful BBC television version of the novel first shown in 1995 declares too that "though it's about many things, it principally about sex, and it's about money: those are the driving motives of the plot" (Birtwistle, *The Making of Pride and Prejudice* v). *Pride and Prejudice* has a connected and coherent narrative with a beginning, a middle, and an end. The novel begins in the right place, with the arrival on the scene of the two young men whose love for Elizabeth and her sister Jane is the main theme of the novel, and it ends in the right place with their marriage. It is the traditional happy ending. The relationships of Elizabeth and Darcy, Jane and Bingley, Charlotte and Collins, and Lydia and Wickham, develop the theme of money and marriage, with its social and economic implications. Through the marriages the theme of the importance of money in marriage is revealed and the moral penchant of the novelist is also given a focus. One can cite also the words on the theme of money and marriage from the unfinished sketch of Austen's novel, *The Watsons,* to refer to her attitude to marriage:

> To be so bent on marriage—to pursue a man merely for the sake of situations—is a sort of thing that shocks me! I cannot understand it. Poverty is a great evil, but, to a woman of education and feeling, it ought not, it cannot be the greatest—I would rather be a teacher at a school, than marry a man I did not love.

(IV) NARROW WORLD/SOCIETY/MANNERS

The novel as a literary form, broadened out in Scott's hands, to mirror a whole roaring world, great events, and crowds on the march. In Jane Austen's delicate hands it becomes a miniature, 'on which I work with so fine a brush as produces little effect after much labour.' When Scott built up his world he laid hands on almost everything but the tea-tables;

and it was out of tea-tables and other domestic oddments that Jane Austen created her own little world. It was the one she knew intimately, and so she chose quite deliberately to remain in it. J.B. Priestly observes in "On Jane Austen," "She banished from it nine-tenths of life, and gave us people who never work or fight or die, or starve or go crazy, a world in which a shower of rain is an event, in which there are no wars nor politics nor commerce nor furious passions nor violent deaths. This she had to do in order that her delicate and subtle comedy might be played in peace. She made all her characters cosy and comfortable in order that they might feel at home, and talk away and thus display themselves to us. What she asks us to observe are the little egotisms and absurdities of this life, and she knew very well that we should care nothing about such things unless we met them in an atmosphere of leisure and comfort and security, round a tea-table and not a camp-fire or a death-bed. She creates fiction out of material that might easily be the substance of a correspondence between two ladies living in the most retired parts of the country" (Littlewood I: 451). Jane Austen's societies are restricted in their class composition, though the vague fringe suggests mobility, upwards and downwards. The societies portrayed are neither small, nor enclosed, nor static. Jane Austen's imagination could not have been confined to a few families in a village, but demands the material of social changes and renewals. Warren Roberts observes in *Jane Austen and the French Revolution*: "Improvement was a theme in *Sense and Sensibility* and *Pride and Prejudice*, and indeed in much of the literature of the seventeenth and eighteenth centuries" (53).

Warren Roberts observes in *Jane Austen and the French Revolution*: "*Pride and Prejudice* is a very different matter. Austen's social ideas are worked out in this novel with a richness and complexity that was strikingly new, setting it apart from its predecessor. A conservative argument was sustained so successfully and positively and was so organic to the story as to make one wonder if ideological underpinnings were there from the beginning. I do not believe this was the case, but that in 'First Impressions' Austen happened to have an ideal vehicle for developing a Burkean social argument. The pride and prejudice theme, undoubtedly present in 'First Impressions', lent itself to a completely different type of development than the sense and sensibility theme, this time the polarities could be tested against one another and a synthesis between them achieved in a way that was no longer merely personal, but social as well. On the personal level, the errors of the hero and heroine were exposed; one was prideful, the other prejudiced. But then Darcy's pride was shown to have a positive side, and the inadequacy of Elizabeth's outlook and judgment was revealed. Once she recognized her mistaken view and saw him in a truer light the doors swung open for the inevitable romantic ending" (Roberts 47). It was in the way that Austen shows how mistaken first impressions were that neither Darcy nor Elizabeth were exactly as they seemed; it was also how Austen invests the story with a different level of meaning adding a new dimension. As Alistair Duckworth has beautifully shown, Darcy became a Burkean figure. As if looking down at Elizabeth, with a smile that she recognized, Darcy is part of a family tradition and he connects, through his ancestors, to the very building and grounds of Premberley; he is part of a continuity that was architectural, familial and social. His concern for Pemberly transcends his interest in its operation, as seen in his regarding himself as a trustee who was not the 'entire master,' but the 'life-renter' of the estate—a nice Burkean conception, as Duckworth points out, just as he also notes that Darcy had a Burkean regard for his ancestors. The estate, then, was something to be carefully and well managed, and also to be handed down from generation to generation. It was also something to be improved, which Elizabeth, perhaps paradoxically, could help bring about. Precisely because she came from a different social stratum than Darcy and belonged to a family line that was running out, she was all the more capable of appreciating the tradition of Darcy's family and helping to maintain it. Darcy stood for permanence, while Elizabeth represented an energy that could translate into improvement. Through marriage the two were synthesized.

As represented by Darcy, the aristocracy is not a closed caste, but open to infusions of life from below. Not only did he marry down in the social sense, but also related easily and successfully to people of different classes than his own. When Elizabeth imagined herself as mistress of Pemberley during her first visit, and wondered if she hadn't made a mistake in rejecting Darcy's proposal, she thought of her aunt and uncle, the Gardiners, and 'recollecting herself' decided that she had made the right decision. "My aunt and uncle would have been lost to me: I should not have been allowed to invite them" (*PP* 246). When Darcy appeared unexpectedly he was friendly and thoughtful to Elizabeth's aunt and uncle, offering Mr Gardiner the use of his stream any time he might choose, along with his own fishing tackle. Only knowing what Elizabeth had told them about Darcy they were surprised at such generosity, and wondered afterwards if he had been serious in the offer. In fact, he had been, partly because they were Elizabeth's aunt and uncle but also because he was polite and found them nice and agreeable people. That Mr Gardiner was a lawyer from London certainly did not prejudice Darcy; pride he certainly did have, but not the type that made him disdainful of those beneath him socially. We read in the final paragraph of *Pride and Prejudice* that with the Gardeners' Darcy and Elizabeth alike "were always on the most intimate terms" (*PP* 388). As Duckworth has said, "the three classes of (Austen's) fictional world—nobility, gentry, and trade—come together finally in the park at Pemberley" (quoted in Roberts 50).

"The worlds of *Sense and Sensibility* and *Pride and Prejudice* were basically stable, undoubtedly reflecting Austen's social awareness in the 1790s, when she wrote the early versions of these novels.... In *Pride and Prejudice* there are signs of social strain, as seen in phrases like 'such times as these.' I think that language of this type was an interpolation, used by Austen when she made the revisions of 1811-12, to dramatise and give urgency to her Burkean argument. The two estates in this novel, Longbourn and Pemberley, were not unsound. It was true that Mr Bennet did not manage

Longbourn, but one of the reasons was the absence of a male heir. The problems that were attached to this estate did not derive from internal weakness, but from the legal consequences of having only daughters. And Pemberley, as we have seen, was well and responsibly managed" (Roberts 52). Roberts further says, "In *Pride and Prejudice* there was a synthesis of different elements through Elizabeth's and Darcy's marriage, thereby infusing new energy into the social body. This happened in a way that was normal in the old, traditional and stable society. New families had long married into old families, and Elizabeth's marriage to Darcy was consistent with that pattern" (52). Austen maintains the same outward silence toward England's military struggle with France as toward the great political events of the day. Aside from a few passing references to military service, the novels contain no descriptions of a war that lasted, with one brief period of relief, from 1793 to 1815. Commenting ironically on *Pride and Prejudice,* Austen said it needed 'to be stretched out here and there' with a serious chapter or perhaps something unconnected with the story, such as one on 'the history of Buonaparte' (*Letter* 199-300). This was what other novelists had done, and it was precisely what she decided not to do, having chosen to limit her setting to the English country village. Roberts observes: "Austen's decision not to discuss the war was completely consistent with her view of herself as a novelist, and it was an artistic decision. And yet, it might have been more than that. Her letters are as free of military news as her novels are of passages describing the war. Given this paucity it might appear that living in the rural quiet of southern England Austen was sufficiently removed from the war that she hardly felt its impact. Another possibility is that as a creature of her sex and social station she so occupied herself with daily rituals, ceremonies and trivialities that she simply did not care about the war" (68). There are no direct references to the war in *Pride and Prejudice,* but there is an important area of allusion and innuendo that does relate to England's wartime experience. We have seen that during the eighteenth century there was a definite animus against standing army, and that 'No barracks' was a common cry. The soldiers who became part of a vastly larger wartime army after 1793, and were billeted most heavily in southern England, made their presence felt in *Pride and Prejudice.* Austen did not raise the old cry of 'No barracks' or declaim against the large army on English soil, but the soldiers stationed at Meryton did turn the eyes of susceptible young ladies in the Netherfield drawing room. Catherine and Lydia collected gossip about the nearby Militia, learning that several officers had dined with their uncle, and that Colonel Forster might be married. Having a romance with an officer was what they hoped for, as became clear when Lydia devised the scheme to vacation at Brighton so she could follow Wickham's regiment, which was being transferred to a camp close to that resort town. Elizabeth's *response,* when she heard of the scheme, is interesting: "Good Heaven! Brighton, and a whole campful of soldiers, to us, who have been overset already by one poor regiment of militia..." (*PP* 220). Her fears were well grounded: the menace that she associated with the army camp was only too real as events soon proved. The trip to Brighton created a sense of impending disaster, which clearly connected to the army camp. And it would seem that Elizabeth's fears were partly based on past experience, as she had already seen Meryton 'overset' by soldiers and had learned of their ways in chance meetings and monthly balls. So Austen did not protest against the billeting of soldiers among the civilian population, but she did show what could happen as a result. The innuendo builds slowly, until by the time Elizabeth's sisters and mother go to Brighton there is little question that something will go wrong, something connected with the army camp.

Pride and Prejudice begins in the village of Longbourn, near the small town of Meryton in Hertfordshire, then to London, on the way to Hunsford near Westerham in Kent, back to Longbourn, because of events taking place in Brighton and London, then to Derbyshire and home again. Public gatherings give Jane Austen an opportunity to begin, retard, and confuse the development of love, to satirize social manners and morals, and to analyse the interactions of group roles and relationships. She seems to balance an interest in depth and surface, manners and character, or structure and ethics, so evenly that it is hard to say which concern is primary. The novelist only shows social groups through the individuality of event and characters, but such individual life establishes general social truths. Jane Austen's constant request that her characters should know their own feelings makes plain her preoccupation with the human heart.

The stories turn on social limit and social change, so the groups which carry on the business of introductions and interchanges reflect intimacy and novelty. Rituals often seem to be designed or developed in order to combine the two. It is in public that Jane Austen's men and women have to get to know each other, and have to endure the hazards and inconveniences of social encounters. Public life is rough and smooth, rude and polite. It may be too polite for intimacy to flourish quickly, as Charlotte Lucas points out in one of those individually voiced opinions which can both hide and discover the author's judgement. In her prudent, matter-of-fact and expert manner, she points out the need for women to snatch every opportunity offered by dinner-parties, balls, round-games, or cards: "But though Bingley and Jane meet tolerably often, it is never for many hours together; and as they always see each other in large mixed parties, it is impossible that every moment should be employed in conversing together. Jane should therefore make the most of every half hour in which she can command his attention" (*PP* 22).

Jane Austen's satire on vulgarity and mercenariness is not restricted to the social climbers. The have-nots may be greedy, but the haves behave as if they were have-nots. The aristocrats are criticized strongly, both in the dullness of the Dalrymples in *Persuasion* and the offensiveness of Lady Cathernine de Bourgh in *Pride and Prejudice.* Darcy's disdain has to be turned against his own aunt, as well as against Elizabeth's mother, as she too shows off, flatters and domineers. Lady Cathernine's loudness is beautifully audible in the drawing room at Rosings, where it is encouraged by her sycophants. Decorum is fragile and easily broken. The hearts and minds of the characters are implicitly shown in the broad comedy of manners, and the serious characters are involved in a complex social response, which the novelist does not explicitly analyse. As Elizabeth is enjoying herself in conversation with Colonel Fitzwilliam, who is talking so agreeably 'of Kent and Hertfordshire, of travelling and staying at home, of new books and music' that she is better entertained than she has ever been 'in that room before,' her hostess is jealous and curious of the unusual 'spirit and flow.' So is Darcy. He just looks curious, but his aunt does 'not scruple to call out' with aristocratic bullying brashness:

> "What is that you are saying, Fitzwilliam? What is it you are talking of? What are you telling Miss Bennet? Let me hear what it is." "We are speaking of music, Madam," said he, when no longer able to avoid a reply. "Of music! Then pray speak aloud. It is of all subjects my delight. I must have my share in the conversation, if you are speaking of music. There are few people in England, I suppose, who have more true enjoyment of music than myself, or a better natural taste. If I had ever learnt, I should have been a great proficient. And so would Anne, if her health had allowed her to apply. I am confident that she would have performed delightfully." (*PP* 173)

The social collision continues, with Lady Catherine snubbing Elizabeth:

> I have told Miss Bennet several times, that she will never play really well, unless she practises more; and though Mrs Collins has no instrument, she is very welcome, as I have often told her, to come to Rosings every day, and play on the piano forte in Mrs Jenkinson's room. She would be in nobody's way, you know, in that part of the house.' Mr Darcy looked a little ashamed of his aunt's ill breeding, and made no answer. (*PP* 173)

Mind and sensibility are discriminated, and social leadership comically displayed. Elizabeth and Darcy talk about musical diffidence as an emblem of social diffidence, to be interrupted by the rude demands and commands of the hostess, which Elizabeth neatly foils by returning to the piano. Lady

Catherine repeats her inane flattery of Anne, who "would have been a delightful performer, had her health allowed her to learn," Darcy neither replies nor shows any response, and Elizabeth receives the unqualified 'instructions on execution and taste' with 'all the forbearance of civility.' The clash of manners and minds is carefully patterned. Once more the group is given a central subject, that of music. This time we have no rise into unbearable conflict, because only one person is behaving badly, and the courtesy of the others makes its own quiet rebuke and preserves the polite surface of the evening. Not until Lady Catherine actually enters Longbourn, to offend as a guest just as she has offended as a host, and threatens Elizabeth's personal life, it does not become necessary to breach decorum and make the elementary intellectual effort to defeat her. The release of this later conflict in the shrubbery owes something to the tension and control of the earlier scenes at Rosings. The local scenes make it clear that decorum and courtesy are expensively bought, and we are not surprised when the novel comes to show that the payments cannot be kept up. Barbara Hardy observes in *A Reading of Jane Austen*: "Domination and submission, flattery and condescension, rudeness and decorum give symmetry to many groups. The comic criticism of class and rank is crossed and controlled by a sense of character. If we are in danger of supposing that Mrs Bennet's bad manners are accounted for by her low origin, we see Lady Catherine's even greater offensiveness. If we are in danger of feeling too sharply Elizabeth's social shame at her parents' behaviour, we see Darcy put through the same experience. If we come to criticize Darcy's diffidence, we see its advantage over his aunt's assertiveness. In a novel where pride is a conspicuous theme, the social groups frequently illustrate its forms and functions" (126-27).

Pride and Prejudice ends with good-tempered tolerance and reconciliation. Jane Austen expressly disclaims revolutions and conversions. Things are a little improved in the Bennet household, Mr Bennet is drawn to Pemberley, informally, 'when he was least expected,' Catherine and Mary improve, for convincingly practical reasons. The characters of Wickham and

Lydia 'suffer no revolution,' remain within the orbit of the Darcy and Bingley aid, generally at a convenient distance. We can imagine the unmiraculous reconciliations with Miss Bingley, paying off 'every arrear of civility to Elizabeth' and being 'almost' as attentive to Darcy as before, and Lady Catherine de Bourgh descending to test the conduct of Mrs Darcy and inspect the pollution of Pemberley. Threats are banished, and when Bingley buys an estate within thirty miles of Pemberley, there is stability and civilization in a small company of friends. Jane Austen's last sentence quietens any discomfort at the admission of Lady Catherine, the banishment of the Wickhams, and the apparent neglect of Mrs Bennet. This harmony is nice but not proud: "With the Gardiners, they were always on the most intimate terms. Darcy, as well as Elizabeth, really loved them; and they were both ever sensible of the warmest gratitude towards the persons who, by bringing her into Derbyshire, had been the means of uniting them" (*PP* 388). The novel ends with a deliberated and impartial gesture to social tact.

Pemberley echoes the worthiness of Squire Allworthy's (*Tom Jones*) seat. Its beauties and prospects are seen through Elizabeth's eyes. The houses in *Pride and Prejudice* are nearly all taken for granted by the author because they are taken for granted by the characters, though environment is given some character by objects and habits. As soon as the characters visit a new place, it is put before the reader. Elizabeth visits Charlotte Collins's new house and is immediately shown round. Mr Collins is a minute guide, self-gratified by possessions, liking to show Elizabeth what she has missed, fishing for praise, and inclined to unselective enumeration:

> After sitting long enough to admire every article of furniture in the room, from the sideboard to the fender, to give an account of their journey and of all that had happened in London, Mr Collins invited them to take a stroll in the garden, which was large and well laid out, and to the cultivation of which he attended himself. To work in his garden was one of his most respectable pleasures; and Elizabeth admired the command of

> countenance with which Charlotte talked of the healthfulness of the exercise, and owned she encouraged it as much as possible. Here, leading the way through every walk and cross walk, and scarcely allowing them an interval to utter the praises he asked for, every view was pointed out with a minuteness which left beauty entirely behind. He could number the fields in every direction, and could tell how many trees there were in the most distant clump. (*PP* 156)

He is the perfect cicerone for the visit to Rosings, and sense is submerged in his anxiety to put the other guests at their ease: "I would advise you merely to put on whatever of your clothes is superior to the rest, there is no occasion for any thing more." His way with things reflects Lady Catherine's more rational superiority: "Lady Catherine will not think the worse of you for being simply dressed. She likes to have the distinction of rank preserved." Rosings is introduced and described through Mr Collins's eyes, voice and values, enumerating 'the windows in front of the house' and relating 'what the glazing altogether had originally cost Sir Lewis de Bourgh.' The owner of Rosings resembles General Tilney in her appreciation of her guest's appreciation. She patronizes through servants, plate and food, especially delighted 'when any dish on the table proved a novelty.' Every object in the drama of Lady Catherine's hospitality, including the fish used in the game of casino and the piano which she offers for Elizabeth's use, is a comic counter in the game of demand-and-supply which she plays so happily, best of all with Mr Collins, who is just the guest the hostess requires. In Mr Collins, Austen depicts a clergyman whose "good opinion of himself, of his authority as a clergyman, and his rights as a rector, made him altogether a mixture of pride and obsequiousness, self-importance and humility" (*PP* 70). A comic figure, his cowing to his patroness in one moment and assuming pious airs in the next makes him an object of ridicule. Here is a clergyman to be laughed at.

When Elizabeth comes to Pemberley, we not only see it through her eyes, but against the background of the visit to Rosings. Jane Austen manipulates those contrasts and parallels through the characters' sensibility. The plentiful and refreshing luncheon, elegantly presented, 'beautiful pyramids of grapes, nectarines, and peaches,' and even the diffident and shy hospitality of Georgiana Darcy, are contrasted with the ostentation of Rosings. The handsome house is a sympathetic habitat in every way. Its saloon has a northern aspect which is cool in summer. Jane Austen is always attentive to temperature—and the sense of space is neither intimidating nor lofty. Like Allworthy's house, it partakes of the handsomeness and honesty of its owner:

> It was a large, handsome, stone building, standing well on rising ground, and backed by a ridge of high woody hills;—and in front, a stream of some natural importance was swelled into greater, but without any artificial appearance. Its banks were neither formal, nor falsely adorned. Elizabeth was delighted. She had never seen a place for which nature had done more, or where natural beauty had been so little counteracted by an awkward taste. (*PP* 245)

Jane Austen makes her heroine appreciate the quality of the furnishings too, as 'suitable to the fortune of their proprietor' and his taste, 'neither gaudy nor uselessly fine,' as she makes the contrast with Rosings. But Jane Austen does not make Elizabeth aware only of Darcy's property and taste. She responds also to a less definable quality in the atmosphere of the house, suggested by the variety and spaciousness. As Elizabeth goes over Pemberley, there is a sense of movement and exhilaration:

> Every disposition of the ground was good; and she looked on the whole scene, the river, the trees scattered on its banks, and the winding of the valley, as far as she could trace it, with delight. As they passed into other rooms, these objects were taking different positions; but from every window there were beauties to be seen. (*PP* 246)

The vivid account of moving through a sequence of large rooms with large windows extending over wide vistas also conveys the heroine's elation. Outside and inside, Pemberley extends her acquaintance with Darcy, and in tangible or intangible ways it offers her a charm and a guarantee. Jane Austen is creating the spirit of a place.

The drama of *Pride and Prejudice* involves Misses with choices. Elizabeth forges her happiness in free refusals of Mr Collins and Mr Darcy, with leisure to amend prejudices and errors. Men are endowed with choice, especially elder sons who've survived their parents and the authority they might exert. Mr Collins, it is true, has to today to his patroness, the formidable Lady Catherine de Bourgh; an earl's younger son, Colonel Fitzwilliam must seek a profession or a cushy marriage; steward's son and scoundrel, Wickham, having blown his patronage, must fortune-hunt with his charm as bait. But men's social esteem is not always birth-bound. Tradesman William Lucas gets knighted; amiable, "good looking," Mr Bingley is "gentlemanlike"; for good sense and decency, tradesman Mr Gardiner earns this same compliment from Mr Darcy. Mr Bennet, with a modest £2,000 a year, is a "gentleman." To Lady Catherine's dismay at Darcy's proposal, Elizabeth replies: "He is a gentleman; I am a gentleman's daughter; so far we are equal" (*PP* 356). Such a daughter does best, however, with a handsome dowry or settlement, of which the Bennet girls are short. Austen has no traffic with the social decorum that keeps women innocent of financial reality. In *Pride and Prejudice* everyone keeps tabs: moral ledgers may be misread; financial ones are assiduously monitored. Women also bring assets of youth, beauty, and sweet temper. The debits correspond: foremost, age. Young Miss Gardiner was a beauty, an attorney's daughter with a fortune of £4,000, the belle of the ball. The middle-aged Mrs Bennet is a joke, no match for Mr Bennet's library. But as for his meagerly endowed, unmarried daughters, only his wife feels any urgency. Yet marriage is "the only honorable provision for well-educated young women of small fortune," as sober pragmatist Charlotte Lucas knows—"their pleasantest preservative from want" (*PP* 122-23). Not to marry by age 28 (she's 27) is to resign to "spinster-hood," pitiful and dependent on male kin (if any).

Most women had no legal standing (a suitor seeks a father's permission). Wealthy widow Lady Catherine is the rare female property-owner. While Wickham's mother seems to have had a spendthrift license, and the Bingley heiress enjoy some liberties, obedience to men (fathers, brothers, husbands) was the sanctioned norm. A rebellious girl (one who eloped, or refused her father's choice of husband) could be sent packing, even disinherited. Mr Collins's insistence that the Bennets shut their doors to truant Lydia is no singular meanness; he bears the social consensus and its discipline. Should Lydia ever tire of Wickham's deadbeat profligacy, she could not divorce him, only he her, with a claim to all her money and property, and any children (and their access to family providence).

Austen's uneasiness about this systemic male priority is coolly issued by the novel's least likeable (officious, rude, meddlesome, arrogant), most financially powerful, most self-possessed woman, Lady Catherine. "I see no occasion for entailing estates from the female line" (*PP* 164), she declares to Elizabeth. Mr Bennet merely jests, "My cousin, Mr Collins,...when I am dead, may turn you all out of this house as soon as he pleases" (*PP* 61). If Elizabeth will accept no marriage of convenience with this "conceited, pompous, narrow-minded, silly" heir (*PP* 135), her mother is the only woman to echo Lady Catherine; and like her, she is stigmatized:

> Jane and Elizabeth attempted to explain to her the nature of an entail. They had often attempted it before, but it was a subject on which Mrs Bennet was beyond the reach of reason; and she continued to rail bitterly against the cruelty of settling an estate away from a family of five daughters, in favour of a man whom nobody cared anything about. (*PP* 62)

Everyone knew that office-holders had to be members of the church, that the power in Parliament was the hereditary House of Lords, that the districts for the elective House of Commons were controlled by conservative landowners like Mr Darcy, whose borough might amount to a few hundred souls: principal families, their employees, and tradespeople dependent on their patronage. Scarcely mentioned in this novel are the new manufacturing cities, teeming with miserably exploited workers, with no parliamentary representatives. In 1800, only 5 percent of Englishmen had the vote. Austen's social idiom was percent of the population: "the little bit (two Inches wide) of Ivory on which I work with so fine a Bruch" is "3 or 4 Families in a Country Village" (letter to her nephew, December 16, 1816). These families are serviced and defended by unnamed, or scarcely named, labourers—noncommissioned soldiers, tenant farmers, maids, cooks, housekeepers, servants, carriagemen—all reduced to agentless syntax, horses were brought, dinners were served, tables were cleared, girls were dressed. Ever polite Elizabeth and Jane refer to their housekeeper only as "Hill" ("Mrs Hill" is the singular courtesy of Austen's narrator).

Women of higher rank incorporate their Christian names in a form that distinguishes Lady Catherine de Bourgh and Lady Anne Darcy, in *Pride and Prejudice,* as titled in their own right. Regardless of their marital status or the rank (if lower) of their husbands, daughters of peers invariably used this form, which marks out Lady Catherine, the wife of a knight, as noble by birth (in this case, as daughters of an earl). Thomas Keymer writes in "Rank": "Scarcely lower in standing were the greatest of the landowning commoners, who had not been touched by—or in some cases had eschewed—the titles of their ostensible superiors. With an estate worth more, at £10,000 a year, than that of many nobles, Mr Darcy represents an important category of rural gentry in Austen's England: men of wealth and lineage for whom plain 'Mr' was a badge of honour...the note of regret with which Lady Catherine de Bourgh describes Darcy's paternal line as 'respectable, honourable, and ancient, though untitled' (*PP* 14) signals her distance from the Tory values often attributed to Jane Austen herself, according to which Darcy's untitled state might even be his highest distinction. Simple esquireship connotes an incorruptible aloofness from the processes of political ingratiation and meretricious reward that had characterized the Whig hegemony of the previous century—a 'peer making age' during which the House of Lords grew in size from 153 in 1688 to 224 in 1780, despite the natural extinction of titles over the same period. After 1780, the younger Pitt's efforts to break the power of the Whig magnates led to increased rates of ennoblement, and brought into being a new body of parvenu peers who diluted the old equation between aristocratic rank and blue blood" (Todd 391-92). Jane Austen's egregious kinsman Sir Egerton Brydges (Bart.) was among many traditionalists affronted, in this process, by Pitt's 'palpable preference of mercantile wealth, and by his inborn hatred of the old aristocracy.' Beneath a character such as Darcy, who holds his own in noble company and impresses inferiors "as one of the most illustrious personages in this land" (*PP* 15), there stretches a long and finely graded continuum of genteel rank that was widely seen as ensuring social stability and cohesion. The obsequious Mr Collins, with only some exaggeration, can "consider the clerical office as equal in point of dignity with the highest rank in the kingdom" (*PP* 18).

Alan Richardson writes in "Reading Practices": "One of the more striking social changes between the end of the seventeenth century in Britain and the beginning of the nineteenth concerns the very provision of books. Changes in printing technology, in paper manufacturing, in copyright law and in the retail book trade made books far more common and readily available over the course of the 'long' eighteenth century. In the world of Austen's novels, the very possession of books can serve as a marker of social pretension and intellectual attainment" (Todd 401). The importance of a 'family library' comes in for explicit discussion in *Pride and Prejudice,* and helps to establish an initial connection between Elizabeth Bennet, who unfashionably prefers reading to card playing, and Mr Darcy, whose library at Pemberley is the 'work of many generations,' extensively augmented by himself (*PP* 8). Caroline Bingley, in contrast, demonstrates both her insipidity and her unsuitability as a wife for Darcy by failing to become caught up in reading, despite her hollow wish for an 'excellent library' such as Darcy's own (*PP* 11). In the novel, however, the social anxieties raised by the increasing availability of books finds voice in the fastidious horror of the fatuous Mr Collins upon discovering he has been asked to read aloud from a novel, 'from a circulating library' (*PP* 14). In contrast to the home library, the contents of which might be carefully monitored by the family patriarch, the circulating library (where books could be borrowed in exchange for a one-time fee or regular subscription) represented the threat of promiscuous reading and individual autonomy of choice.

Richardson writes in "Reading Practices": "Reading is associated throughout Austen's novels with education in the broadest sense, that is, with intellectual and moral development. Yet not just any reading practice will result in such 'improvement.' Mary, Elizabeth's pretentious younger sister in *Pride and Prejudice,* exemplifies the error of reading for superficial knowledge and memorizing set passages for the purpose of showing off" (Todd 402). To 'read great books, and make extracts,' however, does not result in genuine mental growth. Darcy describes the proper method, a bit later in the novel, in completing his formula for a truly accomplished woman as the 'improvement of her mind by extensive reading' (*PP* 8). Reading, for Darcy, should not involve mere acquaintance with a list of classics, much less of anthology pieces, but years of wide reading with an end to attaining habits of mental discipline as well as gaining general knowledge.

Markman Ellis observes in "Trade": "To contemporaries—especially from the point of view of the gentry—the stigma attached to trade meant that no one could remain active in trade and be fully acceptable in gentry society. Much of the social drama of *Pride and Prejudice* plays out the complex consequences of this shame about trade and the origins of wealth" (Todd 419). In notorious scenes with Lady Catherine de Bourgh and Darcy, Elizabeth Bennet has to fight to establish her credentials as a gentleman's daughter, despite the contamination of her mother's background in a professional family. In the imaginary of the Austen novels, as elsewhere in eighteenth-century culture, the acquisition of landed property was the only permanent way to seal the retirement from commerce. Adam Smith took it for granted that "merchants are commonly ambitious of becoming country gentlemen, even though he thought their economic status quite separate" (*Wealth of Nations* I: 411). Historians have debated the extent to which this cultural commonplace was true, without coming to much agreement. One historian estimates that about 11 per cent of the owners of country houses in the period 1760-1819 had purchased them with new money gained from the world of business.

Even so, it was certainly widely believed in the early nineteenth century that a tradesman in possession of a secure fortune must be in want of a country estate. Sir William Lucas serves as an example: having made a tolerable fortune in trade in Meryton, Lucas had been knighted during his service as mayor of the town. Emboldened by the higher status implied by the knighthood, Lucas had developed 'a disgust to his business and to his residence in a small market town' and so had removed to a more rural residence which he grandiosely renamed Lucas Lodge. While Sir William's title and wealth give him a certain claim to gentry status, the novel makes clear to readers that this claim is recent, and insecure. Lucas's trajectory undercuts that of Charles Bingley, who is less advanced along a parallel social progress. Bingley has inherited £100,000 from his father, a fortune that had been acquired by trade in the north of England. With this money, Bingley intends to purchase 'a good house and the liberty of a manor,' so as to establish himself as a gentleman with a landed estate (*PP* 4). Both Charles Bingley and Sir William Lucas remind us that all landed wealth has an origin, and that in a commercial society, trade is likely to figure prominently. Subsequently, both the Bingleys and Lucases express a constant and complex anxiety about their status, which manifests itself especially as disgust for their origins in trade.

The mention of white soup in *Pride and Prejudice* is an excellent example of the way Austen uses food to illustrate character. Based on the expensive ingredients veal stock, cream and ground almonds, white soup originated in the courtly cookery of medieval England and France, when its name was *soupe a la reine.* Mr Bingley is here humorously acknowledging that only the most elegant concoctions suit the notions of his house guests Mr Hurst (who favours French cookery) and Mr Darcy (who can afford a French cook). In this most passing of remarks Mr Bingley displays the attractive qualities of wit, generosity and—slightly more questionable—carelessness about money. When Mr Hurst scorns Elizabeth Bennet because she prefers a plain dish to a ragout, he is condemned and Elizabeth endorsed for their respective tastes by the narrator. The antithesis of French food was English roast beef. "I have more than once been asked at table my opinion of the roast beef of Old England, with a sort of smile, and in a tone as if the national honour were concerned," wrote Robert Southey in the guise of a foreign visitor to Britain in 1807.

In *Pride and Prejudice,* the bounds of Austen's coteries and groups are constantly broken, and their closeness challenged, by fresh arrivals and departures. Her inhabitants are constantly on the move, entering new coteries. To refuse to see the social intrusions and erosions in the novel is to ally ourselves with Mrs Bennet in her quarrel with Darcy. He proposes that the country cannot supply enough subjects for the study of character, 'in a country neighbourhood you move in a very confined and unvarying society'; Mrs Bennet replies that there is just as much alteration of people 'going on in the country as the town,' and Elizabeth, 'blushing for her mother,' explains that Darcy is referring to the relative absence of variety. Of course Darcy himself ignores the comings and goings in which he participates, and even Mrs Bennet cannot confine herself to the prescription of three or four families: 'I know we dine with four and twenty families.' Austen's *Pride and Prejudice* conveys an air of social density beyond the novel's focus. She chooses to vary and enlarge her company. The novel devises the action for an expanded social experience, which tests and instructs the central characters.

(V) MORAL COMEDY

Jane Austen was not a pedagogic novelist like Maria Edgeworth; she did not make it her business to preach a doctrine or illustrate some moral theorem by devising a conclusive chain of events. She saw herself, rather, as a critical observer, an interpreter of what actually goes on; and she adopted the comic view as the most illuminating as well as the one that appealed to her humour. But there are passages in which she summarizes the history enacted, or in which one of her more thoughtful characters formulates his reflections; and what she made of it all is a process of education. Experience such as Elinor's and Marianne's teaches how to live wisely and temperately, and therefore, too, happily. Happiness comes of internal harmony and harmony with the rest of the world. She was a religious woman; but except as a personal quality, reverence, and as a moral sanction, religion is not an active element in the life she portrayed. It is not recorded that Wordsworth and Coleridge were among the poets she read. She was no transcendentalist, but keenly interested in every phase of the life going on around her. The value she set upon a fine personality was no doubt intuitive. Human beings have their duty to others, to society, but especially to themselves. It is through their manner of fulfilling their duties that they show what they are, and what they are is the important matter. In this profound sense of the value of personality she forestalls philosophies of life. Her *Pride and Prejudice* also is an educational novel; but more specifically than its predecessor is it concerned with the problem of achieving a perfect marriage, chief among the personal relations in which the individual asserts and at the same time develops personality. Her irony was far removed from either cynicism or satire; it was conformable with what the average respectable citizen would regard as pure idealism. Jane Austen was, in fact, as good an idealist as her romantic fellow-novelists, or a better. But she was a practical idealist. Her lucid scheme of order and a personal life worth living was one that could be carried out. Everyone has commented on this preoccupation of hers with the subject of love and marriage, and the importance that she ascribes to suitable mating among the supreme things in this earthly existence.

The adult Jane Austen, of course, stuck to her Enlightened faith. Each of her novels is a moral and emotional education to its heroine and, usually, its hero, too. In *Pride and Prejudice*, she holds the differences in the Bennet sisters' education (Elizabeth reads, Lydia doesn't) accountable for the difference in their moral characters. Not without purpose does she consistently put bad grammar into Lydia's mouth and letters. And education became the rational criterion by which Jane Austen matured her original irrational judgment that one must admire people in family or feudal loyalty, simply because they are Stuarts or Leighs. She thus arrived at her moral concept of 'good breeding,' where the literal breeding-stock is no longer all important. Elizabeth Bennet can be better bred than her younger sisters, though all are of the same middle-class family, and Darcy better bred than Lady Catherine though both are of the same aristocratic family. The contempt Jane Austen shows, in her treatment of Lady Catherine, for aristocratic absolutism was already developed when she wrote her juvenile works. Lady Catherine's upper-class insolence to Elizabeth is already sketched in details in the third of the juvenile *Collection of Letters;* Jane Austen had already withdrawn belief from the principle of Stuartism.

It was Jane Austen's habit to leave didacticism, the practice of edification, to certain chosen characters. It was one of their idiosyncrasies, sometimes a virtue, more often a vice. One of the ironies in *Pride and Prejudice* is that the persons most given to the moral instruction of their fellow-beings are the most absurd; they are Mr Collins and Lady Catherine de Bourgh. The only plausible excuse for the existence of such a character as Elizabeth's sister Mary, who anyhow was a missfire, is that she was meant as a sly poke at the heavy school of moralistic novelists. This young woman was always "deep in the study of thorough bass and human nature," and stupefies Elizabeth with her threadbare morality at the harrowing moment when there is every reason to fear worst of Lydia's escapade with Wickham. "This is a most unfortunate affair, and will probably be much talked of. But we must stem the tide of malice, and pour into the wounded bosoms of each other the balm of sisterly consolation." And she goes on: "Loss of virtue in a female is irretrievable...one false step involves her in endless ruin...her reputation is no less brittle than it is beautiful." And more in the same strain. Taken ironically, as she is intended, Mary does provide some amusement, and the satire was probably clear enough to contemporary readers. In the eighteenth century, moralization was a prevalent social infirmity. People were addicted to the public discussion of such questions as a certain class of novelist seemed to regard as the sole justification for writing about human nature. There are many such conversations in Jane Austen's novels; and in *Pride and Prejudice,* where they are usually provoked by the behaviour or some observation of Darcy, they are thoroughly in character. In nothing is that gentleman more Grandisonian than in his conscious pursuit of personal excellence; and it was natural for him to expound himself to Elizabeth, with whom he is in love long before he declares himself he is even fully aware of it.

> "It has been the study of my life to avoid those weaknesses which often expose a strong understanding to ridicule."
>
> "Such as vanity and pride."
>
> "Yes, vanity is a weakness indeed. But pride—where there is a real superiority of mind—pride will always be under good regulation."
>
> Elizabeth turned away to hide a smile.
>
> "Your examination of Mr Darcy is over, I presume," said Miss Bingley; "and pray what is the result?"
>
> "I am perfectly convinced by it that Mr Darcy has no defect. He owns it himself without disguise."

Ernest A. Baker writes in *The History of the English Novel,* "Elizabeth's wit must not blind us to the fact that she is a little too hard on Darcy, as her creator meant her to be. Elizabeth Bennet also has almost as much pride in her as prejudice; and in both her and Darcy, Jane Austen can be seen between the lines championing the cause of honesty and self-respect at the risk of condoning pride. Though for a long while Elizabeth does not give Darcy a chance, she is usually both sane and fair-minded, and her attitude is a contrast to her father's indolent cynicism. Like other clear-sighted critics to the human scene, like Fielding for instance, she had her fits of disillusionment. There is a passage in which she eloquently compares the angelic sweetness and disinterestedness of her sister Jane, cheerfully bearing up against the pain of Bingley's desertion, with her own instinctive distrust of the motives of others" (90).

> You wish to think all the world respectable, and are hurt if I speak ill of anybody. I only want to think *you* perfect, and you set yourself against it. Do not be afraid of my running into any excess, of my encroaching on your privilege of universal goodwill. You need not. There are few people whom I really love, and still fewer of whom I think well. The more I see of the world, the more am I dissatisfied with it; and every day confirms my belief of the inconsistency of all human characters, and of the little dependence that can be placed on the appearance of either merit or sense.

One feels intuitively that it is Miss Austen speaking for herself: Elizabeth Bennet is so like her. Another trait, of a different significance, comes out in the visit to Pemberley, where there are many good paintings: "but Elizabeth knew nothing of the art," and was interested only in the portrait of Darcy and some efforts by his sister. Writing to Cassandra about a visit to the Liverpool Museum and the British Gallery, Jane said: "I had some amusement at each, tho' my preference for Men and Women always inclines me to attend more to the company than the sight."

The Bingley sisters must be set down early as "very fine ladies; not deficient in good humour when they were pleased, nor in the power of being agreeable where they chose it; but proud and conceited" (*PP* 15). And Charlotte Lucas accepts Mr Collins 'solely from the *pure* and *disinterested* desire of an establishment.' By using these words, Jane Austen does in fact emphasize the impurity and interestedness which lie behind Charlotte Lucas's acceptance of the fatuous clergyman; in making the statement so strongly positive the author underlines the severe moral criticism she is making of Charlotte. Lydia

Wickham, newly married and triumphantly describing her wedding to Elizabeth, says, "...I was thinking, you may suppose, of my dear Wickham. I longed to know whether he would be married in his blue coat" (*PP* 319). She puts love on the same level with fashionable clothing—and so casts doubt on the sincerity and profundity of her ability to love. Finally, when Elizabeth Bennet asks Lady Catherine why she may not accept Darcy, Lady Catherine replies: "Because honour, decorum, prudence, nay, interest, forbid it" (*PP* 355). Indeed it is 'interest' rather than anything else which makes Lady Catherine so loath to see Darcy and Elizabeth married—a very strong 'interest' that her own daughter will be her nephew's wife. Darcy is liked in the Netherfield 'neighbourhood' "till his manners gave a disgust which turned the tide of his popularity; for he was discovered to be proud...," the grandeur of the metaphor reflecting the shallowness of those who eagerly admire him because he is handsome, but quickly reject him when his diffidence or pride makes him seem unresponsive. Darcy is at his worst for Elizabeth in his low opinion of the Longbourn people, the Bennets, the Lucas and Philips families; not less so because he is manifestly right. Given his intellectual and moral superiority, Darcy's struggle with himself was bound to be acute, and he holds the reader's sympathies not less than Elizabeth, at any rate on a second perusal of the book. Jane Austen puts in one for herself in a speech that must be credited to Elizabeth, though who was the speaker is left to the reader's intelligence. The talk is about those intricate characters who are "the *most* amusing"; and Darcy observes, "The country can in general supply but few subjects for such a study. In a country neighbourhood you move in a very confined and unvarying society." This irritates Mrs Bennet, who is entirely incapable of understanding him. "I assure you there is quite as much of that going on in the country as in town," she foolishly remarks. It must be Elizabeth Bennet who corrects Darcy's generalization, "But people themselves alter so much, that there is something new to be observed in them for ever." It is not only the protagonists that engross interest, the minor characters are as perfectly studied, in their due perspective. Leaving Mr Collins and Lady Catherine out of account, not as extraneous, however, for together they provide a magnificent comic pendant to the more intense of Elizabeth and Darcy, we may look at the others. The Bennets are a comedy in themselves, and Mary is a failure only because she remains an unfinished sketch. But the two elder sisters, so finely contrasted, and the pair of hoydens, the empty-headed, flirting Lydia, and Kitty who so narrowly escapes the same fate; and their friends, the over-genial, babbling Sir William Lucas, so uplifted with his kinghthood; his womenfolk, and the officers from Meryton; every one is individualized with masterly precision. With such figures may be coupled that amiable, colourless young fellow Bingley, and his insincere sister, and the easy-going scamp Wickham, whose worst faults are left unprobed. Mrs Bennet is a comic production of high order. Silly, incredibly ignorant, and irresponsible, she was a dreadful infliction for those who were in any way dependent upon her. She alone would justify all Darcy's strictures upon the Bennet family, and she must have been to Elizabeth a thorn in the flesh. Yet, she is never made an object of satire. On the contrary, it is an exquisitely kind touch on Jane Austen's part when her namesake, who has regained the laggard Bingley, will not lose a moment before consoling her mother with the glad news. Elizabeth, with less tenderness if equal affection, thinks first of her father, when Darcy's suit is in question, and the interview is one to be read with mixed feelings. The hare-brained, vulgar, incontinent Lydia would be a terrible example of moral and mental recklessness, and can be made to point the lesson which it is easy to draw from this history, that education, discipline, and self-control are all-important, and that parental Laodiceanism bears pernicious fruits. Her father and mother are another Mr and Mrs Shandy (Sterne's *Tristram Shandy*). He has cultivated impassivity as an antidote to his wife's shallow effusiveness, and the attitude has set. Lizzie, the only member of the family who inherits his sense of humour, comprehends him; to his wife he is as inscrutable as Mr Shandy was to his better half. Sterne was one of the classic authors whom Jane Austen knew well enough to quote from.

Denis Donoghue observes in "A View of *Mansfield Park,*" "I think she felt something factitious in *Pride and Prejudice,* as if it were too dazzling to be true, and she was beginning to think a good deal about the nature of truth. In *Mansfield Park,* she would propose a sterner discrimination, even at the risk of being, as she said, 'not half so entertaining.' In *Pride and Prejudice,* life allowed the novelist to declare the marvellous union of Wit and Wisdom, but this was one liberty in a thousand restrictions. The more general rule of life is that Wit and Wisdom are cut adrift and often in that severance Wit becomes corrupt and Wisdom a little dull; and if it must be a choice, then one must choose Wisdom, because (as Jane Austen wrote to Fanny Knight in November, 1814) 'Wisdom is better than Wit, and in the long run will certainly have the laugh on her side'" (Southam, *Critical Essays on Jane Austen* 42). Each of Jane Austen's novels has at least one major occasion on which the demands of Truth are flouted: if in *Sense and Sensibility,* the secret trip of Marianne and Willoughby to Allenham (Ch. 13) which mimes a marital relation to which they have no claim is a case in point, in *Pride and Prejudice,* Lydia's elopement with Wickham is another case.

The two great temptations which lie across the path of truth in Jane Austen's fiction are "charm" and "selfishness." It is possible, of course, for charm to be good, as it is in the miracle of Elizabeth Bennet. But Jane Austen often felt, and particularly after *Pride and Prejudice,* that the dangerous people were those whose charm was at once irrefutable and corrupt. Clearly, she was afraid of charming, worthless, clever men like Wickham. She knew that charm in such men is notoriously beguiling; even Elizabeth was greatly taken by Wickham's charm in Chapters 16 and 17 of *Pride and Prejudice.* The second temptation in the path of Truth is selfishness. Jane Austen was not a pupil of Mandeville or Hobbes but she was sufficiently wry to acknowledge that selfishness, whatever the cause, is a common effect in human action. But if truth means commitment—so her argument would run—the movement of feeling cannot be self-engrossed, it must go out in full acknowledgement of other people. There are many versions of selfishness in Jane Austen's fiction, some deadlier than others. If in *Sanditon,* Sir Edward Denham plans to seduce Clara Brereton and in *Sense and Sensibility,* Marianne shows rudeness to Mrs Jennings, Mr Bennet's systematic contempt in *Pride and Prejudice* is also a kind of selfishness.

Robert Garis observes in "Learning Experience and Change": "JANE AUSTEN'S form is the comic drama of reason, in which the happy ending comes about not through the lucky disappearance of accidental impediments, but through a dramatic action in which one of the leading characters learns something important enough about reality and his own nature to experience a deep change of mind or heart. But she doesn't always succeed in making this learning process dramatic, or convincing, or significant; and it seems to me that some very plain and simple things remain to be said about when, how and why, and with what kind of character, she succeeds or fails" (Southam 60). Learning brings the characters closer to what Jane Austen means by her complex word 'sense.' The two chief meanings of this word are 'seeing well' and 'behaving well' and both meanings are in force in all the novels, but with different degrees of emphasis. When in *Pride and Prejudice* and *Emma* the emphasis is on 'seeing well,' 'behaving well' seems to come about naturally. In *Pride and Prejudice,* learning feels like gaining something positive, eagerly and energetically chosen once it is recognized. Elizabeth in fact falls in love with sense.

Garis writes: "When we emerge into *Pride and Prejudice* from the constricted world of *Sense and Sensibility,* we encounter the character of Elizabeth Bennet with a feeling of enormous release. Freedom, wit, high spirits, physical energy, open affections, the capacity to charm and the frank interest in charming—Jane Austen has given her heroine all these without stint and without a hint of cautious pessimism, in the frank intentions to win our love and approval and the full knowledge that she will succeed. And she rewards her heroine's courageous independence handsomely. Jane Austen was never again to achieve or perhaps to need this exhilaration, which is undoubtedly the most important characteristic of *Pride and Prejudice*. But there is another aspect of freedom in this novel which links it with the far less exuberant *Emma*. In liberating herself from caution, Jane Austen has by no means suppressed or distorted her interest in sense" (Southam 70). Elizabeth Bennet is something of a rebel against pretension and pomposity and pride, but when she learns to love Darcy, she sees his strength of principle and soundness of judgments, even his stiff reserve, not as limitations to her freedom, but as means to her own self-fulfilment. In marrying sense, she gives up neither her ego, her wit nor her playfulness; she can laugh lovingly at Darcy's mannerisms without hurting him or in the slightest degree expressing disrespect for him. In that union of opposites that love makes possible, Elizabeth's satiric playfulness—the one talent and habit she notably shares with Jane Austen—is deepened and made fruitful by love. Garris observes, "Yet these meanings—that Darcy represents sense and that Elizabeth's learning experience amounts to falling in love with sense—aren't at all fully achieved or finely worked. The creative energy was entirely given to making the favourite delightful, and the word 'favourite' is an index both to the novel's charm and to its limitations. The character of Darcy, and the dramatic action of the learning experience and of the whole novel, are only sketches, and often there is a real lack of unity. But a sketch is not a blank, and a lack of unity isn't the same thing as wilful disunity. Darcy's theatrically arrogant, even insolent rudeness at the beginning suits his theatrically dazzling wealth and good looks, but if it isn't, to say the least, very finely adjusted with his sense, one doesn't feel this as false and strained. Jane Austen wanted her favourite to marry 'well' in both senses of the word—'glamorously' and 'wisely'—an ambitious and generous but not self-contradictory undertaking" (Southam 70-71).

The learning experience too is an ambitious and generous sketch. Halfway through *Pride and Prejudice* Elizabeth seems to have learned everything: "I have courted prepossession and ignorance, and drive reason away…. Till this moment, I never knew myself" (Ch. 36). The language rings out clearly in the theatre, and one hears Jane Austen's youthful ambition pretty clearly too; but this is a rather hollow set-piece of self-knowledge. And the physical and psychological action in which Elizabeth learns to love Darcy is full of awkward contrivances. After the coincidental meeting at Pemberley, both Elizabeth and Jane Austen seem to be nervously trying to think of just the right words:

> Such a change in a man of so much pride, excited not only astonishment but gratitude—for to love, ardent love, it must be attributed; and as such its impression on her was of a sort to be encouraged, as by no means unpleasing, though it could not be exactly defined. She respected, she esteemed, she was grateful to him, she felt a real interest in his welfare, and she only wanted to know how far she wished that welfare to depend upon herself, and how far it would be for the happiness of both that she should employ the power, which her fancy told her she still possessed, of bringing on the renewal of his addresses. (Ch. 44)

When she does know this, the language firmly establishes Darcy as the man of sense, but seems perfunctory:

> It was an union that must have been to the advantage of both; by her ease and liveliness, his mind might have been softened, his manners improved, and from his judgment, information, and knowledge of the world, she must have received benefit of greater importance. (Ch. 50)

From this point on all the positive moves toward resolution are theatrical: Darcy's secret exertions about Lydia, Lady Catherine's insolence, Mr Collins's letter, Mrs Bennet's rudeness—we accept it all and enjoy it all, but we are learning nothing, nor is Elizabeth. The one non-theatrical sense is, interestingly enough, a threat to the happy ending: Elizabeth's painful attempt to convince her father of her love for Darcy. The scene is beautifully conceived and in part well executed, and here the theme of falling in love with sense gets its most poignant expression. But Jane Austen hurries through a summary of the learning process:

> at length, by repeated assurances that Mr Darcy was really the object of her choice, by explaining the gradual change which her estimation of him had undergone, relating her absolute certainty that his affection was not the work of a day, but had stood the test of many months' suspense, and enumerating with energy all his good qualities, she did conquer her father's incredulity, and reconcile him to the match. (Ch. 55)

Elizabeth learns to love a man whom she has detested on first acquaintance, doesn't know very well and rarely sees. In *Pride and Prejudice,* the highly recognizable shape of the basic fable telegraphs the ending. Garis writes, "All this is more strikingly true in the learning process. Elizabeth, in thinking about Darcy's letter, must conduct a complicated rational inquiry in which she compares in considerable details the two contradictory reports of Darcy's actions concerning Wickham and her sister; and she must also collect a lot of evidence before she can learn to understand how Darcy's basically principled, generous nature happens to express itself in such misleading ways. Learning that her own admirable love of wit and character-analysis has led her astray is particularly hard, because her mistakes are almost unavoidable: Wickham is an exceptionally open, attractive, likeable and generally well-liked young man who happens to be a liar, and whose lies deceive almost everybody else too; Darcy's behaviour likewise offends nearly everybody; anybody would find him an extremely puzzling man. We too are to some extent misled in all this; the shape of the fable makes us ready and eager to believe the opposite of these 'first impressions' but offers no further help" (Southam 72-73).

John Mullan says in "Psychology": "Between Richardson and Austen, 'virtue' is invariably the leading characteristic of arty novel's heroine. 'All the Good will be unexceptionable in every respect—and there will be no foibles or weaknesses,' wrote Austen in her 'Plan of a Novel.' Escaping such goodness was essential to her psychological realism" (Todd 378). When Elizabeth Bennet and Mr Darcy banter in *Pride and Prejudice* about each other's possible deficiencies, we might hear in the comedy Austen's rejection of the faultlessness of the Richardsonian heroine. This is the significance of Austen's taking the title of her best-known novel from the final chapter of Frances Burney's *Cecilia* (1782). Austen never married; but she thought about loving and marrying as intensely as the sentimental enthusiasts whom she laughed at. Her conception of a genuine union was a loftier one than theirs. They either romanticized love, glorifying it with ecstatic emotionalism, or like Fanny Burney sedately followed the match-making tradition to the conventional goal, a handsome husband, satisfactory marriage settlements, and a happy and elegant home. The conclusion of *Pride and Prejudice* is the achievement of self-knowledge, self-control, and self-respect, and a principal means of such an achievement is a league of perfect sympathy with another who is one's spiritual counterpart. Although D.H. Lawrence writes in "Morality and the Novel" that "Morality in the novel is the trembling instability of the balance" (McDonald, Edward D. Ed, *Phoenix, the Posthumous Papers of D.H. Lawrence.* 1936, London: Heinemann, 1961. 528), the moral in *Pride and Prejudice* is integral to the texture and structure of the novel.

(VI) CHARACTERIZATION

In reading Jane Austen's novels, we are not intended to take all the figures in the same way. Some are offered as full and natural portraits of imaginable people; others, while certainly referring to types of people we might easily have come across, are yet presented with such exaggeration and simplification that our response to them is expected to be rather different. The epigrammatic brilliance of *Pride and Prejudice* relates it in tone to the eighteenth century, as does the characterization. Although Austen's *Pride and Prejudice* is no less serious in intention than any of the others, its method is livelier and more humorous. This is chiefly because Elizabeth is a lively and humorous heroine—unlike Elinor, Fanny, or Anne Elliot—and largely responsible for the tone of the whole novel. But Jane Austen herself appears here as a lively commentator, though only to present material when this cannot be done through Elizabeth. W.A. Craik writes in *Jane Austen: The Six*

Novels: "She (Austen) has to appear more as narrator than she did in *Sense and Sensibility,* first because she has a heroine whose judgement has limitations: she has to make clear what the limitations are, and tell us facts, some of which the heroine cannot tell because it would distort her as it almost distorts Elinor, and some which she cannot know either because her limited judgement does not let her perceive them or because she has no chance to perceive them.... Jane Austen appears as narrator secondly because Elizabeth is only the mam interest of the novel, not the sole one; the title itself shows this: 'pride' and 'prejudice' can easily be made to stand for Darcy and Elizabeth" (63).

As usual, the opening of the novel is a deliberate guide to the whole:

> It is a truth universally acknowledged, that a single man in possession of a good fortune, must be in want of a wife.
>
> However little known the feelings or views of such a man may be on his first entering a neighbourhood, this truth is so well fixed in the minds of the surrounding families, that he is considered as the rightful property of some one or other of their daughters. (*PP* 3)

This is irony at its best and most useful. We hear what the story will be about—courtship and marriage; we have a hint in 'the surrounding families' that this will be the concern of more than one couple, the concern not only of Elizabeth and Darcy, but of Jane and Bingley, Mr Collins and Charlotte, and of Wickham and Elizabeth, Miss King and Lydia by turns; we see what the deeper preoccupations of the novel will be—the moral weight of material and financial matters in personal affairs; and we see how the sense of the family and the neighbourhood which accompany the action will bear on individuals, for most of Jane's troubles (for example) are caused by her family, and the neighbourhood gossip is one of the trials after Lydia's elopement, and it encourages and intensifies Elizabeth's misrepresentations of Darcy. Craik writes, "Jane Austen characteristically finds ways of subordinating her part as narrator; irony is not merely an attitude, it is a method of presentation, organization, analysis and judgment. Her skill in irony is at its greatest here and in *Emma,* where she can be serious without ever being solemn, both in contrast to *Sense and Sensibility,* where the theme is not suitable, while in *Mansfield Park*—particularly the latter half—and in *Persuasion* she is using a different method. Irony is appropriate in *Pride and Prejudice* because the characters are all deficient in some way, even though the intelligent characters may express Jane Austen's judgment for her" (64).

Elizabeth Bennet is the key to *Pride and Prejudice,* both for the personality Jane Austen gives her and the way she uses it. Elizabeth is a much more accomplished piece of work and a much more subtle character than any preceding her. She is a lens through which the action is seen, and like Emma she is a lens with a flaw. The flaw, Elizabeth's faulty judgement, itself, ironically, interprets the events. She does not emerge as the main character until midway through the third chapter, after we have made the acquaintance of all the Bennets, Lady Lucas, the Bingleys and Mr Darcy. She therefore makes her first important appearance in her most important postion, in relation to Mr Darcy, when she overhears him slight her ('not handsome enough to tempt me'). The scene is presented through her eyes, or, rather, through her ears, showing how the greater part of the novel will be done. We see from it that she is acute and attractive, that she has a personal basis for her prejudice, and a strong inclination towards a perverse estimate, even at the risk of being wrong; as she eventually admits

> I meant to be uncommonly clever in taking so decided a dislike to him, without any reason. It is such a spur to one's genius, such an opening for wit to have a dislike of that kind. (*PP* 225-26)

This is her own accurate statement of the case. She therefore may discriminate quite properly on other matters not connected with Darcy or with Charlotte (whom her prejudice favours) and she can be Jane Austen's mouthpiece in the novel. Yet her successes against Lady Catherine, Miss Bingley and Mr Collins cannot counterbalance her failure to understand Wickham, her close friend Charlotte, or Mr Darcy.

Her experiences, and the novel, fall into two parts, the first ending with Darcy's letter which follows his first proposal of marriage. In the first part events reveal themselves through conversation and Jane Austen's comment, Elizabeth's reactions being given with two objects: first, to limit what the reader sees and to regulate what he is to think, as in the opinions on Wickham already mentioned; and second, to show her incorrect conclusions, and direct the reader to the true ones, as in her conversation with Colonel Fitzwilliam:

> "I do not know any body who seems more to enjoy the power of doing what he likes than Mr Darcy."
>
> "He likes to have his own way very well", replied Colonel Fitzwilliam. "But so we all do. It is only that he has better means of having it than many others, because he is rich, and many others are poor. I speak feelingly. A younger son, you know, must be inured to self-denial and dependence.... There are not many in my rank of life who can afford to marry without some attention to money."
>
> "Is this," thought Elizabeth, "meant for me?" (*PP* 183)

Indeed it is, and although it may refer on one level to the Colonel's interest in Elizabeth, it undoubtedly refers on another to what we have seen of Darcy's, which Elizabeth entirely ignores, although he is paying her just as much attention as the Colonel. In the second part of the novel, after she has realized the errors her prejudice has led her into, judgment is directed inwards on herself rather than outwards on to other people, and more of the action takes place in her own mind, less in actual events. If we compare the lively conversations which take place at Netherfield while Jane is ill (Ch. 8) with those which take place during the stay at Pemberley, which involve most of the same people, in the latter the emphasis is all on what Elizabeth feels and perceives, and not on what anyone else says or does because the interest here is in her moral reform and emotional maturity. During and after her stay in Lambton, Elizabeth is presented by the kind of reported thought-process which is Jane Austen's most original method. This method imposes organization on the events and relates Elizabeth's changing feelings firmly and unsentimentally to their context:

> The present unhappy state of the family, rendered any other excuse for the lowness of her spirits unnecessary; nothing, therefore, could be fairly conjectured from *that,* though Elizabeth, who was by this time tolerably well acquainted with her own feelings, was perfectly aware, that, had she known nothing of Darcy, she could have borne the dread of Lydia's infamy somewhat better. It would have spared her, she thought, one sleepless night out of two. (*PP* 298-29)

Darcy parallels Elizabeth. Like her, he is deluded about his own character: "It is I believe too little yielding" (*PP* 58) is his first and favourable way of putting what he finally admits: "I have been a selfish being all my life, in practice, though not in principle" (*PP* 369). Elizabeth is the means of reforming him, as he is of her. Like her also, he is presented differently before and after his first proposal of marriage, and the way it is done is almost the reverse of the way Jane Austen treats Elizabeth. At first Jane Austen gives his actual thought to mark the progress of his attachment, concisely noting its growth and quality:

> No sooner had he made it clear to himself and his friends that she had hardly a good feature in her face, than he began to find it was rendered uncommonly intelligent by the beautiful expression of her dark eyes. (*PP* 23)

> Darcy had never been so bewitched by any woman as he was by her. He really believed, that were it not for the inferiority of her connections, he should be in some danger. (*PP* 52)

> ...they went down the other dance and parted in silence; on each side dissatisfied, though not to an equal degree, for in Darcy's breast there was a tolerable powerful feeling towards her, which soon procured her pardon, and directed all his anger against another. (*PP* 94)

Craik observes, "She (Austen) is forced to use this method by having a remote hero whom she cannot reveal through the heroine—as Mr Knightley is revealed through Emma, or, rather differently, Edmund through Fanny. But for the most part Darcy is seen only through what he does and says and through Elizabeth's interpretation of him, with help from occasional unprejudiced observers like Colonel Fitzwilliam and Mrs Gardiner. Since his language is always correct and often formal, and since Jane Austen herself eschews strong language for worthy characters, small details of facial expression must often reveal strong emotion, particularly when Darcy's thoughts cannot be retailed like Elizabeth's. This is specially the case during his first proposal, where his language is restrained and correct (though his sentiments may not be). Such pharases as 'his complexion became pale with anger', 'he changed colour,' 'a smile of affected incredulity', 'an expression of mingled incredulity and mortification' (191-93) all make an account of his feelings as unnecessary as, if given alongside Elizabeth's, it would be confusing. The irony and a good deal of the comedy of the first part come from the difference between what Mr Darcy means and what Elizabeth thinks he means, and between what Elizabeth's replies intend, and how they appear to Mr Darcy. The misunderstanding is all Elizabeth's doing, though the speeches of both are most skillfully ambiguous" (80-81).

Jane Austen makes Mr Darcy interesting by the same means as she makes Elizabeth charming, which makes them artistically suited to one another, and imposes a pattern on the novel as a whole. Just as Wickham's attentions show Elizabeth's attractions, so Miss Bingley's show Darcy's; Elizabeth is witty in her exchanges with Jane and Colonel Fitzwilliam, and so is Darcy in his with Bingley and Caroline; Elizabeth sensibly refuses to be involved with Wickham, and Darcy deftly extricates himself from Miss Bingley's schemes; and Darcy is seen as the friend and intellectual superior of Bingley just as Elizabeth is of Jane. External events also connect them, even those which, as far as the action is concerned, seem to separate them. Elizabeth rightly thinks

Lydia's elopement is an obstacle to any possible engagement with Mr Darcy; but their common feelings of responsibility for the disaster set them apart from the other characters and strengthen the artistic connexion between them. Craik observes: "Darcy is as good a match for Elizabeth as Mr Knightley is for Emma, the novel is therefore better balanced than *Northanger Abbey* or *Sense and Sensibility,* where the hero and heroine are unequal in intellect and role" (82).

Elizabeth is the focus of the novel, but other characters are none the less important. Elizabeth does not overshadow all others as Emma (*Emma*) does by the way the novel is presented through her. The persons who reinforce and correct her judgment gain considerable influence although playing small parts; Jane Bennet, for example, excessively and entertainingly good-natured, is yet right in her estimate of Mr Darcy, and no more wrong than Elizabeth in judging Charlotte (she is too generous, while Elizabeth is too harsh). These characters who do what might have been the narrator's work are Jane and Charlotte; Mr Bennet, who sums up his daughters, his wife, Mr Bingley and Wickham; Mrs Gardiner, who is right about Darcy, and Bingley, whose humorous comments so illuminate Darcy. These characters are presented in the same way as the major characters, and the novel therefore is moving away from caricature, even though caricatures are used with great effect. These caricatures who have no judgement and can excite no sympathy—Mr Collins, Lady Catherine, Sir William Lucas, and Mrs Bennet—are thoroughly worked in and quite acceptable as a commentary on the main theme. The discordances in *Pride and Prejudice* embody principles and themes. Charlotte's marriage to Mr Collins shows that her moral sense is deficient; Mrs Bennet shows how Jane's setting and connections injure her prospects; so does Sir William Lucas, for he (who has no right to mention such a subject on so slight an acquaintance) first suggests to Darcy the possibility of an engagement between Bingley and Jane, and so shows that though Elizabeth and her father may laugh at him, his folly can be a danger; while lady Catherine shows that by contrast with her own arrogance Darcy's pride is something much more subtle. Here is an example from Lady Catherine which concerns both of them:

> Young women should always be properly guarded and attended, according to their situation in life. When my niece Georgiana went to Ramsgate last summer, I made a point of her having two men servants go with her. (*PP* 211-12)

We already know what happened to Miss Darcy at Ramsgate, and so see that Darcy's pride is much less exceptionable, being concerned with ethics rather than etiquette.

Mr Darcy is the first hero Jane Austen tackles seriously or at much length. He develops like Elizabeth from complacency to self-knowledge and reformation. He is her equal and reforms her in the same process as she reforms him; and although he cannot be seen from inside as she is, and cannot be seen often, Jane Austen makes all his appearances important and significant. She revels his states of mind by giving only their external results to himself and to others. This makes Mr Darcy interesting without taking any of the structural emphasis away from Elizabeth; we can interpret him correctly by what Elizabeth sees, even though she interprets it wrongly.

> "I should never have considered the distance as one of the *advantages* of the match," cried Elizabeth. "I should never have said Mrs Collins was settled *near* her family."
>
> "It is a proof of your own attachment to Hertfordshire. Any thing beyond the very neighborhood of Longbourn, I suppose, would appear far."
>
> As he spoke there was a sort of smile, which Elizabeth fancied she understood; he must be supposing her to be thinking of Jane and Netherfield, and she blushed as she answered,
>
> "I do not mean to say that a woman may not be settled too near her family. The far and the near must be relative, and depend on many varying circumstances.

> Where there is fortune to make the expense of travelling unimportant, distance becomes no evil." (*PP* 179)

Elizabeth's misinterpretation of Darcy's words and smile point out the true meaning—he is thinking of her and of Pemberley, not of Jane and Netherfield—and her reply constitutes direct encouragement, particularly when accompanied by the blush which he misinterprets in his turn.

Character, narrative, and conversation are virtually inseparable. Descriptions of the leading characters throw light on others; Elizabeth, for instance, is seen for the first time as Darcy sees her:

> ...no sooner had he made it clear to himself and his friends that she had hardly a good feature in her face, than he began to find it was rendered uncommonly intelligent by the beautiful expression of her dark eyes. To this discovery succeeded some others equally mortifying. Though he had detected with a critical eye more than one failure of perfect symmetry in her form, he was forced to acknowledge her figure to be light and pleasing; and in spite of his asserting that her manners were not those of the fashionable world, he was caught by their easy playfulness. (*PP* 23)

Summaries of character are rare, and most of the information comes from conversation, where it inevitably illuminates speaker as well as subject:

> "From all that I can collect by your manner of talking, you must be two of the silliest girls in the country. I have suspected it some time, but I am now convinced."...
>
> "I am astonished, my dear," said Mrs Bennet, "that you should be so ready to think your own children silly. If I wished to think slightingly of any body's children, it should not be of my own however."
>
> "If my children are silly I must hope to be always sensible of it."
>
> "Yes—but as it happens, they are all of them very clever.... My dear Mr Bennet, you must not expect such

> girls to have the sense of their father and mother. When they get to our age I dare say they will not think about officers any more than we do. I remember the time when I liked a red coat myself very well—and indeed so I do still at my heart." (*PP* 29)

We see here the ostensible point—the characters of Lydia and Catherine—we see their father's attitude to his children and his wife, and we see her deficiencies and the children's likeness to her—they have, ironically, exactly 'the sense of their mother.' Such information comes only where it is exactly relevant; we hear little more about Lydia until she asks Mr Bingley about the ball at Netherfield:

> Lydia was a stout, well-grown girl of fifteen, with a fine complexion and good-humoured countenance.... She had high animal spirits, a sort of natural self-consequence, which the attentions of the officers, to whom her uncle's good dinners and her own easy manners recommended her, had increased into assurance. (*PP* 45)

This information is necessary to explain such overconfidence in a girl who by the standards of her time ought to have been still in the schoolroom; the whole incident is useful preparation for her much more shameless elopement.

The introductory character-sketch as Jane Austen used it in *Sense and Sensibility* is superseded by more subtle methods which are worked into the structure of *Pride and Prejudice* as a whole. When Mr and Mrs Bennet are sketched in at the end of the first chapter it actually reduces their importance; though they speak first and effectively they are not leading characters; a summary makes it clear that they are not capable of development or much subtlety. Although the news that Mrs Bennet does not understand her husband is some preparation for him to behave unexpectedly vigorously when Lydia elopes, he does not really alter; the elements of his nature merely appear in a new way. Jane Austen begins here to use the method which is at its most perfect in *Emma,* the method first attempted in the later parts of *Northanger Abbey*—where her appearance in *propria persona* as narrator are hardly noticeable, and we never feel consciously that she is directing what we shall think. What the author tells us, what the heroine perceives and the conclusions the heroine then draws, are so mingled that they are hardly separable.

> If he had been wavering before, as to what he should do, which had often seemed likely, the advice and intreaty of so near a relation might settle every doubt, and determine him at once to be as happy, as dignity unblemished could make him. In that case he would return no more. Lady Catherine might see him in her way through town; and his engagement to Bingley of coming again to Netherfield must give way.
>
> "If, therefore, an excuse for not keeping his promise, should come to his friend within a few days," she added, "I shall know how to understand it. I shall then give over every expectation, every wish of his constancy. If he is satisfied with only regretting me, when he might have obtained my affections and hand, I shall soon cease to regret him at all." (*PP* 361)

The first paragraph gives facts, but is just as easily to be read as Elizabeth's assessment of them as Jane Austen's, and it merges easily with Elizabeth's deductions from them which follow. Thus, highly ambiguous facts are often put before us, about which we note consciously only what is relevant at the time:

> "Till I can forget his father, I can never defy or expose *him*."
>
> Elizabeth honoured him for such feelings, and thought him handsomer than ever as he expressed them. (*PP* 80)

We have time to observe only that Elizabeth is thinking illogically, and the idea that Wickham is at this moment 'exposing' Darcy is remarked just sufficiently for the incident to be readily recalled when Elizabeth learns the truth from Darcy's letter:

> She was *now* struck with the impropriety of such communications to a stranger, and wondered it had escaped her before. (*PP* 207)

Craik writes, "The novel thus has the appearance of the inevitability of real life, at the same time and by the same means as it is organized to embody its author's moral plan" (69).

Sense and Sensibility has some good minor characters, notably Mrs Jennings, but those of *Pride and Prejudice* are richer in themselves and even the most comic ones are put to more functional use. Whereas Willoughby came to be enveloped in melodrama, the new "villain," Wickham, is kept almost clear of that—though his lesser villainy goes along with less vitality; and there are no other really bad characters. Lydia Bennet is a robustly successful creation, a girl who, while not vicious, is only a pleasure-loving animal devoid of mind and principle; she is her mother's own daughter. Satire, having less serious human faults to work on, is less sharp and more humorous than it is in *Sense and Sensibility,* but it does not spare the jealous and self-defeating cunning of Miss Bingley, the crude and self-defeating arrogance of Lady Catherine, the several kinds and degrees of imbecility embodied in Mrs Bennet, Mr Collins, and Sir William Lucas, or Mr Bennet's irresponsible often cynical and sometimes callous levity. Mr Bennet, though wins at least our retroactive sympathy when, in warning Elizabeth against marrying a man she could not respect, he touches on the disparity—due of course to his own bad choice—which had caused his retreat into cynicism, the spirit of Jane Austen's early burlesques survives in such mature distillations as Mrs Bennet, Mr Collins (a comic successor of serious clerics in the Richardson-Burney line), and Lady Catherine. Although we cannot imagine such broad caricatures in any of the later novels, they scarcely jar with the less rigorous realism of such a half-Romantic comedy as *Pride and Prejudice,* Some readers may wish that the author's diligent lopping and cropping had included Mary Bennet, whose scraps of threadbare morality, as satire on moralizing in the Richardsonian tradition, fall pretty flat, though she can be said to represent a bookishness as remote from life as her intelligent father's. Such characters resemble some in *Sense and Sensibility* in being "humors," which were

Fanny Burney's very inferior stock in trade: everything, or almost everything, they say reveals one dominant trait, with a consistency which goes beyond the measure of predictability common enough in people of limited intelligence. This relatively elementary kind of characterization, which can of course be very funny, may be seen as a survival of Jane Austen's youthful relish for high colouring. These are the farcical characters, whose motives, as far as Jane Austen investigates them, are interesting as matter for comedy. These—Mr Collins, Lady Catherine and Mrs Bennet—are similar in the way they are presented and the uses they are put to, and are about equally important. Mr Collins obviously functions for our amusement, talking the riotous and illogical nonsense of the minor works:

> Do not make yourself uneasy, my dear cousin, about your apparel. Lady Catherine is far from requiring that elegance of dress in us, which becomes herself and daughter. I would advise you merely to put on whatever of your clothes is superior to the rest, there is no occasion for any thing more. (*PP* 160)

Craik writes, "His proposal to Elizabeth has a literary basis, again like the early works, and its humour derives from literary conventions; Mr Collins assumes that he should be 'run away with by his feelings' and that her refusal is a romantic convention. He also has a serious purpose and many uses to justify his literary existence, and is kept in his place among more subtle delights" (70). As soon as he has arrived, he is eclipsed at Mrs Philips's evening party by another new and interesting visitor, Wickham; after his magnificent proposal he appears but little, and at Hunsford he is in the background to Lady Catherine, and to Elizabeth and Darcy; thereafter he appears only in two letters, one of cousinly consolation for Lydia's downfall, and the other of warning to Elizabeth and her 'noble admirer' not to 'run hastily into a marriage that has not been properly sanctioned' (*PP* 363). A little of Mr Collins goes a long way, though he is useful as well as memorable; he is a link between Longbourn and Rosings, between Elizabeth's family surroundings and Darcy's, and therefore helps to balance Darcy's objections to Elizabeth's family with Elizabeth's objections to Darcy's, while his proposal to Elizabeth gives a chance to see that she acts according to her principles, and that her judgment is sound:

> Mr Collins is a conceited, pompous, narrow-minded, silly man; you know he is, as well as I do; and you must feel, as well as I do, that the woman who marries him, cannot have a proper way of thinking. (*PP* 135)

Lady Catherine is a fit patron for Collins; she is introduced through him, again saving Jane Austen from introducing her in person, and doing it more effectively because she takes on character from what we know of Mr Collins before she appears in person. As she has no prominent habits of speech—being vulgar in more essential ways—she can be subordinated by appearing through what Elizabeth observes of her:

> She enquired into Charlotte's domestic concerns familiarly and minutely, and gave her a great deal of advice, as to the management of them all; told her how every thing ought to be regulated in so small a family as her's, and instructed her as to the care of her cows and her poultry. Elizabeth found that nothing was beneath this great Lady's attention, which could furnish her with an occasion of dictating to others. (*PP* 163)

The replies and reactions she produces are the important thing:

> "Upon my word," said her Ladyship, "you give your opinion very decidedly for so young a person. Pray, what is your age?"
>
> "With three younger sisters grown up," replied Elizabeth smiling, "your Ladyship can hardly expect me to own it." (*PP* 165-66)
>
> "She is very welcome, as I have often told her, to come to Rosings every day, and play on the piano forte in Mrs Jenkinson's room. She would be in nobody's way, you know, in that part of the house."
>
> Mr Darcy looked a little ashamed of his aunt's ill breeding, and made no answer. (*PP* 173)

Such remarks prepare for the splendid scene in which she attempts to browbeat Elizabeth into refusing Darcy. Though just as striking as Mr Collins, she is less useful; her only function to the plot is to precipitate Darcy's proposal by trying to prevent it. But she has other uses; she makes Darcy seem interesting and romantic after a bad start, because she embodies the wealth and power of his connections even before we see his own at Pemberley, but at the same time her indecorous behaviour puts him and his family much more on a level with Elizabeth and hers.

Like Lady Catherine, Mrs Bennet has many of the features of Jane Austen's early work. Her practical use is to be the direct cause of Jane's misfortunes and of Lydia's as well. She appears almost entirely through her own words, and says some of the funniest irrational things in Jane Austen. She is based on a few strong traits given in her first appearance:

> She was a woman of mean understanding, little information, and uncertain temper. When she was discontented she fancied herself nervous. The business of her life was to get her daughters married; its solace was visiting and news. (*PP* 5)

These traits are exercised mainly on Jane's prospects of marrying Bingley, her neighbour Mrs Long and her nieces (no one else ever mentions them), and the entail. Her actions are always consistent with herself, but always surprising because she is consistently irrational: "There is knowing how estates will go when once they come to be entailed" (*PP* 65); "How any one could have the conscience to entail away an estate from one's own daughters I cannot understand" (*PP* 130). She is useful to the reader because she is invariably wrong where there is visible evidence, and can therefore be assumed to be wrong where there is none:

> I beg you would not put it into Lizzy's head to be vexed by his ill-treatment; for he is such a disagreeable man that it would be quite a misfortune to be liked by him. (*PP* 19)

This, for the reader, is as good as praise. These three, Mr Collins, Lady Catherine and Mrs Bennet, show how Jane

Austen can use humour, as opposed to wit, for satiric purposes, an unusual talent.

George Wickham and Lydia are like these farcical characters in being seen wholly from the outside, but they are not as detailed, and have no entertaining qualities apart from their services to the plot. Lydia's elopement is tactfully prepared for in the presentation of Lydia herself. She is the most striking of the sisters after Elizabeth and Jane, which is what her part in the action is, and she makes an impression before either of them:

> Lydia, my love, though you *are* the youngest, I dare say Mr Bingley will dance with you at the next ball.
>
> 'Oh!' said Lydia stoutly, 'I am not afraid; for though I *am* the youngest, I'm the tallest.' (*PP* 8)

After Elizabeth and Jane come home from Hunsford and London she comes more to the fore, until she leaves for Brighton and disgrace: she orders a salad she cannot pay for and buys a hat she does not like because she "might as well buy it as not" and because "there were two or three much uglier in the shop" (219), revealing the same carelessness of consequence and irresponsibility (on a small scale) as eloping with Wickham will do. When Elizabeth tries to persuade her father to forbid the Brighton visit, this, as well as showing the growth of Elizabeth's feeling of moral responsibility, prepares us to expect some kind of disaster. Wickham is treated like Lydia. What is heard of his actions before the elopement—that he has tried to elope with Georgiana Darcy when he has failed to sponge on her brother—is enough to make his conduct there credible, while he is charming, like Willoughby, not so much by his own acts as because another character, Elizabeth, thinks him so. While Willoughby never says or does anything admirable, Wickham is even more emphatically presented as an obvious hypocrite, and the reader always has the evidence for making the true estimate of him that Elizabeth only makes much later. When he first appears his unprompted confidences to Elizabeth are as improper as she later sees them to be, but because the reader tends to see through Elizabeth's eyes and even more because the sudden confidence is in any case a conventional part of the novelist's stock-in-trade, distrust is not roused at the time. His words always contradict his conduct:

> It is not for *me* to be driven away by Mr Darcy. If *he* wishes to avoid seeing *me*, he must go. (*PP* 78)

It is then Wickham who stays away from the ball at Netherfield. Elizabeth herself unconsciously indicates suspicious circumstances, at a point already mentioned:

> Elizabeth honoured him for such feelings, and thought him handsomer than ever as he expressed them. (*PP* 80)

There is a definite pattern in relationships between characters. What Wickham does for Elizabeth, Miss Bingley does for Darcy: Miss Bingley, another hypocrite, while displaying Darcy's wit and right thinking, makes him seem a desirable *parti,* just as Wickham's attentions are proof of Elizabeth's charm.

Bingley and Jane as well as being like each other, each perform a similar function towards Darcy and Elizabeth. Intelligent and right-thinking, both reveal the greater intelligence and subtlety of the more important character. The exchanges between the two men at Netherfield establish—as Jane Austen has already remarked—that "Bingley was by no means deficient (in understanding), but Darcy was clever" (*PP* 16). Bingley's weakness also matches Jane's, he being too easily influenced, while she is too good-natured. He is redeemed as a husband fit for her—the plot has put him in a position where he does not seem to be, when he has allowed Darcy to influence him—when he renews his attentions to her before Darcy has confessed to using his influence to separate them.

It is of course a further mark of the caricatures that they are in some degree ridiculous, proper targets for laughter even if we condemn them too. The laughter implies that in some sense we see them as not seriously mattering. But that is true only if we discriminate between the reader's view and the view taken by figures in the fiction. While Elizabeth sees Mr Collins with contemptuous amusement our view of him as a caricature and her view of him as—within the fictional world—a real person are not noticeably different. When, however, he proposes, and Mrs Bennet's urgent pressure turns the proposal into a genuine threat, then we have to recognize that although he remains a joke for us he has become no joke for Elizabeth. Nor is he a joke for her when Charlotte Lucas marries him. The handling of him as a caricature is a convention between author and readers; the other fictional figures are not party to it. Lady Catherine in the shrubbery, forbidding Elizabeth to become engaged to Darcy, touches the heights of caricature for us—"Heaven and earth!—of what are you thinking? Are the shades of Pemberly to be thus polluted?" But for Elizabeth she is a threat, a very real person; Elizabeth for her own part can confidently judge her to be absurd, but at the same time her power, especially over Darcy, is not easily gauged:

> She knew not the exact degree of his affection for his aunt, or his dependence on her judgment, but it was natural to suppose that he thought much higher of her ladyship than *she* could do. (Ch. 57)

D.W. Harding observes in "Character and Caricature in Jane Austen": "...Jane Austen insists on the reality of the monstrous Mr Collins in two ways; first by showing the real pressure that Mrs Bennet exerts to make Elizabeth marry him; and secondly, and more thoughtfully, by allowing him to secure Charlotte, a real person, and letting Elizabeth gradually realize, once over the first shock of horror, that her friend was after all making a tolerable life for herself in the second-best world that most people except heroines have to inhabit" (Southam 99).

Most of the other characters are handled in the same way as Mr Collins and Lady Catherine, but in less detail. Kitty, Mary, Mr Hurst, and Sir William Lucas are the chief ones. Kitty is not much more than an appendage to Lydia, demonstrating Lydia's vitality by her own lack of it. Mary is more entertaining than she is usually given credit for, another literary burlesque whose language is a delight. One can enjoy "we must stem the tide of malice, and pour into the wounded bosoms of each other, the balm of sisterly consolation" (*PP* 289) without perceiving its orgin (in sentimental fiction and drama), but not this:

> In point of composition, his letter does not seem defective. The idea of the olive branch perhaps is not wholly new, yet I think it is well expressed. (*PP* 64)

Mr Hurst is the gentlemanly bedrock below the gold of Bingley and Darcy. Sir William is the dressing up of several essential pieces of plot, in particular when he awakens Darcy's suspicions about Bingley and Jane, and he is another type of social and moral ineptitude.

This is the earliest novel to have comically treated characters capable of serious conduct, who are limited only by what the plot lets them do. These are Mr and Mrs Gardiner, Colonel Fitzwilliam, Charlotte Lucas, and Jane. These characters are like Mrs Weston in *Emma,* and the pleasant group of naval figures in *Persuasion.* That their personalities are not at all alike shows how Jane Austen can use a deliberately limited method for a wide variety of effects. Though Mr and Mrs Gardiner are slight their judgment is to be respected, and Mrs Gardiner gives Elizabeth necessary and prudent advice about Wickham. Colonel Fitzwilliam tells Elizabeth how Darcy separated Jane and Bingley; he is seen just enough to be a trustworthy witness to the truth of Darcy's letter, and, by being rational and agreeable, shows that Elizabeth is attractive to a man of better sense than Mr Collins or Wickham, and that Elizabeth herself is ready to be attracted by a suitable person—"Elizabeth was reminded by her own satisfaction in being with him, as well as by his evident admiration of her, of her former favourite George Wickham" (*PP* 180); he therefore provides the necessary step between Wickham and Darcy. Charlotte Lucas and Jane, both standing in relation to Elizabeth, are more important. They both show up some deficiency in her while their own deficiencies show up her virtues. Charlotte is an acute observer: she sees that Jane's feelings may be too well concealed:

> Bingley likes your sister undoubtedly; but he may never do more than like her, if she does not help him on.
>
> But she does help him on, as much as her nature will allow. If I can perceive her regard for him, he must be a simpletion indeed not to discover it too.

> Remember, Eliza, that he does not know Jane's disposition as you do. (*PP* 22)

More important, she sees a good while before his proposal that Darcy is paying attentions to Elizabeth, a circumstance which Elizabeth ought to have seen, too. She follows her own precepts when she marries Mr Collins—

> Happiness in marriage is entirely a matter of chance.... It is better to know as little as possible of the defects of the person with whom you are to pass your life. (*PP* 23)

and although the marriage is a surprise to the reader as well as to Elizabeth, it has been prepared for, and so is not at all incredible. Charlotte, like Mrs Gardiner, shows that though Jane Austen's subjects are romantic, her view is a practical one, and she most fairly presents the extenuating circumstances in Charlotte's case, though these do not at all undermine our respect for Elizabeth's standards:

> Without thinking highly either of men or of matrimony, marriage had always been her objects; it was the only honourable provision for well-educated young women of small fortune, and however uncertain of giving happiness, must be their pleasantest preservative from want. (*PP* 122-23)

Jane, like Charlotte, contrasts with and interprets Elizabeth; but she regulates her conduct by a prejudice in favour of people rather than against them. Her engagement to Bingley and their whole courtship—except for its one artificial interruption from Darcy—progresses quickly and agreeably, in sharp contrast to Elizabeth's and Darcy's. She has, however, very little to say and not much to do; she is seen mainly through Elizabeth's opinion of her, and most of what she says is to Elizabeth.

Mr Bennet resembles Charlotte, an acute and rational person warped into moral irresponsibility, she by materialism, her by disillusion and lethargy:

> For what do we live, but to make sport for our neighbours, and laugh at them in our turn? (*PP* 364)

Wit warps his judgement as it does Elizabeth's, but warps it more.

> Lydia will never be easy till she has exposed herself in some public place or other, and we can never expect her to do it with so little expense or inconvenience to her family as under the present circumstances. (*PP* 230)

This is the same kind of argument, though worse, as that with which Elizabeth defends Wickham's paying court to Miss King:

> If it was not allowable for him to gain my affections, because I had no money, what occasion could there be for making love to a girl whom he did not care about, and who was equally poor? (*PP* 153)

Mr Bennet is seen just fully enough for his penitence to be convincing, when Lydia elopes:

> Let me once in my life feel how much I have been to blame. I am not afraid to being overpowered by the impression. It will pass away soon enough. (*PP* 299)

The emotion, convincingly mingled with his customary cynicism, makes him a more solid figure, fit for his coming association with Bingley and Darcy; for the question of his consent to their respective engagements, though a formality, must not be a farce. Craik writes, "Mr Bennet's attitude of *laissez aller* not only makes him an obvious foil for Mrs Bennet, but also forces on the two heroines a freedom of moral choice and conduct which they must have for Jane Austen's purpose, and which all her heroines have. The minor characters are all therefore clearly patterned to bring out the central theme embodied in them and in the two main characters" (77-78).

Around these main characters Jane Austen constructs a recognizable society. It does not embrace so many different elements as *Sense and Sensibility* did—only rural gentry with a glance at the London of the Gardiners—but it shows much greater skill and uses new methods. She makes much use of background characters, those who never appear in person in the action, or who, if they do appear, never speak. This appears here better regulated in Mrs Long and her nieces, who are a barometer of Mrs Bennet's humours:

> ...Mrs Long has promised to introduce him.
>
> I do not believe Mrs Long will do any such thing. She has two nieces of her own. She is a selfish, hypocritical woman, and I have no opinion of her. (*PP* 6)
>
> I do think Mrs Long is as good a creature as ever lived—and her nieces[*sic*] are very pretty behaved girls, and not at all handsome: I like them prodigiously. (*PP* 342)

Other background characters are not the property of one character but represent a kind of society; such are Colonel Forster and his wife with whom Lydia is 'such friends,' who take her to Brighton and epitomize military society; and Mrs Younge, who chaperoned Georgiana Darcy on her ill-fated visit to Ramsgate, and who hides Lydia and Wickham in London, embodying the shabby and shifty milieu from which Wickham has emerged. This is a new use for characters and looks forward to *Emma* and *Mansfield Park* because it reveals situation rather than personality: the Forsters stand for Lydia's Brighton.

Two other devices are practically exclusive to *Pride and Prejudice*; first, the character who appears but never speaks, like Lady Lucas and Mr Philips, who therefore merely gives an impression of a type of company; and second the localized but disembodied public opinion. This latter is necessary because of the public nature of many of the events; Lydia's elopement and subsequent reclamation are things that cannot be kept secret:

> The good news quickly spread through the house; and with proportionate speed through the neighbourhood.
>
> It was borne in the latter with decent philosophy. To be sure it would have been more for the advantage of conversation, had Miss Lydia Bennet come upon the town: or, as the happiest alternative, been secluded from the world, in some distant farm house. But there was much to be talked of, in marrying her; and the

> good-natured wishes for her well-doing, which had proceeded before, from all the spiteful old ladies in Meryton, lost but little of their spirit in this change of circumstances, because with such an husband, her misery was considered certain. (*PP* 309)
>
> Other events could be kept secret, but are not; Wickham's slanders become public and 'every body was pleased to think how much they had always disliked Mr Darcy'. (*PP* 138)

Pride and Prejudice has a main plot admirably suited to Jane Austen's purposes. There is no dissociation here between characters and the things they have to do, as there is in *Sense and Sensibility,* and events always appear to be the natural consequence of the personalities involved. 'Lydia's elopement is the only event seriously influencing the relations between Darcy and Elizabeth which is not the direct result of the behaviour of one of them. Though adequately prepared by her own previous behaviour and Wickham's, it is a stumbling-block for some readers; but it is not as important as it seems, for it has no direct effect on their relationship, except to let us see Darcy actually behaving as the revised character Elizabeth's reproofs have made him. The always very minor clumsinesses in handling are all on the fringes, and are such as in almost any other novelist would pass unobserved; it is only beside the standard of perfection that Jane Austen sets for herself with *Emma* and (where technique is concerned) with *Mansfield Park* that they are noticeable. Colonel Fitzwilliam appears only at Rosings—as a companion for Darcy and a witness to his letter, and as an admirer for Elizabeth; he is never mentioned elsewhere, and this is a casual use of character which she does not usually permit herself even in her early work. A more striking *gaucherie* is Gerogiana Darcy. There is no reason why she should not be at Netherfield, particularly as Darcy hopes she will marry Bingley: she is two years older than Lydia and has already had an establishment in Ramsgate. She seems to be deliberately kept out of the action to satisfy the exigencies of the plot: Wickham can tell irrefutable lies about an absent person, and Darcy can show his esteem for Elizabeth and the Gardiners by introducing them to a hitherto unknown sister.

Craik writes, "A new thing in *Pride and Prejudice* is the handling of groups of characters. There are almost twice as many characters in this novel as in *Sense and Sensibility,* and Jane Austen handles large groups of them at a time, with the minimum of directives from herself" (87). The second chapter of the novel introduces the whole of the Bennet family in conversation, without superfluous exchanges, giving useful information not only about themselves by what they say, but also about their neighbours. The scene is really a conversation between Mr and Mrs Bennet, with the daughters' remarks interpolated, which makes it clear and easy to follow. The interpolations themselves are in a significant order. Elizabeth is most important and speaks first:

> I hope Mr Bingley will like it, Lizzy.
>
> 'We are not in a way to know what Mr Bingley likes', said her mother resentfully, 'since we are not to visit.' 'But you forget, mama,' said Elizabeth, 'that we shall meet him at the assemblies, and that Mrs Long has promised to introduce him.' (*PP* 6)

This shows that she shares her father's sense. Lydia is last and therefore in a position second in importance only to Elizabeth:

> I am not afraid; for though I am the youngerst, I'm the tallest. (*PP* 8)

Kitty's cough brings forward Mrs Bennet's nerves as a force to be reckoned with, and a 'fretful' reply ranges her with her mother. Mary makes clear the force of Mr Bennet's irony; she brilliantly says nothing:

> What say you, Mary? for you are a young lady of deep reflection I know, and read great books, and make extracts.
>
> Mary wished to say something very sensible, but knew not how. (*PP* 7)

Mr Bennet's comments and introductions are as efficient as any from a narrator could be, and are more dramatic, so the scene goes as briskly as if one were reading a play, though more clearly, and with more information, in a shorter time, than any play could bear. This same method is used to give the effect of large parties of people in conversation, of which we hear only the interesting parts out of several exchanges taking place simultaneously; the evenings at Netherfield are excellent examples. While all that is said is relevant to the characters and to how they will behave later, neither the order in which they speak nor what they say is logical, but gives the impression of casual and often interrupted chat. On Elizabeth's second evening there, Miss Bingley, bored with her book, opens the conversation by asking her brother about the proposed ball; the subject soon drops, because from Mr Bingley's words it is clear that no one either agrees with Caroline or cares to argue with her:

> 'I should like balls infinitely better,' she replied, 'if they were carried on in a different manner.... It would surely be much more rational if conversation instead of dancing made the order of the day.'
>
> 'Much more rational, my dear Caroline, I dare say, but it would not be near so much like a ball.' (*PP* 55-56)

What this exchange does is to show that Caroline will be aiming all her behaviour at Mr Darcy, and that as even Mr Bingley is a match for her Darcy will never be taken in. The talk goes on between Miss Bingley and Elizabeth, and it is only when Elizabeth teases him, not when Miss Bingley flatters him, that Mr Darcy speaks himself:

> 'As to laughter, we will not expose ourselves, if you please, by attempting to laugh without a subject. Mr Darcy may hug himself.'
>
> 'Mr Darcy is not to be laughed at!' cried Elizabeth. 'That is an uncommon advantage, and uncommon I hope it will continue, for it would be a great loss to me to have many such acquaintance. I dearly love a laugh.'
>
> 'Miss Bingley', said he, 'has given me credit for more than can be'.... (*PP* 57)

For a few lines there is a rational though still light-hearted exchange between Elizabeth and Darcy, which Miss Bingley's interruption emphasizes by seeming merely a frivolous intrusion:

> 'Your examination of Mr Darcy is over, I presume,' said Miss Bingley;—'and pray what is the result?' (*PP* 57)

In fact, it has no effect on the topic at all, because Mr Darcy simply goes on talking to Elizabeth. The conversation is intimate, but the setting is quite public; we feel Bingley to be ready to speak because we have already heard him, and we assume Mrs Hurst to be listening because we know she is 'principally occupied in playing with her bracelets and rings' (*PP* 55). The remarks we hear do not follow logically from the remarks of each previous speaker, but indicate the drift of each speaker's private thoughts, without holding up the conversation with an account of them.

There is an unfailing naturalness and ease—ease that comes from careful work as well as inspiration—with which Jane Austen builds characters and situations that forward the growth of love while creating both social comedy and suspense. And economy contributes much to the graceful, coherent symmetry of *Pride and Prejudice*. The author's own famous comment on the book is evidence enough of her deliberate avoidance of anything irrelevant to her story (Letter 77, to Cassandra: February 4, 1813):

> The work is rather too light, and bright, and sparkling; it wants shade—it wants to be stretched out here and there with a long chapter of sense, if it could be had; if not, of solemn specious nonsense, about something unconnected with the story; an essay on writing, a critique on Walter Scott, or the history of Buonaparte, of anything that would form a contrast, and bring the reader with increased delight to the playfulness and epigrammatism of the general style. I doubt your quite agreeing with me here. I know your starched notions.

Some references in the letters suggest how real to the author her characters were. One item of general significance is that, while she enjoyed the Liverpool Museum and the British Gallery, her avowed "preference for Men & Women" inclined her, as always, "to attend more to the company than the sight" (Letter, 69: April 18, 1811). So Elizabeth Bennet, thinking of one man if not of people, was indifferent to all portraits but one in the Pemberley gallery. Two years later (Letter 80; May 24, 1813), when Jane and Henry visited an exhibition, she was particularly happy to see "a small portrait of Mrs Bingley," which she described in detail as an exact likeness. But there and at another exhibition she was disappointed in finding nothing like Mrs. Darcy: she could "only imagine that Mr D. Prizes any Picture of her too much to like it should be exposed to the public eye, that he w'd have that sort of feeling—that mixture of Love, Pride & Delicacy."

In *Pride and Prejudice*, as in the other novels, various pairs represent various attitudes towards love and marriage. Although, as we have seen, some readers think Darcy implausibly manipulated, the workings of pride and prejudice are not, like the workings of sense and sensibility, obtrusively moulded in opposed patterns. We may note further that this novel, unlike most of the others, has no mentor whose rational wisdom establishes a point of view and scale of values. But to say that is to realize that the role is tacitly given to the spirited and highly intelligent heroine, who, though she can err grievously, is nevertheless the person through whose eyes and usually reliable mind we assess the other characters and the action. In every respect, in characters, plot, structure, dialogue, tone, *Pride and Prejudice* is very much lighter, brighter, more sparkling, and more maturely competent than its predecessor. Indeed, as its long popularity proclaims, this, more than any of the novels except *Emma*, maintains social comedy among fully realized characters with dramatic verve, frequent subtlety, and a fine blend of wit and serious feeling.

(VII) NARRATIVE ART

In Austen's novels there are different characteristic points of view which are separable and susceptible of analysis. Jane Austen in her novels sometimes stands as apparently objective as the Chaucer of the *Troilus and Creseyde* and sometimes, at the opposite extreme, she sets herself down, in *propria persona,* in the centre of her work with quite as much self-consciousness as the Thackeray of *Vanity Fair.* Andrew H. Wright writes in *Jane Austen's Novels: A Study in Structure*: "She is by turns omniscient and ignorant, humble and sententious, direct and oblique, the dramatist and the teller of tales. Unshackled by more modern theories, her point of view varies; it is sly, often intentionally misleading—or at least very delicately subtle: quite unobtrusive transitions carry the reader from one point of view to another..." (36). Craik writes in *Jane Austen: The Six Novels,* "Jane Austen characteristically finds ways of subordinating her part as narrator; irony is not merely an attitude, it is a method of presentation, organization, analysis and judgment. Her skill in irony is at its greatest here [*Pride and Prejudice*] and in *Emma,* where she can be serious without ever being solemn, both in contrast to *Sense and Sensibility,* where the theme is not suitable, while in *Mansfield Park*—particularly the latter half—and in *Persuasion* she is using a different method. Irony is appropriate in *Pride and Prejudice* because the characters are all deficient in some way, even though the intelligent characters may express Jane Austen's judgment for her" (64).

As usual, the opening of the novel is a deliberate guide to the whole:

> It is a truth universally acknowledged, that a single man in possession of a good fortune, must be in want of a wife.
>
> However little known the feelings or views of such a man may be on his first entering a neighbourhood, this truth is so well fixed in the minds of the surrounding families, that he is considered as the rightful property of some one or other of their daughters. (*PP* 3)

This is irony at its best and most useful. We hear what the story will be about—courtship and marriage; we have a hint in 'the surrounding families' that this will be the concern of more than one couple, the concern not only of Elizabeth and Darcy, but of Jane and Bingley, Mr Collins and Charlotte, and of Wickham and Elizabeth, Miss King and Lydia by turns; we see what the deeper preoccupations of the novel will be—the moral weight of material and financial matters in personal affairs; and we see how the sense of the family and the neighbourhood which accompany the action will bear on individuals, for most of Jane's troubles (for example) are caused by her family, and the neighbourhood gossip is one of the trials after Lydia's elopement, and it encourages and intensifies Elizabeth's misrepresentations of Darcy.

If Austen is sometimes a chronicler of the past, at others she is a narrator of the present. Although Austen poses as a neutral observer, Wright writes in *Jane Austen's Novels* that neutrality is quite impossible for Austen as "she will not let the facts speak for themselves, for she does not believe that facts can be articulate" (38). After the delicious dialogue of the first chapter of *Pride and Prejudice* the author sums up the characters of Mr and Mrs Bennet:

> Mr Bennet was so odd a mixture of quick parts, sarcastic humour, reserve, and caprice, that the experience of three and twenty years had been insufficient to make his wife understand his character. *Her* mind was less difficult to develope. She was a woman of mean understanding, little information, and uncertain temper. When she was discontented she fancied herself nervous. The business of her life was to get her daughters married; its solace was visiting and news. (*PP* 5)

Here, in very economical compass, is an accurate sketch of both the characters, drawn by someone who has a complete insight into them. Yet the chapter has begun with some grandiloquent statements as to the marriageability of rich young men; statements which cannot represent the author's opinion. Actually, the reader can at this point only guess that Mr and Mrs Bennet are being truly described, but the guess can be grounded on the conversation which they have just completed. And we notice what Jane Austen withholds: she does not tell us of Mr Bennet's wanton irresponsibility nor of Mrs Bennet's malevolent selfishness; the author simply states some conditions from which these can follow.

Of the relationship between Darcy and Bingley the reader gets an analytical account:

> Bingley was endeared to Darcy by the easiness, openness, ductility of his temper, though no disposition could offer a greater contrast to his own, and though with his own he never appeared dissatisfied. On the strength of Darcy's regard Bingley had the firmest reliance, and of his judgment the highest opinion. In understanding Darcy was the superior. Bingley was by no means deficient, but Darcy was clever. (*PP* 16)

Again Jane Austen omnisciently presents insights into her characters; and, as there is no suggestion in any of her language or syntax that she is not being altogether straight forward, we accept this statement at its face value. On the other hand, in recording Mr Bennet's early history, the author, while apparently giving an objective account, actually shifts rapidly from one point of view to another:

> Had Elizabeth's opinion been all drawn from her own family, she could not have formed a very pleasing picture of conjugal felicity or domestic comfort. Her father captivated by youth and beauty, and that appearance of good humour, which youth and beauty generally give, had married a woman whose weak understanding and illiberal mind, had very early in their marriage put an end to all real affection for her. Respect, esteem, and confidence, had vanished for ever; and all his views of domestic happiness were overthrown. But Mr Bennet was not of a disposition to seek comfort for the disappointment which his own imprudence had brought on, in any of those pleasures which too often console the unfortunate for their folly or their vice. He was fond of the country and of books; and from these tastes had arisen his principal enjoyments. To his wife he was very little otherwise indebted, than as her ignorance and folly had contributed to his amusement. This is not the sort of happiness which a man would in general wish to owe to his wife; but where other powers of entertainment are

> wanting, the true philosopher will derive benefit from such as are given. (*PP* 236)

The mention of Elizabeth in the first sentence suggests that the author is preparing to present the heroine's impressions of her father; this is the case: in the following paragraph, the viewpoint is that of Elizabeth. But here Jane Austen relates certain facts of which Elizabeth cannot have such direct knowledge; in fact, the author is speaking, and she even introduces several sententious phrases: '...that appearance of good humour which youth and beauty generally give' must be admitted as an objective truth if we are to accept the fact that an intelligent man would marry a silly woman; 'those pleasures which too often console the unfortunate for their folly or their vices' is stated with such moderation and straightforwardness that we must believe it; but the last sentence must be immediately suspected if we reflect on Jane Austen's diction: the ambiguous word 'entertainment' which in the eighteenth century meant both 'support, sustenance,' and 'that which affords interest or amusement' (*N.E.D.*); and her mention of 'the true philosopher,' the slightly grand epithet for something much more ordinary—a characteristic method of achieving an ironic purpose.

Occasionally, Jane Austen summarizes an incident or series of incidents in such a way as to disclose certain reactions which could be known only to the omniscient narrator. After William Collins's proposal to Charlotte Lucas, this paragraph occurs:

> Sir William and Lady Lucas were speedily applied to for their consent; and it was bestowed with a most joyful alacrity. Mr Collins's present circumstances made it a most eligible match for their daughter, to whom they could give little fortune; and his prospects of future wealth were exceedingly fair. Lady Lucas began directly to calculate with more interest than the matter had ever excited before, how many years longer Mr Bennet was likely to live; and Sir William gave it as his decided opinion, that whenever Mr Collins should be in possession of the Longbourn estate, it would be highly expedient that both he and his wife should make their

> appearance at St. James's. The whole family in short were properly over-joyed on the occasion. The younger girls formed hopes of *coming out* a year or two sooner than they might otherwise have done; and the boys were relieved from their apprehension of Charlotte's dying an old maid. (*PP* 122)

Andrew H. Wright writes, in this context, in *Jane Austen's Novels: A Study in Structure*: "This pretends to be an objective narrative by an omniscient scribe; objectively, it is 'a most eligible match'; objectively, 'the whole family were properly overjoyed'; and the girls speak of '*coming out.*' Actually, the surrounding circumstances make it quite clear that the author has identified herself with the viewpoint of the Lucases, while maintaining the pose of narrator—and this in order to achieve the purpose of mocking the pretensions of this trades-family" (51).

After Darcy's departure from the neighbourhood of Longbourn, Wickham freely tells the story of the former's wrong doings to him—a story which previously he revealed only to Elizabeth.

> The whole of what Elizabeth had already heard, his claims on Mr Darcy, and all that he had suffered from him, was now openly acknowledged and publicly canvassed; and everybody was pleased to think how much they had always disliked Mr Darcy before they had known anything of the matter. (*PP* 138)

Wright comments: "In the first part of this paragraph Jane Austen identifies herself with Wickham's viewpoint, in that—rather than speaking of an allegation or even one version of a story—she uses the word 'acknowledged'. Yet this acknowledgment is rendered suspect by the hint which she then gives of the people of the neighbourhood: 'everybody was pleased to think' contains an ambiguity in the leading verb; they could either be taking pleasure in the thought, or they could *choose* to recollect what they do. Both meanings existed then, as now" (51).

On their return to Longbourn after being married, Lydia and Wickham are described with partial objectivity; their actual words of greeting are not heard:

> Their reception from Mr Bennet, to whom they then turned [after greeting Mrs Bennet], was not quite so cordial. His countenance rather gained in austerity; and he scarcely opened his lips. The easy assurance of the young couple, indeed, was enough to provoke him. Elizabeth was disgusted, and even Miss Bennet was shocked. Lydia was Lydia still; untamed, unabashed, wild, noisy, and fearless. She turned from sister to sister, demanding their congratulations, and when at length they all sat down, looked eagerly round the room, took notice of some little alteration in it, and observed, with a laugh, that it was a great while since she had been there. (*PP* 315)

The beginning and the ending of this paragraph contain what might be observed by a perceptive and evaluating witness. But the author does also take us directly into the minds of Elizabeth and Jane. Wright observes: "Who, then, describes Lydia with the five devastating adjectives? The reader might attribute the thought to either of the Miss Bennets; but upon reflection one realizes that Jane Bennet would never censure so wholly—and in fact the adjectives have such a literary tone that they probably emanate from the narrator rather than from the mind of Elizabeth. There is at least a question as to what viewpoint is used in the sentence" (52).

The early relationship between Fitzwilliam Darcy and George Wickham is never directly presented to the reader; the time scheme of the book forbids it: the action of *Pride and Prejudice* takes place long afterwards: but there are other important reasons: George Wickham gives the first version, which much maligns the squire of Pemberley—and so reinforces Elizabeth's prejudice; Darcy then, in the famous, letter to Elizabeth, gives the true version which discloses at once the measure of his honourable discretion, the softening of his pride, the unimpeachability of his behaviour to Wickham, and the strength of his affection for the girl. In fact, letters provide a very effective method of indirect reportage.

Austen is never more than ostensively objective. When, however, she intrudes herself indirectly, she casts aside all pretence. In Derbyshire, Elizabeth Bennet first awakens to the true nature of her sentiment for Darcy—but she is called away suddenly on account of the elopement of Lydia and Wickham. She hates to go, and she "sighed at the perverseness of those feelings which would now have promoted its continuance [their acquaintance] and would formerly have rejoiced in its termination." Then the author steps in:

> If gratitude and esteem are good foundations of affection, Elizabeth's change of sentiment will be neither improbable nor faulty. But if otherwise, if the regard springing from such sources is unreasonable or unnatural, in comparison of what is so often described as arising on a first interview with its object, and even before two words have been exchanged, nothing can be said in her defence, except that she had given somewhat of a trial to the latter method, in her partiality for Wickham, and that its ill-success might perhaps authorize her to seek the other less interesting mode of attachment. Be that as it may, she saw him go with regret.... (*PP* 279)

Deep within Jane Austen, as the delineation of Wickham shows, is a distrust of appearance; and Elizabeth has learned from her experience with the Meryton lieutenant to look beyond surface to essence, so it is natural that she should not fling herself immediately at Darcy; it is inevitable, in the terms of the story itself, that 'gratitude and esteem' should be now more highly valued by her: but they do not preclude love.

Andrew H. Wright writes in *Jane Austen's Novels: A Study in Structure*: "Related to the personal and impersonal intrusion by the author is her penchant for sprinkling in her works—or rather sayings that seem to have the authority of maxims but which may have little weight so far as Jane Austen's own thinking is concerned. Actually, maxims usually express the common-sense point of view; and Jane Austen is full of that kind of sense—but she goes far beyond it; and hovering about every single piece of homely wisdom is the ironic qualification" (68-69). The famous first sentence of *Pride and Prejudice,* "It is a truth universally acknowledged, that a single man in possession of a good fortune, must be in want of a wife" is meant to have ironic qualification and it is shown both in the orotundity of the diction, and by contrast with what is said in the following sentence—that the concern is to be not with the universe but with a 'neighbourhood', not with the totality of mankind, but with 'the surrounding families.'

Very much of Jane Austen's work is in dialogue form; she is a master-dramatist—with a perfect ear, a perfect sense of timing, a shrewd instinct for climax and anti-climax. And when one thinks of Jane Austen's novels one is apt to remember most clearly such conversations as that between Mr and Mrs Bennet on the subject of the new tenant at Netherfield Park.

A close attention may be given at one particularly ironic dialogue, that between Lady Catherine de Bourgh and Elizabeth Bennet, on the subject of Mr Darcy.

> "You can be at no loss, Miss Bennet, to understand the reason of my journey hither. Your own heart, your own conscience, must tell you why I come."
>
> Elizabeth looked with unaffected astonishment.
>
> "Indeed, you are mistaken, Madam. I have not been at all able to account for the honour of seeing you here."
>
> "Miss Bennet," replied her ladyship, in an angry tone, "You ought to know, that I am not to be trifled with. But however insincere you may choose to be, you shall not find *me* so. My character has ever been celebrated for its sincerity and frankness, and in a cause of such moment as this, I shall certainly not depart from it. A report of a most alarming nature, reached me two days ago. I was told, that not only your sister was on the point of being most advantageously married, but that *you,* that Miss Elizabeth Bennet, would, in all likelihood, be soon afterwards united to my nephew,

> my own nephew, Mr Darcy. Though I *know* it must be a scandalous falsehood; though I would not injure him so much as to suppose the truth of it possible, I instantly resolved on setting off for this place, that I might make my sentiments known to you." (*PP* 353)

Lady Catherine's self-ignorance is colossal: she is to be trifled with, her 'sincerity and frankness' are immediately impugned, when Elizabeth retorts,

> If you believed it impossible to be true...I wonder you took the trouble of coming so far. What could your ladyship propose by it? (*PP* 353)

The conversation results in a complete rout for Lady Catherine—she goes away "most seriously displeased", having failed to exact any promise from Elizabeth not to marry Darcy. Retrospectively, this interchange gains in irony, for we learn in the concluding pages that the heroine's refusal to make such a promise to Lady Catherine is reported by her Ladyship to Darcy himself—and this gives strength to his hope that he might be accepted.

One sign of a distance between Jane Austen and her heroines is found in the arrangement of their thought patterns—a slight abridgement takes place, perhaps some clarification as well, so that the reader can grasp what the heroine does not. There are, for example, Elizabeth Bennet's slowly self-modified impressions of Darcy's letter:

> Her feelings as she read were scarcely to be defined. With amazement did she first understand that he believed any apology to be in his power; and steadfastly was she persuaded that he could have no explanation to give, which a just sense of shame would not conceal. With a strong prejudice against every thing he might say, she began his account of what had happened at Netherfield. She read, with an eagerness which hardly left her power of comprehension, and from impatience of knowing what the next sentence might bring, was incapable of attending to the sense of the one before her eyes. His belief of her sister's insensibility, she instantly resolved to be false, and her account of the real, the

worst objections to the match, made her too angry to have any wish of doing him justice. He expressed no regret for what he had done which satisfied her; his style was not penitent, but haughty. It was all pride and insolence.

But when this subject was succeeded by his account of Mr Wickham, when she read with somewhat clearer attention, a relation of events, which, if true, must overthrow every cherished opinion of his worth, and which bore so alarming an affinity to his own history of himself, her feelings were yet more acutely painful and more difficult of definition. Astonishment, apprehension, and even horror, oppressed her. She wished to discredit it entirely, repeatedly exclaiming, "this must be false! This cannot be! This must be the grossest falsehood!"—and when she had gone through the whole letter, though scarcely knowing any thing of the last page or two, put it hastily away, protesting that she would not regard it, that she would never look in it again.

In this perturbed state of mind, with thoughts that could rest on nothing, she walked on; but it would not do; in half a minute the letter was unfolded again, and collecting herself as well as she could, she again began the mortifying perusal of all that related to Wickham, and commanded herself so far as to examine the meaning of every sentence.... She put down the letter, weighed every circumstance with what she meant to be impartiality—deliberated on the probability of each statement—but with little success. On both sides, it was only assertion. Again she read on. But every line proved more clearly that the affair, which she had believed it impossible that any contrivance could so represent, as to render Mr Darcy's conduct in it less than infamous, was capable of a turn which must make him entirely blameless throughout the whole. (*PP* 204-05)

The sequence of thought here is evidently more obvious to the reader than to Elizabeth herself—from disdainful disbelief to somewhat reluctant acceptance. This is artistic objectivity.

Besides, Jane Austen's very omniscience argues that "a single point of view could not comprehend the intent of the novels fully: the many shifts in viewpoint indicate a completeness and a detachment which none of the characters can possibly share" (Wright 82). For instance, Elizabeth Bennet is unable to apprehend the true nature of Darcy's feeling for her until some time after his open declaration of love; the declaration itself is a stunning surprise—but not to the reader, who has already glimpsed the progress of the hero's feelings. Thus, very early in the story, while Jane Bennet languishes ill at Netherfield Park, Darcy reacts as follows to Elizabeth:

> Though he had detected with a critical eye more than one failure of perfect symmetry in her form, he was forced to acknowledge her figure to be light and pleasing; and in spite of his asserting that her manners were not those of the fashionable world, he was caught by their easy playfulness. Of this she was perfectly unaware.... (*PP* 23)

Though *Pride and Prejudice* is no less serious in intention than any of the others, its method is livelier and more humorous. This is chiefly because Elizabeth is a lively and humorous heroine—unlike Elinor, Fanny, or Anne Elliot—and largely responsible for the tone of the whole novel. But Jane Austen herself appears here as a lively commentator, though only to present material when this cannot be done through Elizabeth. W.A. Craik writes in *Jane Austen: The Six Novels*: "She (Austen) has to appear more as narrator than she did in *Sense and Sensibility,* first because she has a heroine whose judgement has limitations: she has to make clear what the limitations are, and tell us facts, some of which the heroine cannot tell because it would distort her as it almost distorts Elinor, and some which she cannot know either because her limited judgement does not let her perceive them or because she has no chance to perceive them. Charlotte's acceptance of Mr Collins is an example. Elizabeth cannot know that

Mr Collins has proposed to Charlotte on the sly, but we must not only know it, but must know why Charlotte accepted him—'solely from the pure and disinterested desire of an establishment'—then we can see how far Elizabeth has been misled in her estimate of Charlotte. The account is as far as possible through Charlotte herself, but 'pure and disinterested' is a lively, concise and ironic comment from the author. Jane Austen appears as narrator secondly because Elizabeth is only the main interest of the novel, not the sole one; the title itself shows this: 'pride' and 'prejudice' can easily be made to stand for Darcy and Elizabeth (63). Barbara Hardy observes in *A Reading of Jane Austen*: "In *Pride and Prejudice,* in spite of Jane Austen's delight in her heroine, her direct commentary is still sober and grave, though it has lost the spite and sourness of *Sense and Sensibility*. Once more, the appreciations can be made within the novel, by Elizabeth Bennet, whose point of view prevails. It is here that we find, for the first time, the mature development of that free indirect style which allowed Jane Austen to use the third person as a sensitive register of her characters' mind, feelings and personality. But much of the commentary is dry, caustic and not playful" (174). It is as if all the playfulness has gone into Elizabeth Bennet, leaving none over for the narrator:

> This is not the sort of happiness which a man would in general wish to owe to his wife; but where other powers of entertainment are wanting, the true philosopher will derive benefit from such as are given. (*PP* 236)
>
> Upon the whole, therefore, she found, what has sometimes been found before, that an event to which she had looked forward with impatient desire, did not in taking place, bring all the satisfaction she had promised herself. (*PP* 237)
>
> Sometimes it is neutral, as in this curt avoidance of description: It is not the object of this work to give a description of Derbyshire, nor of any of the remarkable places through which their route thither lay; Oxford, Blenheim, Warwick, Kenilworth, Birmingham, &c. are sufficiently known. (*PP* 240)

At the end the author's solitary 'I' appears: "I wish I could say, for the sake of her family, that the accomplishment of her earnest desire in the establishment of so many of her children, produced so happy an effect as to make her a sensible, amiable, well-informed woman for the rest of her life" (*PP* 385). Hardy comments in *A Reading of Jane Austen*: "It is not, as in *Sense and Sensibility*, that we feel ourselves in the presence of an occasional superfluity of irony, but rather that the author has withdrawn as far as possible, reserving her commentary and using her most neutral tones" (174).

Austen had to discover the proper tone of voice for different kinds of narrative; not merely for occasional passages of emotional urgency but also for the sustained course of grave, circumstantial relation of events. A sense of this difficulty may be lightly expressed in her own half-mocking criticism of *Pride and Prejudice* as rather "too light, and bright, and sparkling; it wants shade; it wants to be stretched out here and there with a long chapter of sense, if it could be had; if not, of solemn specious nonsense, about something unconnected with the story; an essay on writing, a critique on Walter Scott, or the history of Buonaparte, or the playfulness and epigrammatism of the general style" (*Letters* 299-300). There are several shafts of satire in this one sentence, and not all of them directed against *Pride and Prejudice,* but that phrase 'playfulness and epigrammatism' exactly hits off the character of its narrative style, its charm and its limitations.

(VIII) STYLE

F.R. Leavis says, "The great novelists...are all very much concerned with 'form'; they are all very original technically, having turned their genius to the working out of their own appropriate methods and procedures. But the peculiar quality of their preoccupation with 'form' may be brought out by a contrasting reference to Flaubert. Reviewing Thomas Mann's *Der Tod in Venedig,* D.H. Lawrence adduces Flaubert as figuring to the world the 'will of the writer to be greater than and undisputed lord over the stuff he writes', This attitude in art, as Lawrence points out, is indicative of an attitude in life—or towards life. Flaubert, he comments, 'stood away from life as from a leprosy'. For the later Aesthetic writers, who, in general, represent in a weak kind of way the attitude that Flaubert maintained with a perverse heroism, 'form' and 'style' are ends to be sought for themselves, and the chief preoccupation is with elaborating a beautiful style to apply to the chosen subject" (Littlewood II: 300). Mary Lascelles writes in "Some Characteristics of Jane Austen's Style":

> "Manner of writing, with regard to language"—that is Johnson's definition of style, in the *Dictionary*; and to illustrate it he quotes Swift: "Proper words in proper places make the true definition of a *stile.*" It is in this comfortably limited sense, and almost unmindful of the wider implications suggested by modern criticism, that I propose to use the word here. (Littlewood II: 260)

Austen had to discover the proper tone of voice for different kinds of narrative; not merely for occasional passages of emotional urgency but also for the sustained course of grave, circumstantial relation of events. A sense of this difficulty may be lightly expressed in her own half-mocking criticism of *Pride and Prejudice* as rather "too light, and bright, and sparkling; it wants shade; it wants to be stretched out here and there with a long chapter of sense, if it could be had; if not, of solemn specious nonsense, about something unconnected with the story; an essay on writing, a critique on Walter Scott, or the history of Buonaparte, or the playfulness and epigrammatism of the general style" (*Letters* 299-300). There are several shafts of satire in this one sentence, and not all of them directed against *Pride and Prejudice,* but that phrase 'playfulness and epigrammatism' exactly hits off the character of its narrative style, its charm and its limitations.

Baker comments in *The History of the English Novel*: "Irony is the soul of Jane Austen's comedy; the comic aspects of life are the ironical aspects, visible to good sense in its contemplation of erroneous judgments and bigoted or merely indolent persistence in error, of the contradiction between our desires and the good that we desire" (88). Andrew H. Wright writes in *Jane Austen's Novels: A Study in Structure*: "*Sense and Sensibility* is a study of opposites; *Pride and Prejudice* is not: it is much more complex; for, as one examines the book, one is struck with the facts that Pride leads to Prejudice and Prejudice invites Pride; and that both have their corresponding virtues bound up withm them" (32). Indeed, a key to the ironic significance of the book lies in the following conversation between Elizabeth and Bingley:

> "Whatever I do is done in a hurry... [he says] and therefore If I should resolve to quit Netherfield, I should probably be off in five minutes. At present, however, I consider myself as quite fixed here."
>
> "That is exactly what I should have supposed of you", said Elizabeth.
>
> "You begin to comprehend me, do you?" cried he, turning towards her.
>
> "Oh! Yes—I understand you perfectly."
>
> "I wish I might take this for a compliment; but to be so easily seen through I am afraid is pitiful."
>
> "That is as it happens. It does not necessarily follow that a deep, intricate character is more or less estimable than such a one as yours."
>
> "Lizzy," cried her mother, "remember where you are, and do not run on in the wild manner that you are suffered to do at home."
>
> "I did not know before," continued Bingley immediately, "that you were a studier of character. It must be an amusing study."
>
> "Yes, but intricate characters are the *most* amusing. They have at least that advantage." (*PP* 239)

Elizabeth puts it light-heartedly; but on the ironic level *Pride and Prejudice* concerns itself with Intricacy and Simplicity as those terms apply to personality. Each has its virtues and each its defects: they are contradictory, and the supreme irony is that Intricacy, which is so much deeper, carries with it grave dangers unknown to Simplicity. Like Elizabeth and Darcy, and Jane and Bingley pairs, there is a third pair, Charlotte and Wickham, who are the focus of this deeper meaning: they are a comment on Elizabeth and Darcy, whose breadth and depth involve them in the dangers of *Pride and Prejudice*. If the central couple is flanked on the one side by the unexceptionable Bingley and Jane, it is flanked on the other by Charlotte and Wickham, both of whom have a great deal of the cleverness of the two main characters, but whose concern for worldly success undermines their virtue. *Pride and Prejudice* is thus concerned with the contradictions of human personality—one might say, the price of intelligence.

Lloyd W. Brown observes in "Jane Austen's Imagery": "Jane Austen's personal comments suggest that she is not averse to imagery as such. She is primarily interested in the complete integration of verbal patterns with the multiple levels of her irony. And accordingly, her figurative language is diversified, ranging from the burlesque of florid style to the analytic and the emotive. Indeed, far from being 'unmetaphorical,' Jane Austen's style is remarkable for the aptness of figurative epigrams that illuminate the essence of situation or personality" (Littlewood II: 368). After Darcy's marriage a disappointed Miss Bingley prudently 'paid off every area of civility' to his bride (*PP* 387). When we turn to the inept users of imagery we find that they are distinguished from each other as well as from unimaginative persons who shun images. The unimaginative Mr Collins uses threadbare metaphors. Mr Collins introduces himself to the Bennets in a burst of hoary cliches: he has always wished to 'heal the breach' between himself and the Bennets, and he now hopes that they will not 'reject the offered olive branch' (*PP* 62-63). Mary Bennet is widely read, but lacking the florid imagination she is restricted to Mr Collins' brand of petrified images. Hence, as she sees it, Lydia's elopement is an unfortunate affair, but "we must stem the tide of malice, and pour into the wounded bosoms of each other, the balm of sisterly consolation" (*PP* 289).

Some of Jane Austen's fictional principles are enunciated by Elizabeth in early conversations at Netherfield. One concerns the village world of the novels (Ch. 9):

> "Yes; but intricate characters are the most amusing. They have at least that advantage."
>
> "The country," said Darcy, "can in general supply but few subjects for such a study. In a country neighbourhood you move in a very confined and unvarying society."
>
> "But people themselves alter so much, that there is something new to be observed in them for ever."

Some later remarks from Elizabeth touch the lighter side of Jane Austen's satirical creed. She agrees with Darcy that the wisest and best of men "may be rendered ridiculous by a person whose first object in life is a joke," but, she says: "I hope I never ridicule what is wise or good. Follies and nonsense, whims and inconsistencies *do* divert me, I own, and I laugh at them whenever I can." We may note that, as usual, Elizabeth's feminine instinct is drawn to the natural and individual, Darcy's masculine mind to the rational and general.

Throughout the book the main vehicle of characterization, comedy, and satire is dialogue; narration and description are given largely to placing conversation in its setting and summarizing characters' thoughts and feelings. The talk of Elizabeth and Darcy especially carries frequent ambiguities of meaning and tone which, whether in or outside the speaker's consciousness, are left to the perceptive reader to interpret, with or without a hint from the author. And many things are said which, in addition to being appropriate at the moment, recall or anticipate things said or done earlier or later. One brief and straightforward example shows the unregenerate Darcy revealing, with unconscious irony, the armour of self-assurance which Elizabeth is destined to pierce with more than a hidden smile.

We noticed, in Elizabeth's heated replies to Darcy's first proposal, some unexpected examples of complicated syntax, and once in a while we come upon a speech which sounds like a remnant from the first version of the book. One example is Elizabeth's exhortation to her father to put some restraint upon Lydia (Ch. 40). Apropos of Lady Lucas' offering condolence and aid in regard to Lydia's elopement, Elizabeth's comment to Jane begins with entire naturalness and shifts into the formal rhetoric of Fanny Burney and Dr. Johnson (Ch. 47):

> "She had better have stayed at home" cried Elizabeth; "perhaps she meant well, but under such a misfortune as this, one cannot see too little of one's neighbours. Assistance is impossible; condolence, insufferable. Let them triumph over us at a distance, and be satisfied."

The Bingley sisters must be set down early as "*very fine ladies*; not deficient in good humour when they were pleased, nor in the power of being agreeable where they chose it; but proud and conceited." And Charlotte Lucas accepts Mr Collins "solely from the *pure* and *disinterested* desire of an establishment." By using these words, Jane Austen does in fact emphasize the impurity and interestedness which lie behind Charlotte Lucas's acceptance of the fatuous clergyman; in making the statement so strongly positive the author underlines the severe moral criticism she is making of Charlotte.

Syntactical anti-climax is no new thing in Jane Austen. One remembers the most famous lines in "The Vanity of Human Wishes" in which the great 'Swedish Charles' is thus described: "He left the name at which the world grew pale,/ To point a moral or adorn a tale." Lydia Wickham, newly married and triumphantly describing her wedding to Elizabeth, says, "...I was thinking, you may suppose, of my dear Wickham. I longed to know whether he would be married in his blue coat" (*PP* 319). She puts love on the same level with fashionable clothing—and so casts doubt on the sincerity and profundity of her ability to love. Finally, when Elizabeth Bennet asks Lady Catherine why she may not accept Darcy, Lady Catherine replies: "Because honour, decorum, prudence, nay, interest, forbid it" (*PP* 355). Indeed it is 'interest' rather than anything else which makes Lady Catherine so loath to see Darcy and Elizabeth married—a very strong 'interest' that her own daughter shall be her nephew's wife.

If the dominant trope of *Northanger Abbey* is the (missing) simile and the dominant trope of *Sense and Sensibility* is the broken synecdoche, *Pride and Prejudice* has a generous mixture of tropes, including metonymy and metaphor. But strong rhetorical functions link these tropes. In our hearing, Elizabeth resorts to the proverbial: "There is a fine old saying, which everybody here is of course familiar with—'keep your breath to cool your porridge'" (*PP* 24). This is a strikingly "low" expression, an "old saying" (unutterably vulgar in itself according to Chesterfield, a breach of rhetorical manners according to Blair). Margaret Anne Doody writes in "Turns of Speech and Figures of Mind," "Elizabeth deploys her 'saying' as a deliberately vulgar challenge to Darcy. Will he take this ebullition as a proof that the speaker 'has kept bad and low company'? The references to breath and base food can also remind Darcy of Elizabeth's physicality. In *Pride and Prejudice,* abstractions tend to collapse back into physical counterparts or causes, reminders of physical embodiment and body, organic or inorganic" (*A Companion to Jane Austen* 174). We can see this if we compose a quick florilegium of memorable lines: "[Your nerves] are my old friends" (*PP* 5); "what are men to rocks and mountains?" (*PP* 154); "every savage can dance" (*PP* 25). Dancing savages, rocks, plates of porridge—these things wait in the physical world for the breathing participant in life. Almost everything becomes physical and to a certain degree intimate. Elizabeth goes into Derbyshire to pick up "petrified spars," an unconsciously chosen image of what Darcy's love for her (so she fears) will have become. Feelings and experiences find embodiment in physical entities; practically everything is actually or potentially an active agent. Anthony Blackwall admits the effect of giving human qualities to animals and animal qualities to inanimate objects: "Those are admirable and very beautiful *Metaphors* when the Properties of rational Creatures are apply'd to Animals, and those of Animals to Plants and trees: This way of treating a Subject gives Life and Beauty to the whole *Creation*" (Blackwall 1725: 164).

"Life and beauty" are qualities "instinctively desired by Elizabeth Bennet and by some of those around this memorably 'rational Creature,' who has life enough to spare for those around her. The animation of abstract nouns, a particularly Austenian forte, is found here in the conversation of characters as well as in authorial narration. Yet in *Pride and Prejudice* Austen undertakes not only the animation of abstractions but a touch of true prosopopoeia, giving animation to nonhuman but not abstract subjects; we find a higher number of personifications of physically objects than in the other two early novels" (*A Companion to Jane Austen* 174). Mr Darcy early meditates "on the very great pleasure which a pair of fine eyes in the face of a pretty woman can bestow"—Elizabeth's eyes are energized and active, benevolently bestowing something (the antitype of Lady Catherine de Bourgh). Even in the view of an inimical rival Elizabeth's very clothes have an active power: a gown is "not doing its office" but a muddy petticoat also "escaped my notice" (*PP* 36). A gown may not *do* its office, a petticoat may escape. This device lends a sense of physical immediacy and of activity to the whole, thus centering our reading, even when Elizabeth isn't there, on the animated and animating qualities of the heroine herself.

In Mr Bennet's plea to his daughter near the end of the novel we find a surprising mixture of what may be personification with cautious synecdoche. "I know your disposition, Lizzy.... Your lively talents would place you in the greatest danger in an unequal marriage" (*PP* 376). What a surprising utterance! Mr Bennet thinks his favourite daughter would be capable of—in danger of—committing adultery, if her lively *talents*, unappreciated, looked outside the marriage for exercise and refreshment. The "talents," seem to be personified; they threaten to be cut off from Elizabeth as in synecdoche, yet they are most essentially related to her and thus rather a metonym than the amputated entity a synecdoche suggests. Mr Collins has absurdly imagined that Elizabeth's liveliness might be cut off, asphyxiated, while leaving her essentially the same—her father knows better. Elizabeth's "lively talents" are connected to her body and instincts, her sexuality. Surprisingly, Mr Bennet's insight brings into the end of the novel a reminder of Elizabeth's resemblance to Lydia—even though the plot has officially made the maximum effort to persuade us of their difference. Lydia too cannot be amputated from her family, Mr Bennet's initial conventional efforts notwithstanding.

The rhetoric of *Pride and Prejudice* characteristically searches for the universal, a turn introduced, parodied, and examined in the famous first sentence: "It is a truth universally acknowledged...." Throughout the narrative, characters are given to large-scale generalizations; words such as "every," "none," "nobody," "always", "never," tumble out on all sides. "*Every* savage can dance" (*PP* 15); "*Nothing* could be more delightful!"; "to her he was only the man who made himself agreeable *no where;*" "*Whatever* bears affinity to cunning is despicable" (*PP* 40). The tendency to pronounce universal truths, inadvertently parodied by Mary Bennet and Mr Collins, is widespread. Such a colloqually philosophic tendency preempts the search for truth and fosters both pride and prejudice. Hasty and dismissive, universalizing is amusingly and subtly counteracted by the reiterated animation of the world found in the novel's tropes, and the constant suggestion of physical present and enjoyable reality.

Andrew Wright observes in "Aspects of Style in Jane Austen": "One of the most interesting facts about Jane Austen's style is that it is almost entirely unmetaphorical, except when more or less adverse criticism is meant. Miss Lascelles is, I think, the first critic to make this point; and conjectures that she is '*shy* of figurative language' because of its tendency to become cliche and because 'it cannot *fossilize* without turning into a lie'" (Littlewood II: 314). There is plenty of evidence to support this conjecture. For instance, Jane Austen writes to Anna about one of the characters in the latter's novel:

> Devereux Forester's being ruined by his Vanity is extremely good; but I wish you would not let him plunge into 'a vortex of Dissipation'. I do not object to the Thing, but I cannot bear the expression;—it is such thorough novel slang—and so old, that I dare say Adam met with it in the first novel he opened. *(Letters* II: 404)

In *Pride and Prejudice,* Darcy is liked by those in the Netherfield 'neighbourhood' "till his manners gave a disgust which *turned the tide* of his popularity; for he was discovered to be proud...", the grandeur of the metaphor reflecting the shallowness of those who eagerly admire him because he is handsome, but quickly reject him when his diffidence or pride makes him seem unresponsive. Mr Collins is, of course, full of figures. He says in his letter to Mr Bennet that he hopes the latter will not 'reject the offered olive branch,' a cliche which even Mary discovers to be 'not wholly new'. And writing to Mr Bennet after hearing of Lydia's elopement, he says: "Let me advise you...to console yourself as much as possible, to *throw off* your unworthy child from your affection for ever, and leave her to reap the fruits of her own heinous offence." There is nastiness as well behind Lady Catherine de Bourgh's famous mixed metaphor on the prospect of Elizabeth's marriage to Darcy: "Heaven and earth!—of what are you thinking? Are the *shades* of Pemberley to be thus *polluted*?" (*PP* 357).

Jane Austen develops her use of free indirect speech—though not so far as in *Mansfield Park* or *Emma*—as well as the scintillating dramatic dialogue for which the book is famous. And what is not so often noticed as that brave comedy is, is the habitual vivid energy and economy of phrase like that when, invited to Brighton "Lydia flew about the house in restless ecstacy." We notice the open vowel sounds, as one might say of Lord Tennyson. For the most part the texture of both dialogue and narrative is—allowance being made for a standard of elegance—informal, spontaneous, and easy. It warrants the author's comment on "the playfulness and epigrammatism of the general style." The social gifts of Bingley's sisters are summed up in a manner which suggests their brittle smartness: "Their powers of conversation were considerable. They could describe an entertainment with accuracy, relate in anecdote with humours, and laugh at their acquaintance with spirit." Mrs Bennet of course is constantly quotable. The clever Mr Bennet enjoys his own fastidious ironies, chiefly at the expense of his wife and daughters, but Mr Collins, the pompous toady, is a prime butt for parody: "You judge very properly...and it is happy for you that you possess the talent of flattering with delicacy. May I ask whether these pleasing attentions proceed from the impulse of the moment, or are the result of previous study?" (Ch. 14). Even the amiable but hardly brilliant Bingley is given one gem: "I declare I do not know a more awful object than Darcy, on particular occasions, and in particular places; at his own house especially, and of a Sunday evening when he has nothing to do" (Ch. 10). Somerset Maugham writes in his essay, "*Pride and Prejudice*": "No one has ever looked upon Jane Austen as a great stylist. Her spelling is peculiar and her grammar often shaky, but she had a good ear. I think the influence of Dr Johnson can be discerned in the structure of her sentences. She is apt to use the word of Latin origin rather than the plain English one, the abstract rather than the concrete. It gives her phrase a slight formality which is far from unpleasant: indeed it often adds point to a witty remark and a demure savor to a malicious one" (Littlewood I: 464-65). Maugham further comments in "*Pride and Prejudice*": "Her dialogue is probably as natural as dialogue can ever be. To set down on paper speech as it is spoken would be very tedious, and some arrangement of it is necessary. Since so many of the speeches are worded exactly as they would be today, we must suppose that at the end of the eighteenth century young girls in conversation did express themselves in a manner which would now seem stilted" (Littlewood I: 465). We can see, for example, what Jane, speaking of her lover's sisters, remarks:

> They were certainly no friends to his acquaintance with me, which I cannot wonder at, since he might have chosen so much more advantageously in many respects.

Maugham writes: "I have said nothing yet of what to my mind is the greatest merit of this charming book: it is wonderfully readable—more readable than some greater and more famous novels. As Scott said, Miss Austen deals with commonplace things, the involvements, feelings, and characters of ordinary life; nothing very much happens and yet when you reach the bottom of a page you eagerly turn it in order to know what will happen next; nothing very much does and again you turn the page with the same eagerness. The power of making you do this is the greatest gift a novelist can have and I have often wondered what creates it. Why is it that even when you have read the novel over and over again your interest never flags? I think with Jane Austen it is because she was so immensely interested in her characters and in what happened to them and because she profoundly believed in them" (Littlewood I: 465).

The action is organized not only by what happens, but by where it happens; the place itself is relevant to what occurs. Though all are rural gentlemen's estates (except London, which is rather passed through than used), Longbourn, Rosings and Pemberley—in ascending order of magnitude as well as in order of appearance—are distinguished by significant physical characteristics. Longbourn itself is not described, except when it is too late to affect our view of it, when we hear that it has a hermitage, and 'a prettyish kind of a little wilderness' (*PP* 352) for Lady Catherine to inspect. It is one of a group of small estates, including Netherfield and Lucas Lodge, in a neighborhood of small gentry and of trade, as Sir William Lucas and the proximity of Meryton bear out. Rosings is clearly superior socially:

> [Mr Collins] was so much struck with the size and furniture of [Mrs Philips's drawing room], that he declared he might almost have supposed himself in the small summer breakfast parlour at Rosings. (*PP* 75)

But its real attractions are moderate:

> Every park has its beauty and its prospects; and Elizabeth saw much to be pleased with, though she could not be in such raptures as Mr Collins expected the scene to inspire. (*PP* 161)

This is a background in sympathy with Lady Catherine and with Darcy, who shows at Rosings the unattractive qualities he shares with his aunt. The well-arranged parsonage emphasized the pomp and suggests the lack of taste of the mansion. After this, Longbourn seems a setting not out of keeping with the folly and vulgarity Elizabeth recognizes in her family, though the place is not in itself vulgar, being a residence fit for the gentleman Mr Bennet is. Pemberley is all the more splendid by contrast; its natural beauty shows the combination in Mr Darcy, as in his house, of nature and taste:

> It was a large, handsome, stone building, standing well on rising ground, and backed by a ridge of high woody hills; and in front, a stream of some natural importance was swelled into greater, but without any artificial appearance. Its banks were neither formal, nor falsely adorned. Elizabeth was delighted. (*PP* 245)

The general organization of material resembles *Sense and Sensibility*. The plan seems less skilful but is more so, because the manipulation is not obtrusive in itself; a good many of the points of construction have therefore been dealt with in discussion of character. The longest dialogues occur at Mr Collins's proposal—a glorious exhibition of himself and not much more than a monologue—and at Lady Catherine's attempt to forbid Elizabeth to marry Darcy. This, although greatly heightened, is a real exchange of personalities. Elizabeth scores a practical triumph over Lady Catherine, unlike Elinor, who can only be said to score a moral one over Lucy. The exchanges between Elizabeth and the other characters are all brief; the one chance for a long one, where Darcy might explain away Elizabeth's prejudices against him is deliberately put aside by the device of the letter. This is less obviously dramatic, but essentially more probable and satisfactory. The reader, like Elizabeth, needs time to take in all this information, and if it were given in person the interview would require most improbable self-control in Mr Darcy. Willoughby's confession by contrast tells nothing new, but gives a new aspect of what we know already, while the violence and incoherence with which he tells it make him more attractive (though no more estimable). The longest of the conversations are those between Darcy and Elizabeth after their engagement, which are merely a review of what has gone before, giving an agreeable view of the relationship between them, which is necessary since they have been at cross-purposes or under some restraint for the whole of their acquaintance. This represents an advance on *Sense and Sensibility*, where we have no such evidence of the good understanding between

Elinor and Edward Ferrars, which is merely assumed to exist. Craik writes, "Such an account of a developing relationship is a new technique; it is even more necessary in *Emma,* where a number of minor dilemmas are still to be resolved even after Emma and Mr Knightley have come to an understanding, and Elizabeth teasing Darcy sounds very like Emma teasing Mr Knightley" (87).

"I doubt," says Dr Chapman, if J.A. was conscious of having a style of her own. Outside her dialogue it is not highly individual; it is just the ordinary correct English that, as Johnson had said, "everyone now writes" (*Jane Austen: Facts and Problems* 209). As to Chapman's viewpoint, Andrew Wright observes in "Aspects of Style in Jane Austen": "I believe he underrates her on this point. It seems to me fully apparent that Jane Austen is as thoroughly original (or 'new', in Eliot's sense) in her style as she is in the other aspects of her work. Indeed, as Bacon told us long ago, style cannot be regarded as a peripheral matter. Like her literary forebears she uses stylistic devices (even including those usually associated with the term 'irony') for many purposes, both ironic and unironic—from mere delightful *jeux d'esprit* to solemn considered judgments" (Littlewood II: 317). Wright justly observes, "So far as style is concerned, Jane Austen's irony is much more pervasive than the usual rhetorical categories will allow. Understatement and antiphrasis by no means account for all the ironies in her diction and syntax. But other categories—however useful in an analysis of this kind—betray their own inadequacies at the moment when the light thus shed reveals further, deeper, subtler shadows: for style, more perhaps than any other aspect of a novel, is a finally indissoluble unity, a fabric which cannot be cut up without destroying the harmony of the whole. It is because of this fact that such difficult but useful words as 'tone' and 'texture' are so often applied to style. And, however difficult it may be to analyse the whole style of a lyric poem, the task is plainly impossible in a novel—unless one is willing to read perhaps a thousand pages of explication; and this is no doubt more trouble than it is worth. One recourse, and it is a pleasant one, is to read the novels themselves, bearing in mind the 'transparent vesture'...which, as much perhaps as anything else, is responsible for Jane Austen's front rank among the English novelists" (Littlewood II: 317). Mary Lascelles writes in "Some Characteristics of Jane Austen's Style":

> Among Jane Austen's readers, some must surely have wondered why nobody has yet looked curiously into her 'manner of writing, with regard to language. This was not surprising in those days when the fullest critical account of her could dismiss the subject in a single bland denial: "She has no remarkable distinction of style"; but it is surprising now, when even those critics who say they do not like her admit her fine workmanship. Again, that these antagonistic readers should be satisfied once they have made the admission—"When I call her writing truthful and apt, I have said all that should be said in praise of it"—this is natural enough; but surely it is strange that her admirers should be willing to take for granted this element in her art, letting it pass as "mere technical accomplishment"—all the stranger since she allows us to learn something of her own preferences and opinions as to 'proper words in proper places.' (Littlewood II: 260)

(IX) *PRIDE AND PREJUDICE* AND FEMINISM

Margaret Kirkham writes in "Jane Austen and Contemporary Feminism": "Jane Austen grew up and became a novelist in the 1790s, when feminist/antifeminist controversy was strong and when the novel itself was of particular importance to the debate. Since the publication of *Pamela* in 1740-41, questions of feminist concern such as the moral status and education of women and the right basis of marriage and authority within the family, had formed an important part of the ethical subject matter of fiction, but by the end of the century women themselves had found a public voice as novelists. After the 1770s and 1780s, when Mary Wollstonercraft's *Mary* (1788) and Fanny Burney's *Evelina* (1778) appeared, the novel was at least as important as the treatise, conduct book, or educational work in defining women's attitudes toward the rights and duties of their own sex" (Littlewood II: 169).

While it would be misleading to speak of a well-defined school of eighteenth-century feminist thought in England, it is possible to see some development of ideas and practical concern, going back to Mary Astell's feminist treatises written between 1694 and 1705, continuing in the lives, letters, and other writings of the learned ladies associated with the bluestocking salons, and emerging in a more controversial way in fictional and theoretical works by women at the end of the century.

Margaret Kirkham writes in "Jane Austen and Contemporary Feminism", "Eighteenth century feminism begins with questions about the moral and spiritual status of woman with which, from the beginning, improvement in female education was associated as the main practical concern. By the end of the century, philanthropy, often of an educational kind, had also become important. Ray Strachey speaks of Mrs Trimmer and Hannah More as founders of the women's movement, though it would have shocked them to know it. Hannah More, despite her conservative sympathies, adopted a 'revolutionary role' by 'marking out a new sphere for the young women of the middle classes,' from which 'their revolt against their own narrow and futile lives followed' (Strachey 13). Women novelists, even where, unlike Jane Austen, they showed no understanding of feminist moral argument, fulfilled a similar role simply by becoming published authors" (Littlewood II: 169-70).

But Austen does show a clear and consistent commitment to the rational principles on which woman, not having been denied powers of reason by providence, must learn morals in the same way as men and must therefore be taught to think. As Janet Todd (*A Wollstonecraft Anthology* 10) points out, Mary Wollstonecraft, by the time she wrote *A Vindication of the Rights of Woman,* saw the 'revolutionary implication' of teaching women to think and made it apparent.

The feminist claim that women had the same moral nature and capacity as men and should be educated accordingly always carried a long-term political implication, but the demand for constitutional right, even at the time of the French Revolution, when it became explicit in Condorcet, Olympe de Gouges, and Wollstonecraft, was not in the forefront of English feminist writings. By 1794 Condorcet was dead in a prison cell and de Gouges at the guillotine. Englishwomen might well feel that improvement in the status and education of their sex was not one of the benefits to be had of the Revolution.

Margaret Kirkham writes in "Jane Austen and Contemporary Feminism," "Enlightenment feminism is sometimes spoken of as though it had no English roots and as though those who supported the Revolution were, in general, feminists. Such beliefs do not bear scrutiny, for feminism cut across other political, national, and religious interests, and it is worth remembering, when considering Mary Wollstonecraft's ideas in relation to the Austen novels, that *Vindication* draws on an English feminist tradition in which women of orthodox religion, not associated with revolutionary politics, have their place, as Wollstonecraft acknowledges in her respectful treatment of Hester Chapone" (Littlewood II: 170-71).

Arnold Kettle, in his 1951 essay on *Emma,* saw Jane Austen's 'highly critical concern over the fate of women in her society' as a 'positive vibration', and it has since become common to notice a degree of feminist concern in Austen but not to associate it with the central 'moral interest' that Leavis, in 1948, saw as 'the principle of organization and the principle of development' in all her work, nor to connect Austen's criticism of romantic writers with Wollstonecraft's attack on Rousseau and his followers. The re-publication of Wollstonecraft's writings, with those of others, has made it easier to place Austen, as moralist, in the context of national feminism.

Kirkham observes: "In England, Jane Austen declined to concern herself with the *femme de genie,* concentrating, like Wollstonecraft, on ordinary women of the middle class, whose lives are unexceptional, though her heroines have more than their share of intelligence. Austen follows *Vindication* in the belief that 'women...may have different duties to fulfil; but they are *human* duties,' to be regulated in accordance with rational principle" (Littlewood II: 171). Austen shows no interest in 'performing heroinism' except as the subject of satire.

Jane Austen was ready to publish her first novel in the year that Mary Wollstonecraft died. Had Cadell accepted *First Impressions,* it would have come out in 1798 when Godwin's *Memoirs* provoked a storm of hostile criticism against Wollstonecraft and her ideas. Between 1798 and 1803 her reputation was destroyed and her ideas made unspeakable. The Reverend Richard Polwhele, in *The Unsex'd Females,* divided literary women into feminist goats and modest sheep, between whom there could be no connection. He thought it a sign of the corruption of the age that women's work should be considered on its merits, like men's, and saw 'the sparkle of confident intelligence' as, in itself, a mark of immodesty in a female author.

Among early reviewers, Scott shows an uneasy awareness of Austen's feminist morals, while Whately reveals a more sympathetic understanding, but neither discusses it overtly, perhaps because it could not be discussed without resurrecting discreditable scandal and misunderstanding. By the mid-nineteenth century, no one thought of connecting Austen and Wollstonecraft as feminist moralists, and in the mid-twentieth, 'the enduring problem of Jane Austen criticism' was defined as 'scale versus stature; the slightness of the matter and the authority of the manner'. As more has become known about Wollstonecraft as 'female philosopher' and about the rational feminism of her time, it has become easier to place the Austen novels in a context of feminist ideas, where the 'enduring problem' can be seen in a new light.

Kirkham writes in "Jane Austen and Contemporary Feminism":

> Trilling, in 1957, spoke of Emma Woodhouse as having a moral life, as a man has a moral life...quite as a matter of course, as a given quality of her nature. It is

> because the Austen heroines, not only Emma, are shown as representatives of 'human' rather than 'feminine' nature, learning morals as rational beings were intended to learn them, that we may speak of her as a feminist moralist, connected with Wollstonecraft in opposing the antifeminist view most powerfully expressed in *Emile*. (Littlewood II: 173)

In 1813, writing to Cassandra about *Pride and Prejudice,* Austen had parodied some lines from Scott's *Marmion*: "I do not rhyme to that dull elf/ Who cannot image to himself." This became in Austen's words: "I do not write for such dull elves/ As have not a great deal of ingenuity themselves" (*Letters* 298) and was said in connection with the observation that, in the proofs of *Pride and Prejudice,* there were still "a few typical errors; and a 'said he, or a said she' would sometimes make the dialogue more immediately clear". Margaret Kirkham in "Scott's Review of *Emma*" observes, "Perhaps Jane Austen should have stressed the 'said he' and the 'said she' of it a little more than she did, for not all her readers have been bright elves, and some of the brightest have, through habituation to linguistic convention perhaps, rather than pride or prejudice, found it difficult to take what 'he' says and what 'she' says as at the heart of the comedy and the moral involvement of the Austen novels" (*Jane Austen, Feminism and Fiction* 77). Janet Todd observes in "Jane Austen, Politics and Sensibility":

> If Austen would not on the one hand assent to the naivety required for revolutionary change or any decided amelioration of personal and social conditions, she would not on the other settle comfortably into the pieties of home and hearth. She remained always the poker of the sceptical fire, suggesting that changes might make things worse but that things might already be deplorable, that children were not always loved or deserving of love, and that oppressed women might be as bitter or bad as dominating men and might do well for themselves and society by keeping their honest feelings under control. (Littlewood II: 436)

Margaret Kirkham observes in *Jane Austen, Feminism and Fiction*:

> None of the Austen heroines is more attractive than Elizabeth Bennet, none more clearly possessed of intelligence and warm affections, but as she develops she effectively destroys the role she is supposed to play. The result is that she begins to look too much like a heroine without a part, a real-life character, not a creature in print, and this will not do, for her extreme, and improbable, good luck in marriage is acceptable only if it is properly distanced from life by the formal requirements of plot and part. That is why Jane Austen spoke of *Pride and Prejudice* as 'too light and bright and sparkling', and why she developed new ways of dealing with the heroine's role, so that the plot should no longer turn on a major reversal of her beliefs or judgment. The later heroines may make mistakes, sometimes serious ones like Emma's and their author continues to mock their absurdities, but they are conceived, from the start, as the central and most enlightened minds of the novels in which they appear. They no longer (except incidentally) miscast themselves, their difficulties arise from a miscasting imposed upon them by the society in which they live, where intelligent young women of the middle class have no role appropriate to their abilities. (92)

In the novel, "the main thrust of irony is against the errors of law, manners and customs, in failing to recognize women as the accountable beings they are, or ought to be; and against those forms of contemporary literature which render them 'objects of pity, bordering on contempt', by sentimentalizing their weaknesses and making attractive what ought to be exposed as in need of correction. Austen's adherence to the central convictions of Enlightenment feminism becomes more marked and more forceful, and the scope of her comedy is enlarged, not by taking in a wider social spectrum, but by widening and deepening the range of allusive irony" (Kirkham 92).

In *Pride and Prejudice,* the central heroine, Elizabeth, is given both a good head and a warm heart; Jane Bennet, in whom heart is stronger than head, is pushed away from the centre, though without being censured. In *Pride and Prejudice,* the sympathetic character of Mr Bennet, and his warm affection for his second daughter, had made the morally independent role of Elizabeth all too easy. At various key moments, Austen's novels echo the Enlightenment-inflected rhetoric of contemporary debates about gender politics and the position of women. In *Pride and Prejudice,* desperately trying to convince Mr Collins that "no means no" after his unwelcome proposal, Elizabeth Bennet asserts her right to autonomous choice by describing herself in Wollstonecraftian terms: "Do not consider me now as an *elegant female* intending to plague you, but as a *rational creature* speaking the truth from her heart" (*PP* 109, emphasis added). "Rational creature," as a definition of the human individual, can be found in countless eighteenth-century sermons, or in John Locke's much-reprinted *Some Thoughts Concerning Education* (1693), where the humanist principle that "Children are to be treated as rational Creatures" underpins his educational regime (Locke 1989: 115). But Elizabeth's opposition between rationality and elegance suggests a more specific immediate referent. In *Vindication of the Rights of Woman,* Wollstonecraft reappropriates Locke's pharse in defense of women's rationality: "My own sex, I hope, will excuse me, if I treat them like rational creatures, instead of flattering their *fascinating* graces"; and her stated aim is "to show that elegance is inferior to virtue, that the first object of laudable ambition is to obtain a character as a human being, regardless of the distinction of sex" (Wollstonecraft 1989: 75). Economically, Elizabeth is far from independent. As the closest male relative, under the law of entail, it is Mr Collins rather than herself or her sisters who is heir to her father's estate. But Elizabeth asserts her moral and intellectual independence, at least, and reaches for Wollstonecraftian rhetoric in order to do so.

The denial of the body in Austen's fiction has necessitated the active assertion of the epistemic myopia that Sedgwick terms "unknowing" (Sedgwick 1993: 23-51). In *Pride and Prejudice*, the embodied exuberance that constitutes Elizabeth Bennet's beguiling charm also threatens to render her a monitory figure, her physical exertions and forthright wit potentially comprising her performance of genteel femininity. Walking three miles to Netherfield in order to attend to the ailing Jane, Elizabeth's physicality distinguishes her from the etiolated ideals of decorum endorsed by conduct literature, her "weary ancles [sic], dirty stockings and [...] face glowing with the warmth of exercise" (*PP* 32) rendering her contemptible to Miss Bingley and Mrs. Hurst (Johnson 1988: 75). The questionable nature of her actions is indicated by the ambivalence of Darcy's response, "divided between admiration of the brilliance which exercise had given her complexion, and doubt as to the occasion's justifying her coming so far alone" (*PP* 33). In an equally corporeal display, Miss Bingley invites Elizabeth to join her in strolling about the drawing room, thereby allowing Darcy to attend to her figure. The alluring intent of this contrivance is acknowledged by its intended audience. Refusing Miss Bingley's invitation to join them, Darcy remarks:

> You either chuse this method of passing the evening because you are in each other's confidence and have secret affairs to discuss, or because you are conscious that your figures appear to the greatest advantage in walking;—if the first, I should be completely in your way;—and if the second, I can admire you much better as I sit by the fire. (*PP* 56)

A reader of Tyler's School of "Gentle Jane" might echo Miss Bingley's response, "Oh, how shocking"!—perceiving the "abomination" of Darcy's speech to be constituted less by the acuity of his observation than the forthright nature of its expression. Elsewhere, however, it is the frankness of Elizabeth and Darcy's dialogue that constitutes the defiance and vulnerability that enables their eventual intimacy. The fact that their most affectively charged exchanges take place alone and in secret further pushes their courtship "to the verge of an impropriety unique in Austen's fiction" (Johnson 1988: 90).

Granting that Lydia Bennet's hat-shopping constitutes the Regency equivalent of a Jimmy Choo fetish is not to deny that Austen depicted both the pleasures and dangers of female sexuality (Swendson 2005: 66). Lydia is depicted imagining herself amidst the military finery of Brighton:

> She saw with the creative eye of fancy, the streets of that gay bathing place crowed with officers. She saw herself the object of attention, to tens and scores of them at present unknown. She saw all the glories of the camp, crowded with the young and the gay, and dazzling with scarlet; and to complete the view, she saw herself seated beneath a tent, tenderly flirting with at least six officers at once. (*PP* 232)

Lydia's sensual reverie locates her within a teeming mass of the "young and gay" whose mobility recalls such dangerously alluring figures as Henry Crawford, with his "great dislike" of "any thing like a permanence of abode" (*MP* 41) and Lady Susan, whose lack of fixed address signals her status as "the most accomplished Coquette in England" (*MW* 248). Lydia's vision of "tenderly flirting" with an array of officers is characterized by a hyperbole that underscores her naiveté, her "tender" addresses reflecting the equal tenderness of her years. While gesturing towards the parental indulgence that enables Lydia's folly, Austen does not downplay the scandal of her elopement with Wickham. Through Darcy's moral and financial intervention, Lydia is spared the fate of the two Elizas who haunt *Sense and Sensibility*, the mother's disgrace repeated by the offspring of her "guilty connection" (*SS* 208). She is nonetheless yoked to a demonstrable cad, whose affection for her "was just what Elizabeth had expected to find it; not equal to Lydia's for him". Even in this "lightest and brightest" of Austen's novels, she neither shies from displaying the desiring body, nor the effects of its improper employment, allowing Lydia to adsorb the potentially damning critique of Elizabeth's physical and psychological freedoms (Johnson 1988: 77). Warren Roberts observes in *Jane Austen and the*

French Revolution: "Austen clearly felt that genteel females cared too much about appearances and clothes, making them their own worst enemies, and she objected to the countless influences and pressures placed on girls to make attracting men their main goal in life. From beginning to end her novels are filled with flirtatious females, all of whom are flawed for that reason. Typically, they are vain, shallow, selfish and calculating" (165).

For most women, romance is the luxury of novels like *Pride and Prejudice*; and Collins is still a better bet than Wickham (who in the 1995 BBC mini-series solaces a loveless match with drink and spousal abuse). Wolfson writes in "Re: Reading *Pride and Prejudice*": "If Austen's formal design sets Charlotte, Mrs Bennet, and Lydia as foils to Elizabeth's rational independence, the ledger of *Pride and Prejudice* gives a fuller account, of matches blind, pragmatic, calculating, acquisitive, in sum the probability for most of Austen's female readers, even in the gentry. Austen's romance-plot—the woman who marries up and happily—is exactly Wollstonecraft's worry about novels, fictions that make female readers "restless and anxious", exciting an "overstretched sensibility" that "prevents intellect from attaining that sovereignty which it ought to attain to render a rational creature...content with its own station" (1792, IV: 83). The woman of rational contentment ("I am not romantic, you know," says Charlotte, *PP* 125) is the antithesis of the bright and sparkling heroine around whom the romance of *Pride and Prejudice* builds, in promise without compromise" (*A Companion to Jane Austen* 120-21). What credits this romance is that its terms are not entirely utopian. Here is Elizabeth musing on the prospect of "connubial felicity" as Mr and Mrs Darcy: "It was an union that must have been to the advantage of both; by her ease and liveliness, his mind might have been softened, his manners improved, and from his judgment, information, and knowledge of the world, she must have received benefit of greater importance" (*PP* 312). This is an opinion of sexual character—the man has judgment, information, and knowledge; the woman, a teasing, softening influence—so tuned to gender norms that Wollstonecraft could have taken it as a case in point. As Austen's most lovable and sympathetically defective patriarch, Mr Bennet puts a father's imprimatur on it all: "I know that you could be neither happy nor respectable, unless you truly esteemed your husband, unless you looked up to him as a superior." Although he means that someone of "lively talents" risks "the greatest danger in an unequal marriage" (*PP* 376) the hierarchy is marked. Elizabeth may show how "a woman may take liberties with her husband" (*PP* 388), but the grant is still his. Austen's anti-Romanticism, which is an aspect of her feminism, makes her a critic of the 'Good Man' and of the Great Critic who admired his author. In her own novels, Austen criticizes the belief that women's problems are to be solved by benevolent patriarchs. She does this by showing patriarchal figures as at best defective, like Mr Bennet, and at worst vicious, like General Tilney. While Mr Collins, after rejecting a novel, is reading aloud to the Bennet ladies in the drawing room at Longbourn, it must have been during just such a passage that Lydia, "a stout well-grown girl of fifteen" interrupted him to inform her mother of some interesting gossip about the regiment quartered nearby. In both Wollstonecraft and Austen there is the same objection to the sentimental treatment of girls as 'angels'; it makes them less than rational human beings and it invites hypocrisy, since everyone who has much to do with them knows that girls are not really much like angles anyway. Some may be taught to affect an angelic demeanour, and some men may like it, but observers and analysts of human nature ought not to be deceived. Two of her early novels—*Northanger Abbey* and *Pride and Prejudice*—develop out of well-established burlesque plots. But such burlesque plots, which turn on the early folly of the heroine, make it difficult to establish her as the central moral intelligence of the novel in which she appears.

The heaviest shades fall on bookish, spinster-bound Mary, obtuse in social display, laughable in intellectual ambition, her learning good only for arid maxims, and stupid, even heartless moralisms—a bluestocking satire (of course Marsha Hunt wears glasses in the 1940 Robert Z. Leonard film). Yet Mary is more than a little Austenian, and what she's learned from books (say, Blair's *Lectures on Rhetoric and Belles Lettres*) is on the same page as the moral business of *Pride and Prejudice*:

> By all that I have ever read, I am convinced that [pride] is very common indeed, that human nature is particularly prone to it, and that there are very few of us who do not cherish a feeling of self-complacency on the score of some quality or other, real or imaginary. Vanity and pride are different things, though the words are often used synonymously. A person may be proud without being vain. Pride relates more to our opinion of ourselves, vanity to what we would have others think of us. (*PP* 20)

This could have been Austen's own conviction about *Pride and Prejudice.*

This is a novel, Claudia Johnson proposes, of "experiment with conservative myths," tuning these "to accommodate what could otherwise be seen as subversive impulses and values" into a vehicle of "incisive social criticism" (1998: 75). How to measure the lures and limits of fiction is a question not only about the probabilities of what happens in *Pride and Prejudice*; it is also a question for its readers. And it never seems settled. "Also read again, and for the third time at least, Miss Austen's very finely written novel of *Pride and Prejudice*," wrote Scott in his journal, March 14, 1826 (1890, 1: 155). For Austen's readers, too, impressions mean and matter because they are never final impressions. This is the deep pleasure not only in reading, but in rereading *Pride and Prejudice.*

Austen contended not only with market forces but also with Enlightenment critiques of female education. Mary Wollstonecraft and Hannah More, though sharply at odds about the "rights of women," agreed on novels as junk-reading. Heating sensations at the expense of reason, corrupting language, judgment, and social expectations, this was reading at its least educative. A gentleman could expect to be handed a university education and, if needed, a career. A girl's education tended to cease around the age of eight; her "finishing" was aimed at winning a hand in marriage with advantage of "accomplishments, the only improvement they are excited, by their station in society, to acquire" remarked Wollstonecraft in exasperation (*A Vindication of the Rights of Woman* 1792, 131). The curriculum was "a thorough knowledge of music, singing, drawing, dancing, and the modern languages"—so chirps Miss Bingley, with a dig at Elizabeth's legible deficiencies.

Elizabeth has no particular care for this business or for the attendant fashions, ribbons, and bonnets. She bounds three miles across dusty fields, springs over puddles and stiles, appalls Bingley's sisters with her muddy petticoat and ruddy complexion; her eyes are bright from exercise. She will freckle and tan from touring outdoors with the Gardiners, and a walk of several miles with Darcy will clinch their engagement. Austen collates this aberration from female "accomplishments" with Elizabeth's character as a reader. If Enlightenment rationalists worried about novels, novelist Austen redeems this pleasure as a rational pursuit in *Pride and Prejudice* (though she satirizes it elsewhere), saving her lash for "accomplished" ladies such as Miss Bingley, to whom a book is no more than a prop of self-promotion:

> Darcy took up a book: Miss Bingley did the same;... Miss Bingley's attention was quite as much engaged in watching Mr Darcy's progress through *his* book, as in reading her own; and she was perpetually either making some inquiry, or looking at his page. She could not win him, however, to any conversation; he merely answered her question, and read on. At length, quite exhausted by the attempt to be amused with her own book, which she had only chosen because it was the second volume of his, she gave a great yawn and said, "How pleasant it is to spend an evening in this way! I declare after all there is no enjoyment like reading! How much sooner one tires of any thing than of a book!—When I have a house of my own, I shall be miserable if I have not an excellent library."

> No one made any reply. She then yawned again, threw aside her book, and cast her eyes round the room in quest of some amusement.... (*PP* 54-55)

Susan J. Wolfson writes in "Re: Reading *Pride and Prejudice*: What think you of books?" writes: "Against this yawning calculator, Austen plots Elizabeth's happiness on an arc of genuine readings, from first impressions and prejudices, to reflections and revisions, to rereading and surer comprehensions, to union with a man of equal capacity" (*A Companion to Jane Austen* 115).

It is an early cue that Darcy has a "more substantial" view of female merit than social accomplishments: "the improvement of her mind by extensive reading" (*PP* 390). He and Elizabeth flirt in volleys about reading, whatever the text. He grumbles that the "confined and unvarying society" of a country neighbourhood "can in general supply but few subjects for...study;" she rectors, "but people themselves alter so much, that there is something new to be observed in them for ever" (*PP* 42-43). And then on to books, *per se*:

> "What think you of books?" said he, smiling.
>
> "Books—Oh! No.—I am sure we never read the same, or not with the same feelings."
>
> "I am sorry you think so; but if that be the case, there can at least be no want of subject. We may compare our different opinions." (*PP* 93)

Even so, Elizabeth registers Austen's double-bind about female bookishness. "I am *not* a great reader," she rebuffs Miss Bingley's sarcasm (*PP* 37). In Austen's book, no woman is seen in formal schooling or mentored study; none aims to inhabit a library (save Mary), let alone become a professional author.

For better or worse, the marriage market is the prime investment for careful female reading and self-improvement, with failure punishable by social death. The famous single-paragraph first sentence of *Pride and Prejudice* sets the ethos in a spare 23-word proverb: "It is a truth universally acknowledged, that a single man in possession of a good fortune, must be in want of a wife" (*PP* 3). Susan J. Wolfson writes in "Re: Reading *Pride and Prejudice*": "If Austen's wit is that such a truth is just pride of local prejudice, her darker social text is that for a single woman, the hope declared *a truth* is all that matters. The syntactical rhyme of "in possession of" and "in want of" is a social poetics, no metaphysical philosophy. Deftly tuning irony with social realism, Austen's purchase on the suspect terrain of novel-reading is a "marriage-plot" with a difference, worked out through comparisons of difference: love at first sight; hate at first sight; schemings and inertia, infatuation and anxiety. Matches sad and happy, proposed and rejected, imagined and realized, become a moral measure of character—*moral* not as orthodoxy but as existential trial amid passions, impressions, interpretations, reviews, and not the least, pride and prejudices" (*A Companion to Jane Austen* 115).

Vivien Jones observes in "Feminisms," "'Feminism' is not a term that Austen would have understood. She would have been perfectly familiar, however, with the concept for individual rights and, more specifically, the rights of woman, as developed by women writers sympathetic to the ideals of the French Revolution and enshrined most famously in the title of Mary Wollstonecraft's *Vindication of the Right of Woman* of 1792" (*A Companion to Jane Austen* 282). In their different ways, Margaret Kirkham's *Jane Austen, Feminism and Fiction* (1983), Claudia Johnson's *Jane Austen: Women, Politics, and the Novel* (1988), and more recently, Peter Knox-Shaw's *Jane Austen and the Enlightenment* (2004), take a similar view, identifying Austen with an essentially progressivist position. For Knox-Shaw and Johnson, the influence of Enlightenment skepticism on Austen's thinking produces liberal "centrist views," sympathetic to issues of gender inequality: in Johnson's phrase, Austen "defended and enlarged a progressive middle ground" (Knox-Shaw 2004: 5; Johnson 1988: 166). Kirkham goes further, claiming close kinship between Austen and Wollstonecraft as "feminist moralists of the same school," who shared "the common line of feminist concern and interest, stretching back to Mary Astell at the very end of the seventeenth century" (Kirkham 1983: xi).

(X) *PRIDE AND PREJUDICE*: A PSYCHOANALYTIC READING

In the early part of the 20th century, the assurance of the self-description was disturbed by Sigmund Freud's book, *The Interpretation of Dreams* (1900), which described a discovery that would be the centerpiece of a new discipline, Psychoanalysis. Psychoanalytic theory after Freud divides into two strands, one called object relations, the other neo-Freudianism. The object relations theory favours a model that does without instincts almost altogether and concentrates instead on the way the self-interacts with its social world. The theory of identification, which places greater emphasis on social relations at the expense of the instinctual drives, was especially important to the object relations school of psychoanalysis that came into being after World War II in Britain and America and is associated with such names as Melanie Klein, D.W. Winnicott, and Margaret Mahlar. Jessica Benjamin's work in *Like Subjects, Love Objects* (1995) and *Shadow of the Other* (1998) as with her earlier *The Bonds of Love* (1988), has been focused, perhaps more explicitly than any earlier psychoanalytic thinker, on the phenomena of human relations we call love. Winnicott saw "relating though identifications" and the "use of an object" as successive developmental stages in the drama of human affections: for Benjamin they are more like positions, simultaneous and intermittent potentialities of the psyche, and this perception enables her to extend his thinking more explicitly into the realm of ethics.

The traditional focus of psychoanalysis on the processes occurring within the individual psyche can certainly throw some light on *Pride and Prejudice*. Its understanding of projection, in which 'the subject attributes tendencies, desires, etc., to others that he refuses to recognize in himself' is an example (Laplanche and Pontalis, *The Language of Psychoanalysis* 351). This might suggest why Elizabeth makes no progress in her avowed design of understanding Darcy, of painting a portrait or taking sketch of his nature. Her declared aim is always being undercut and subverted by her unconscious wishes. One might say that Elizabeth denies Darcy's subjectivity at the same time as she professes to invite it to speak. Elizabeth disowns parts of herself and bestows them instead on Darcy. For it is plain that Elizabeth, who is 'determined to dislike' Darcy (as she tells Charlotte, in the half-jest), herself enacts just that "implacable resentment" she attributes to him—building on that first insult and making everything else she hears from or about him, feed into this original orientation. In a series of encounters, Elizabeth attributes to Darcy the very emotions that are driving her—pride and prejudice among them. Her anger at his words about her family's behaviour enables her to forget or displace her own sense of shame, or rather it converts that shame into anger against him. Her hatred of her mother, for example, which Darcy's presence makes her experience most keenly, is naturally projected onto him. Thus this 'Mr Darcy' is for Elizabeth not someone who is perceived in his own right (so to speak) but someone who plays a role in her psychological life, as receptacle of her own projections and needs. It seems the same is true of Darcy's relations to Elizabeth. In a different way, he attributes his own desires to her, so that up to the proposal, as he later confesses, he believes that she wishes for, and is even 'expecting his addresses' (*PP* 369). Just as it was taken for granted that a young man in possession of a fortune would seek a wife, Darcy assumes that a young lady in want of a fortune would accept a husband with one: but this is not all. As Elizabeth realizes, listening to him in the proposal scene, she has no real presence to him: he is, in effect, though speaking in her company, conducting an inner dialogue with himself. His passion for her contains no element of perception of her as an independently existing being.

Among the important terms in the study of neurotic symptom formation are fixation, splitting introjection, and projection. If introjection brings in something from someone else, creating an ideal of that person within oneself, projection throws out something from within oneself and makes it seem as if it is a trait of someone else. Toney Tanner writes in *Jane Austen* that *Pride and Prejudice* is most importantly "about prejudging and rejudging. It is a drama of recognition—recognition, that act by which the mind can look again at a thing and if necessary make revisions and amendments until it sees the thing as it really is" (105). All too often what happens when people respond to others in *Pride and Prejudice* is more nearly akin to what psychologists as early as David Hume would call "projection," not taking, but putting into, the attribution to others of what we feel or desire ourselves. The novel opens with the words: "It is a truth universally acknowledged, that a single man in possession of a good fortune, must be in want of a wife." This is the narrator assuming a voice in order to expose how widespread is the attribution to others of what we ourselves wish. The Mrs Bennets of this world bestow their own desires on the young men who are their object. "Is that his design in settling here?" (*PP* 4): Mr Bennet's reply crisply exposes the absurdity of what Rachel Brownstein in "*Northanger Abbey, Sense and Sensibility, Pride and Prejudice*" calls this 'gossip's fantasy,' but it is inveterate (Copeland, *The Cambridge Companion to Jane Austen* 50). Conflating another's interests with one's own desires is so endemic that Austen seems to feel it requires no complicated irony: Charlotte Lucas, for example, in her 'kind schemes for Elizabeth' at Hunsford lets her own ambitions for her husband's preferment displace her initial focus on her friend (*PP* 181). When, in an unusual moment, Lady Catherine actually perceives that Darcy is low-spirited (after the rejection of his proposal by Elizabeth) she has no difficulty in attributing it to his unwillingness to leave Rosings, thus substituting her own desires for the marriage with Miss Anne, for his (*PP* 210).

The "projection" is specifically noted when the newly married Lydia and Wickham are due to come on to Longbourn. "Their arrival was dreaded by the elder Miss Bennets; and Jane more especially, who gave Lydia the feelings which would have attended herself, had *she* been the culprit, was wretched in the thought of what her sister must endure" (*PP* 315). Elizabeth earlier has imagined how 'miserable' Lydia will be "when she first sees my aunt" (*PP* 305): both projections amusingly at odds with Lydia's own aplomb when she eventually arrives on the scene. More critically, when

Charlotte declares that '[h]appiness in marriage is entirely a matter of chance,' Elizabeth assumes that this is being put forward in the same spirit in which she herself delights in sometimes professing opinions she does not hold (*PP* 23). And when Elizabeth says that Darcy 'has a very satirical eye' (*PP* 24) her interpretation of the meaning of his gaze owes more, it becomes clear, to her own temperament and expectations than it does to his.

The self-scrutinising aspect of Darcy's nature is examined through his friendship with Bingley. The relation of Elizabeth and Mrs Gardiner, as Claudia Johnson points out in *Jane Austen: Women, Politics and the Novel,* is a model of "rational friendship, where domination plays no part" (85). On the other hand, Bingley's persuasibility and Darcy's intellectual superiority disturb the balance of their relationship, and make it possible for Darcy to treat Bingley as a surrogate, proxy or experimental self. It is suggested that his plans for his sister and Bingley influence his endeavour to separate his friend from Miss Bennet "without meaning" that they should. But one might go further: not all of Darcy's cautions about judging objectively can guard him from using Bingley as part of his own internal system of defence-making Bingley's separation from Jane Bennet do duty for his own wish to break free from Elizabeth. "Towards *him* I have been kinder than towards myself" (*PP* 191): the maladroitness of this remark in the proposal scene betrays the confusion into which he has been led. Hence, as he recognizes, he finds himself seduced by 'unworthy' motives, since he obeys his unconscious wishes rather than his own principles in keeping the knowledge of Jane's being in London from Bingley.

Pride and Prejudice is certainly about knowing, knowing oneself and other people, as well as about money and sex. "Till this moment, I never knew myself" (*PP* 208): in the BBC film, the painful process through which Elizabeth Bennet comes to understand that she has been mistaken about Darcy is given very short shrift—thrown away in a bedroom scene in which Jane and Elizabeth pour into each other's bosom the balm of sisterly consolation—but it fills a critical chapter in the novel, as everyone acknowledges. At the same time, this is only half the story. Accounts that represent Elizabeth merely as a thinking being, rather than as a selfhood, a locus of subjective experience, both conscious and unconscious, tend to leave out a whole dimension of the readerly experience of the novel—the perennial fascination of what is actually going on in those dialogues between Darcy and Elizabeth. Wiltshire comments in "*Pride and Prejudice,* live and recognition" in *Recreating Jane Austen,* "Moreover, 'knowing' in the novel, I suggest, is very intimately bound up with its understanding of what it is to love someone. The novel is certainly about love, even if it is no more exclusively about the romantic love that consumes the other in its own yearnings than it is about 'sex' as an appetite. But the fundamental weakness of such readings is that their conception of what it is to 'know' another person is psychologically naive" (102).

The account of Darcy's motives would be open to the familiar criticism that one is "psychoanalyzing" the characters as if they were "real" people. An objection like this rests upon rather unreflective notions about the reality of actual people. When one says that other people are 'real' one is not referring to their physical presence near or around one. Their 'reality' refers to the degree to which they are present to us, and thus must refer to the degree they become real in our thoughts and imaginations. Wiltshire writes: "The kind of novel Jane Austen writes depends upon the reader identifying in turn and sometimes virtually simultaneously with several characters. But the "caricatures" in *Pride and Prejudice*—Collins, Mrs Bennet, Lady Catherine, Lydia have no meaningful interaction with the outside world of others' feelings, and thus are stuck in a set of repetitive behavioural styles. They correspond, I suggest, to the presence of some "real" people in our mental landscape. Such people (politicians, celebrities, for example, but also acquaintances) occupy a space in the inner theatre like that of the caricature, for in the economy of our psychological lives we cannot spare the energy to lend them an inner being. Instead they serve as objects: objects onto which we may project, or into which we may invest, atavistic propensities of our own.

We may think of them as wholly bad, or as buffoons, or admire them as heroes and heroines. We make do, in other words, with partial and stereotyped notions of others. The novel is populated with some figures who have only one gesture (Sir William Lucas) or a limited repertoire of personality traits (Bingley), who thus correspond to the far off and nearer figures in the inner world, and with others who come closer to that full, complex emotional life we usually ascribe to ourselves" (103). It is one of its pleasures that Mr Bennet, whom we are in the habit of understanding in one mode, emerges, as when he speaks to Elizabeth about marriage, as a person in another. But in ordinary life almost all of our internal representations of others are partial, prejudiced, incomplete. Few, very few, actual people, one ventures to assert, are present to us as 'real,' their feelings and motives as fully and unequivocally known to us as those of the protagonist of a novel, as an Elizabeth Bennet. The novel's representation of people corresponds to modalities of the psychological life, in which others are present to us largely as what psychoanalysis calls "internal objects."

Psychoanalysis classically studied and illuminated the way that selves make use of other selves, fantasizing about them, incorporating them into their own psychic life. It is as if the self radiates out, and the phenomena of the external world, other people, were only visible in its own light. In this context, Wiltshire observes: "But through psychoanalysis's intense focus on the individual in whom they are enacted, the discourse itself tended to reproduce precisely that solecism—the focus on the operations of the monadic individual psyche—in its own theoretical writings. It seemed to suggest that this is all that need be said about normal human relations, that others exist for a human subject wholly as receptacles and vehicles for their psychic needs, or as 'objects' for their impulses" (105-06). Jessica Benjamin argues that this concentration on 'object relations' very largely does reflect the nature of human psychological life. But, she insists, there are moments when we get beyond this—when we see others as existing outside ourselves with their own 'equivalent centres of self' (a phrase from George Eliot she uses as an epigraph). Drawing on Hegel's concept of the master-slave relation, she argues that, most of the time, our relationships with others are relations of 'domination,' in which we make psychological (ab)use of them. Darcy is using Elizabeth in this way in his first proposal—he addresses her not as an individual being but, as Rachel Brownstein puts it, as just another girl with a vulgar mother. He is in 'the bonds of love,' so overwhelmed by 'the utmost force of passion' (*PP* 198) that he is in fact oblivious to the person he is addressing—a classic instance of love as domination.

This is the psychological state commonly called 'romantic' love. Romantic love is obsessed with the other person and idealises them, but does not perceive them as other to the self. On the contrary, it merges self and other. It reproduces some aspects of the infant's earliest relation to the mother, in which the mother is only present to the infant, as a supplementary self, serving the immature ego's emotional needs. The patient in classical analysis makes use of the psychoanalyst in the same way, the analyst's neutral demeanour facilitating the patient's freedom to employ her for whatever psychological purposes he or she requires. But Benjamin argues, after Winnicott, that something beyond this must occur for the patient to truly develop. Benjamin calls this the moment of "recognition." This recognition that the other person is what she calls a "like subject," just as much a fully human being as I am myself, this shift into the realm of the intersubjective, involves a momentous psychological, and epistemological, alteration. The "love" of the "outside other," as Benjamin puts it, is "a continuation under more complex conditions of the infant's original fascination with and love of what is outside, her appreciation of difference and novelty" (*Like Subjects* 41).

"Recognition" is an obviously helpful term in the context of *Pride and Prejudice* because it chimes in with the novel's emphasis on the visual. To recognize someone in this larger, deeper sense, though, is not just to see him or her clearly, as an object might be seen, but simultaneously to love them and respect their own nature. Nor is it merely "that act by which the mind can...make revisions and amendments until it sees the thing as it really is," as Tanner describes it. An act of the whole being, not just of the mind, it names that capacity to respond to the other person not merely as a repository for one's own desires, hopes, fears, anxieties and dreams, but as a wholly different (and equivalently human) other person, a 'like subject.' But, as Benjamin repeatedly emphasizes, this can never be a permanent or continuous capacity of the psyche: the moments in which one sees the other in their own light fall constantly under siege to the inveterate human propensity to shadow that other with one's own inner needs and hidden purposes. Recognition is momentarily plucked out of the continual common traffic of reciprocal domination.

Benjamin's concept suggests that Jane Austen thinks through the category of 'knowing'—knowing someone else—as an emotional, even erotic, as well as an epistemological ideal. Such a notion of recognition, then, takes in more than knowledge, philosophically understood: and on the other hand it is rather different from our usual conception of 'understanding' another person. Benjamin makes reference to the French philosopher Emmanuel Levinas's concept of 'alterity,' which clarifies the distinction. The two writers have in common a belief that acknowledgment of the other is at the heart of ethics. In Levinas's thinking, an ethical relation to the other (the 'Altrui') is to their alterity, but this is not to be obtained through 'empathy' or the enveloping of others in our own sympathetic feeling, the route of 'understanding.' Recognition of another in this sense is simply the dispersion of one's own self-understanding onto another. This mode is exemplified in the novel pre-eminently by Jane Bennet. But Jane's sympathy for others is not recognition of their difference from herself: on the contrary, it is guaranteed by her assimilation of everyone else to herself, qualified by her inability to acknowledge that others have radically different being from her own. If Elizabeth is to reach recognition of Darcy's otherness, and he of hers, it must be by a quite different path.

Pride and Prejudice is a novel in which much is not told. What is not commented upon, amplified, or contextualised, is crucially important; interruptions, breaks and what is withheld from our understanding often contribute decisively to the novel's intellectual and emotional excitement. Early in *Pride and Prejudice,* when Charlotte Lucas expresses her cynical opinion of marriage, Elizabeth replies: "You make me laugh, Charlotte; but it is not sound. You know it is not sound, and that you would never act this way yourself" (*PP* 23). Their dialogue ceases at this point. How Charlotte responds to this—whether she replies, whether she smiles wryly, whether she raises her eyebrows—is unknown, since the next paragraph turns immediately to another topic, Mr Darcy's beginning to find Elizabeth 'an object of some interest.' The effect is that the reader is left to take up Elizabeth's opinion as his or her own, pockets as a piece of knowledge what has later to be painfully repaid.

The pruning away of material—the absence of many indications of facial expression, of guiding commentary from the narrator, even of scene setting—has critical consequences for the reading of Elizabeth and Darcy's dialogues leading up to the proposal scene. In that scene, the changing expressions on Darcy's face play an important role in the reader's understanding of the drama. But in earlier exchanges almost the only facet of physical representation recorded is that Darcy 'smiles' quite commonly before speaking. Except for one instance at Hunsford what is not recorded is whether Elizabeth notices these smiles, what effect they have on her, if and how they disturb her fixed idea of him. This means that when it comes to the interpretation of Mr Darcy, the reader is more or less on his or her own, or guided by Elizabeth's responses.

"What most satisfies us in reading the dialogue in *Pride and Prejudice*," wrote Reuben Brower, "is Jane Austen's awareness that it is difficult to know any complex person, that knowledge of a man like Darcy is an interpretation and a construction, not a simple absolute." One might call the narrative of *Pride and Prejudice* a hologrammic narrative, a hologram being a picture which, observed from a different direction, reveals itself to contain a quite different representation. The hologrammic switch from one to another point of view corresponds to differing dispositions of the self.

It is pertinent to note that Benjamin insists that recognition is not a stable position or capacity. "Alienated forms of complementarity...in the best of circumstances alternate with recognition." The moment of recognition of the other is always giving way to repudiation or to some form of narcissistic identification or idealization. When we read from Elizabeth's position we are ensconced in the psychological state in which the other is negated. But we do catch glimpses of the possibility of reading from outside her position in which Darcy appears differently. On the other side, the novel allows the reader quite plainly to see that Darcy himself, broadly speaking, 'sees' Elizabeth from inside his own needs and desires —that indeed is the central irony of the text at this point. The alternation between one and the other reading is the formal equivalent of what Benjamin calls the "other's liability not to survive, the inevitable failure of recognition."

Darcy's letter is a formal turning point in *Pride and Prejudice,* because for the first time he comes forward in an independent voice, unconstrained by the social occasion, cut free from those responses of Elizabeth that have coloured the reader's attention to him so far. His letter forces Elizabeth to recognize that he exists outside her assumptions about him. Whilst his inner life has been given a kind of notional presence earlier in the novel through brief (and perhaps rather coy) acknowledgements of his sexual feelings, now he becomes established as an entity with depth and complexity.

Elizabeth is now invited to see him as a being whose psychological and moral life is constituted largely by his family, as she keenly feels her own to have been. Forced to attend continuously to the other's thought processes, Elizabeth is overwhelmed. The shift from one convention, third person narrative, to the other, the novel in letters, enacts the abrupt change that takes place in the reader's consciousness. In one account, Darcy's letter 'seizes the female reader and turns her into the objects of its force and her own hatred.' Some may indeed feel that their response has been highjacked, so decisive is the reversal of sympathy from Elizabeth to Darcy at this point. Relating through identifications now gives way, in mimicry, to something like incipient recognition.

Next day Darcy, after loitering in the park, hands Elizabeth the letter. The focus is on Elizabeth, as she reads his words, not being able to take them in: she reads the letter at first much as she has heard his proposal, in a mode of psychological refusal. Gradually, and painfully, she is forced to accept the plausibility, and then the likelihood, of what he says. The novelist, by presenting the letter without narrative framing in one chapter and then reviewing the letter through Elizabeth's consciousness in the next, takes the reader through that travail of reading and rereading, that cumulative assault on previous conviction that is Elizabeth's experience.

Sigmund Freud spent most of his life studying the boundary and the dynamic movements between the conscious self or ego and the unconscious, which he later came to call the id. Darcy's letter is a wonderful instance of an assault on the ego being sustained, not resented. Not only the material information in the letter, but the moderation of its tone, and the evidence of the writer's struggle towards impartiality, contribute to its power to convince Elizabeth. His letter contains no reproaches, nor does it make any attempt at reconciliation. Most importantly, except perhaps at the opening, it does not retaliate. Darcy is himself, as he later confesses, "tortured" by her rebuke about his manner, but it is his pride, paradoxically, that saves him from detesting her very name.

In his politically "radical" reading of the novel, Edward Neill has argued indeed that the relation of Darcy and Elizabeth is conducted always within "the master-slave dialectic." "We never leave the terms of the master-slave relationship (whichever way things happen to tilt)" he writes. He understands Darcy as enjoying his power over Elizabeth, and "succumbing to his desire to master her." Several acute contemporary feminist critics besides Neill also read the second half of the narrative as the story of Elizabeth's subjugation by or surrender to Darcy's wealth, authority and superior judgement. They see this, and the happy marriage with which the novel ends, as registering Austen's own, if temporary, capitulation to that patriarchal system which invests all males with more power than females. They see Elizabeth as dwindling into a wife.

Austen never presents Darcy as if he were to be understood as wholly within the space of Elizabeth's psychology, as a lovably equal object. Whilst Elizabeth is amused, for example, at his assumptions about Bingley (and despite telling herself she mustn't yet tease him, comes very close to it) Darcy's inflexibly demanding supergo (the 'I' in these sentences that instructs some other part of the self) is still being reinscribed: "I was obliged to confess one thing, which for a time, and not unjustly, offended him. I could not allow myself to conceal that your sister had been in town three months last winter, that I had known it, and purposely kept it from him" (*PP* 371). The contrast between Elizabeth's impulses to playfulness and mischief and Darcy's inflexible need to act rightly and to be square with his conscience is sustained. This is not a relationship in which each mirrors the other but of distinct subjectivities whose very alterity is the ground of their rapport. This means that, since the novel's point of view continues to be mostly Elizabeth's, Darcy remains out of reach, an enigma, other, to the end. This in turn may explain why for so many readers, he remains a focus of fantasy.

The novel's play on the visual, with treating the other as an object, and as other than an object, is most brilliantly articulated in the sequence at Pemberley in which Elizabeth Bennet contemplates Darcy's portrait, "...it is the apotheosis of the novel's complex understanding on the nature of recognition. Partly because it has been led up to by the novel's reiterated association of visuality and knowledge, this moment, as most readers and critics feel, has significance out of proportion to its duration" (Wiltshire 122). Miss Bingely's early attempts to tease Darcy about Elizabeth's low connections—"Do let the portraits of your uncle and aunt Philips be placed in the gallery at Pemberley" (*PP* 52-53) have followed from Darcy's assertion that an artist 'taking' a picture of Elizabeth would find it difficult to catch the expression of her eyes. A portrait, unlike a 'sketch,' or 'picture' then has already been loaded with public, dynastic, implications. "At last it arrested her—and she beheld a striking resemblance of Mr Darcy, with such a smile over the face, as she remembered to have sometimes seen, when he looked at her." "As she stood before the canvas, on which he was represented, and fixed his eyes upon herself, she thought of his regard with a deeper sentiment of gratitude than it had even raised before; she remembered its warmth, and softened its impropriety of expression" (*PP* 250-51).

The moment when Elizabeth contemplates the portrait is a textual representation of the psychic capacity Jessica Benjamin names 'recognition.' It is difficult to give graphic form, to convey to the reader in writing, the real presence of the unspoken psychological transactions which crisscross the consulting room; hence "recognition" in Benjamin's work, like "use" in Winnicott's, remains a shade abstract, theoretic. But the portrait scene in the novel offers a kind of condensed, symbolic representation of the meaning of that insight into a rare capacity of human interaction when others are encountered as equals. It is an aesthetic rehearsal for that drama of recognition which the following chapters of the novel will play out in detail, and it is followed, in one of the novel's, more daring moments, a short paragraph later, by the reappearance of Darcy himself.

Softened by her thinking about him, Elizabeth is able to 'see' what she had previously not seen, to know something, it is suggested, about Darcy that she had not previously known. In a literally magical moment, the portrait becomes animated. In the presence of art we become enchanted into the belief that the past is alive at the same moment as we are ourselves and *Pride and Prejudice* looks at us with its own eyes. Elizabeth envisages Darcy as a real other being whose smile now becomes the living index of that otherness whose significance she had formerly disregarded. As Rachel Brownstein writes: "What she loves, and sees, is what goes on between them."

Submission, if it occurs, is rather a necessary tendering of self in return for the other's regard. If Elizabeth allows herself to be looked at, puts herself momentarily in the position of the looked at, the object, she is simultaneously the subject of the action and the subject who is acting. It would be hard indeed to find a more compressed figuration of the interplay of alterity, submission and possession that makes up the drama of recognition. The gaze she now sees in the portrait, and the gaze she returns, is not one of domination, but of love.

7 Characters in *Pride and Prejudice*

ELIZABETH BENNET

Although almost every one of Jane Austen's novels has been the declared favourite of Sunday readers, but there can be no doubt that *Pride and Prejudice* has always been the one most widely read and most often re-read. It is also the one that has chiefly invited dramatization, for both stage and film, partly perhaps because of its abundance of bright dialogue and its highly dramatic symmetry of structure. On the other hand, critics who do not allow irresistible charm to sway their judgment might say that, while *Pride and Prejudice* is far richer and more mature than *Northanger Abbey* and *Sense and Sensibility*, and has many more speaking characters than either, it is still a simple, slender tale which has almost too ideal a pattern and seldom achieves the realistic complexity, density, and subtlety of *Mansfield Park* and *Emma*. But few could disagree with the author's avowal, made when she received the first copy of "my own darling child": "I must confess that I think her (Elizabeth Bennet) as delightful a creature as ever appeared in print, and how I shall be able to tolerate those who do not like *her* at least I do not know" (Letter 76: January 29, 1813). Elizabeth is not, like the heroines of conventional fiction, endowed in a transcendent and flawless degree with beauty and all the virtues of heart and head; she is a thoroughly human mixture, above the average in her perceptive interest in people (complicated people), in independence, candour, in gaily satirical wit, in balance of sense and sensibility—in short, very much like her creator. And she is the mainspring of the plot: along with her own personal development, it is through her and her effect on Darcy that her sisters (and also Charlotte Lucas) achieve the appointed end of comedy, marriage.

Although all the Bennet girls claim a great share of the reader's interest and attention, none calls forth our admiration so much as Elizabeth, whose archness and sweetness of manner render her a very attractive object in the familypiece. She is in fact the Beatrice of the tale; and falls in love on much the same principles of contrariety. At first glance, perhaps the two elder Bennet sisters, Jane and Elizabeth, may seem to vie with each other for primacy in *Pride and Prejudice*; but Elizabeth is definitely the heroine: not only does she explicitly represent one of the words of the title of the story; she also quite thoroughly dominates the action—and, by comparison, Jane is a shadowy accessory. The relationship of Jane Bennet to Bingley, which parallels that of Elizabeth and Darcy, is treated much less fully, partly because it is much simpler, but partly because it is intended to be a comment on that of her younger sister and the proud man from Derbyshire.

Elizabeth has no particular care for the attendant fashions, ribbons, and bonnets. She bounds three miles across dusty fields, springs over puddles and stiles, appalls Bingley's sisters with her muddy petticoat and ruddy complexion; her eyes are bright from exercise. She will freckle and tan from touring outdoors with the Gardiners, and a walk of several miles with Darcy will clinch their engagement. Austen collates this aberration from female "accomplishments" with Elizabeth's character as a reader. To say that Darcy is proud and Elizabeth prejudiced is to tell but half the story. Pride and prejudice are faults; but they are also the necessary defects of desirable merits: self-respect and intelligence. Moreover, the novel makes clear the fact that Darcy's pride leads to prejudice and Elizabeth's prejudice stems from a pride in her own perceptions. So the ironic theme of the book might be said to centre on the dangers of intellectual complexity. Jane Bennet and Bingley are never exposed to these dangers; they are not sufficiently profound. But the hero and the heroine, because of their deep percipience, are, ironically, subject to failures of perception. Elizabeth has good reason to credit herself with the ability to discern people and situations extraordinarily well: she understands her family perfectly, knows William Collins from the first letter he writes, comprehends the merits and deficiencies of Bingleys almost at once, appreciates Lady Catherine de Bourgh at first meeting. Her failures are with 'intricate' people who moreover stand in a relationship of great intimacy to her: Charlotte Lucas, George Wickham, Fitzwilliam Darcy. And the book is given an added dimension because it shows that intimacy blurs perceptions: intelligence fails if there is insufficient distance between mind and object.

Charlotte Lucas is 'a sensible, intelligent young woman, about twenty-seven...Elizabeth's intimate friend.' But we very soon know that in an important respect she differs from Elizabeth—though Elizabeth herself does not know this fact. When, very early in the first volume, they discuss the possibility of an attachment between Jane and Bingley, Charlotte says Jane should make some efforts in this direction; but Elizabeth reminds her friend that Miss Bennet hardly knows him. This, however, does not deter Charlotte:

> I wish Jane success with all my heart; and if she were married to him tomorrow, I should think she had as good a chance of happiness, as if she were to be studying his character for a twelve month. Happiness in marriage is entirely a matter of chance. If the dispositions of the parties are ever so well known to each other, or ever so similar before-hand, it does not advance their felicity in the least. They always continue to grow sufficiently unlike afterwards to have their share of vexation; and it is better to know as little as possible of the defects of the person with whom you are to pass your life. (*PP* 23)

But Elizabeth does not believe this statement:

> You make me laugh, Charlotte: but it is not sound. You know it is not sound, and that you would never act in this way yourself. (*PP* 23)

She refuses to believe Charlotte because a natural kindness and affection have blinded Elizabeth to the demerits of her friend; it is because, in the nature of things, involvement (which is so necessary and desirable, in Austenian terms) carries with it the inevitable consequence of obscuring the marvellous clarity and depth of understanding so necessary in personal association.

There is no evidence that Charlotte misunderstands William Collins, but there is much to show that Elizabeth does comprehend him perfectly. '"Can he be a sensible man, sir?"' (*PP* 64) she asks her father rhetorically after hearing the orotund phrases of the clergyman's letter. Nor is she wrong. At the Netherfield Ball, after dancing with him twice, 'the moment of her release from him was exstacy,' but she derives some consolation in discussing his demerits with Charlotte. The next morning he proposes marriage to Elizabeth, and of course she refuses him summarily. Then she is flabbergasted to learn that Charlotte has accepted Mr Collins's subsequent proposal of marriage to her.

> She had always felt that Charlotte's opinion of matrimony was not exactly like her own, but she could not have supposed it possible that when called into action, she would have sacrificed every better feeling to wordly advantage. Charlotte the wife of Mr Collins, was a most humiliating picture! (*PP* 125)

And now, for the first time, she begins to see Charlotte as she really is: and 'felt persuaded that no real confidence could ever subsist between them again.' Elizabeth has learned something from this experience, as is demonstrated in her conversation with Jane not long afterwards:

> Do not be afraid of my running into any excess, of my encroaching on your privilege of universal good will. You need not. There are few people whom I really love, and still fewer of whom I think well. The more I see of the world, the more am I dissatisfied with it; and every day confirms my belief of the inconsistency of all human characters, and of the little dependence that can

> be placed on the appearance of either merit or sense. I have met with two instances lately; one I will not mention (it is Bingley's 'want of proper resolution'); the other is Charlotte's marriage. It is unaccountable! In every view it is unaccountable! (*PP* 135)

Desperately trying to convince Mr Collins that "no means no" after his unwelcome proposal, Elizabeth Bennet asserts her right to autonomous choice by describing herself in Wollstonecraftian terms: "Do not consider me now as an *elegant female* intending to plague you, but as a *rational creature* speaking the truth from her heart" (109, emphasis added).

The famous first encounter between Elizabeth and Darcy is comically disastrous; it occurs at the assembly where Darcy says to Bingley of Elizabeth, who is sitting down: '"She is tolerable; but not handsome enough to tempt *me*; and I am in no humour at present to give consequence to young ladies who are slighted by other men."' And as a natural result, 'Elizabeth remained with no very cordial feelings towards him' (*PP* 12). But at Netherfield, where she has gone to nurse the ailing Jane, Elizabeth makes her extraordinary and attractive personality felt so strongly that Mrs Hurst and Miss Bingley take an immediate dislike to her; so strongly that she finds Darcy staring at her.

> She hardly knew how to suppose that she could be an object of admiration to so great a man; and yet that he should look at her because he disliked her, was still more strange. She could only imagine however at last, that she drew his notice because there was a something about her more wrong and reprehensible, according to his ideas of right, than in any other person present. The supposition did not pain her. She liked him too little to care for his approbation. (*PP* 51)

However, when she refuses to dance with him and says, '"despise me if you dare,"' he replies in unmistakable accents, '"Indeed I do not dare"' (*PP* 52). But the insult of the Ball fresh in her mind, she does not like him; she is even willing to overweigh the negative evidence, which now presents itself first from Darcy himself, then from the plausible and attractive Wickham. In the conversation at Netherfield, during which Elizabeth makes her well-known remark, that '"I hope I never ridicule what is wise and good,"' she finds from Darcy that '"My good opinion once lost is lost for ever"'—a chilling comment which she acknowledges to be a defect, but not a laughable one. Then she meets Wickham, and finding him charming, very easily believes his allegations that Darcy has behaved abominably, that the latter has cast the young lieutenant from a promised living in the church, that in fact both Darcy and his sister suffer from very excessive pride. Elizabeth is vexed and even angry when Wickham fails to appear at the Netherfield Ball, again not trying to suppose that there may be something to be said on Darcy's side. Even so, there are signs that she willy-nilly succumbs to his charms—in the pertness of her conversation while they are dancing:

> 'It is *your* turn to say something now, Mr Darcy. *I* talked about the dance, and *you* ought to make some kind of remark on the side of the room, or the number of couples.'
>
> He smiled, and assured her that whatever she wished him to say should be said.
>
> 'Very well. That reply will do for the present. Perhaps bye and bye I may observe that private balls are much pleasanter than public ones. But *now* we may be silent.'
>
> 'Do you talk by rule then, while you are dancing?'
>
> 'Sometimes. One must speak a little, you know. It would look odd to be entirely silent for half an hour together, and yet for the advantage of *some*, conversation ought to be so arranged as that they may have the trouble of saying as little as possible.'
>
> 'Are you consulting your own feelings in the present case, or do you imagine that you are gratifying mine?'

> 'Both,' replied Elizabeth archly; 'for I have always seen a great similarity in the turn of our minds. We are each of an unsocial, taciturn disposition, unwilling to speak, unless we expect to say something that will amaze the whole room, and be handed down to posterity with all the éclat of a proverb.' (*PP* 91)

However, when she questions him about Wickham, he keeps silent—nor can she understand him, as she readily admits before their dance is finished. It is an artful irony of Jane Austen's that Miss Bingley immediately thereafter tells her that Wickham is entirely in the wrong, and Darcy in the right, in the breach between the two men. Elizabeth disbelieves her for two reasons: first, because she has correctly sized Miss Bingley up as an entirely unreliable source of information; and second, perhaps, because she wants to dislike Darcy in order to avoid any entanglement which will cost her freedom. Nevertheless, she feels mortified when she realizes that Darcy is overhearing Mrs Bennet boast that Jane and Bingley will soon be engaged.

In the second volume, the relationship of Darcy and Elizabeth is resumed in Kent, at Rosings and at Hunsford, the parsonage to which William Collins has taken his new wife. Everything is unpropitious, so far as Elizabeth herself is concerned: she has agreed to visit Charlotte only because of the memory of their close friendship—'all the comfort of intimacy was over.' Mr Collins is just as senseless as ever; Miss de Bourgh is '"sickly and cross. Yes, she will do for him [Darcy] very well. She will make him a very proper wife"'; and Lady Catherine is quite as insufferable as Wickham has promised. Amongst all these displeasing people comes Darcy, who adds to her annoyance by looking confused when she asks whether he has seen Jane in London (for she suspects that he has warned Bingley off her); and, despite his calls at the parsonage and their 'chance' encounters in Rosings Park, her prejudice against him increases, for she finds apparent corroboration of her suspicions in the conversation with Colonel Fitzwilliam, during which he recounts the fact that Darcy has told him of saving an intimate friend recently from a very imprudent marriage.

And so she is bowled over when Darcy tells her he loves her:

> In vain have I struggled. It will not do. My feelings will not be repressed. You must allow me to tell you how ardently I admire and love you. (*PP* 189)

But she is more than astonished: she is gradually angered by the tone and implication of his remarks:

> His sense of her inferiority—of its being a degradation—of the family obstacles which judgment had always opposed to inclination, were dwelt on with a warmth which seemed due to the consequence he was wounding, but was very unlikely to recommend his suit. (*PP* 189)

So—and not without recrimination for '"ruining, perhaps for ever, the happiness of a most beloved sister"' and for his ill-treatment of Wickham—she refuses and dismisses the proud Mr Fitzwilliam Darcy.

But this is not the end; indeed it is only the beginning of Elizabeth's very gradually successfully efforts to know herself thoroughly. The next day she is handed Darcy's justly famous letter, written in proud tones and offering some new light not only on the Jane-Bingley business but upon the supposed unfairness to Wickham's claims. As to the first, Darcy says he thought Jane seemed not much attracted to Bingley, whereas Bingley was strongly attached to Jane; and furthermore, Darcy acknowledges an objection to Miss Bennet's family—two considerations which led him both to conceal from Bingley the fact of Jane's presence in London and to persuade his friend that she did not feel much affection for him. As for Wickham, the young Meryton militiaman resigned all claim to a living, in return for which Darcy gave him £3000 to study law. Three years later, the incumbent of the living, the claim to which Wickham had resigned, died; and Wickham, having lived a dissipated and extravagant life in London, sought it. Darcy refused, and Wickham abused him violently; but more than that, sought Georgiana Darcy out, and persuaded her to elope with him—though the plot was prevented. Elizabeth reads the letter with great astonishment and—at first—with little comprehension. She is, however, even more completely stunned by the account of Wickham, and her first impression is to disbelieve Darcy on that score too. But then, in reflecting on Wickham's behaviour at Meryton (especially with regard to his sudden betrothal to the rich Miss King), she is inclined to think it very probable that Darcy is telling the truth after all.

> She grew absolutely ashamed of herself. Of neither Darcy nor Wickham could she think, without feeling that she had been blind, partial, prejudiced, absurd.
>
> 'How despicably have I acted!' she cried.—'I, who have prided myself on my discernment!—I, who have valued myself on my abilities! who have often disdained the generous candour of my sister, and gratified my vanity, in useless or blameable distrust.—How humiliating is this discovery!—Yet, how just a humiliation!—Had I been in love, I could not have been more wretchedly blind.' (*PP* 208)

In this dramatic moment of self-revelation she has the honesty to see that there may be some justice in what Darcy has said about Jane, for 'she felt that Jane's feelings, though fervent, were little displayed, and that there was a constant complacency in her air and manner, not often united with great sensibility' (*PP* 208). She has learned much from the letter, very much indeed; but Jane Austen is too perceptive a reader of character to suppose that all comes clear at once: it is by a marvellous irony that Elizabeth is made to reflect, '"Had I been in love, I could not have been more wretchedly blind"'; nor, though Elizabeth does know herself henceforth much better, does she yet know herself completely.

It is even true that her attitude toward the letter is to undergo a further change when she has had a better chance to think of it with some coolness. She almost completely reverses her first excited opinion:

> His attachment excited gratitude, his general character respect; but she could not approve him; nor could she for a moment repent her refusal, or feel the slightest inclination ever to see him again. In her own past behaviour, there was a constant source of vexation and

> regret; and in the unhappy defects of her family a subject of yet heavier chagrin. (*PP* 212)

So, in a half-way stage in her thinking and feeling, she yet refuses to look squarely at the consequences of a commitment to Darcy; she still rebels against involvement. Nevertheless, her uncompromising honesty causes her to realize that there is much justice in his views about her family—all of them but Jane.

Elizabeth does not see Darcy again until the unexpected encounter at Pemberley, to which she has gone with the Gardiners on vacation. Presumably she has had an opportunity to absorb the lesson of the letter; at least she is now more willing to believe good things about him—from Mrs Reynolds, for instance, who is the housekeeper of Pemberley and has only warm praise for her master, whom she has known since he was four years old—'"and he was always the sweetest-tempered, most generous-hearted, boy in the world"' (*PP* 249). Already softened towards Darcy by such unstinted praise, she meets him by chance (he has returned home a day early) and finds him more civil to her than ever before, unfailingly kind to the Gardiners, and urgently desirous to '"introduce my sister to your acquaintance."' She likes Georgiana, and after the meeting takes occasion to reflect on her own not very clear feelings:

> She certainly did not hate him. No; hatred had vanished long ago, and she had almost as long been ashamed of ever feeling a dislike against him, that could be so called. The respect created by the conviction of his valuable qualities, though at first unwillingly admitted, had for some time ceased to be repugnant to her feelings; and it was now heightened into somewhat of a friendlier nature, by the testimony so highly in his favour, and bringing forwards his disposition in so amiable a light, which yesterday had produced. But above all, above respect and esteem, there was a motive within her of good will which could not be overlooked. It was gratitude. Gratitude, not merely for having once loved her, but for loving her still well enough, to forgive

> all the petulance and acrimony of her manner in rejecting him, and all the unjust accusations accompanying her rejection.... She respected, she esteemed, she was grateful to him, she felt a real interest in his welfare; and she only wanted to know how far she wished that welfare to depend upon herself, and how far it would be for the happiness of both that she should employ the power, which her fancy told her she still possessed, of bringing on the renewal of his addresses. (*PP* 265-66)

Jane Austen is able to indicate something of the complexity of Elizabeth's mind, and the continued resistance which she is still putting up against the release of her own strong feelings.

A crisis is called for, something which will break the placidity of her reflections; and this comes in the stunning news that Lydia Bennet and George Wickham have eloped; in her anguish Elizabeth blurts the story out to Darcy, who is most consolatory and kind. Nevertheless, when she leaves Derbyshire—as now she must, hurriedly—she is certain she will never see him again. She feels genuine regret on departure: and her feelings have ascended to another level. Elizabeth has little leisure to reflect on her own feelings for several weeks. Then she begins to regret telling Darcy about the elopement, for now that Lydia and Wickham are to be married, she feels that the first tawdry adventure might have been concealed from him, who would so strenuously disprove—though no doubt he would not under any circumstances ally himself to a family connected in any way with the despicable Wickham.

> She began now to comprehend that he [Darcy] was exactly the man, who, in disposition and talents, would most suit her. His understanding and temper, though unlike her own, would have answered all her wishes. It was an union that must have been to the advantage of both; by her ease and liveliness, his mind might have been softened, his manners improved, and from his judgment, information, and knowledge of the world, she must have received benefit of greater importance. (*PP* 312)

But now, she thinks, it is too late: such an alliance can never be—until she discovers that it has been Darcy who has been mainly instrumental in arranging the marriage between Lydia and Wickham, through motives which she must interpret in but one way: 'Her heart did whisper, that he had done it for her.' But she still cannot quite believe that he would ever consent to be the brother-in-law of Wickham, even for her. Nevertheless, she refuses—with keen disdain—to promise Lady Catherine de Bourgh not to accept a proposal of marriage from Darcy: an interview which, as Darcy says, '"taught me to hope...as I had scarcely ever allowed myself to hope before"' (*PP* 367). And so they are betrothed, at last.

Warren Roberts observes in "Women and the Family": "Elizabeth Bennet is an anti-Evelina type in a completely different sense than Catherine Morland, not a burlesque of the 'young girl who enters the world' but the opposite of Burney's shy, bashful, uncertain heroine. Austen revealed a feminist point of view in *Pride and Prejudice* not by commenting ironically on the 'advantages' of female ignorance and then exposing male ignorance, but through a positive, independent heroine" (*Jane Austen and the French Revolution* 180). It is obviously because of the spirited heroine, that *Pride and Prejudice* is the most captivating of Jane Austen's variations on the Cinderella theme. Elizabeth, to be sure, is not a real Cinderella but (as she declared in her grand duel with Lady Catherine de Bourgh) the daughter of a gentleman, a gentleman, however, far below Darcy in station and income. Her chief handicap is her "low connections." Her foolish and ill-bred mother and youngest sisters and her uncle Philips (a Meryton attorney) and his wife must, as Darcy says of Jane and Elizabeth, "very materially lessen their chance of marrying men of any consideration in the world." The social gulf between Darcy and Elizabeth is in accord with the facts of contemporary life, it is not merely a fictional convention; but social divisions had been a great resource for novelists from Richardson onward and were to be through much of the nineteenth century, notably for Trollope. Thus, *Pride and Prejudice* puts formidable obstacles in the way of a happy culmination, and suspense is aggravated and prolonged by other obstacles that develop in the course of the story through the emulation of the character of Elizabeth Bennet. Margaret Kirkham observes in *Jane Austen, Feminism and Fiction*:

> None of the Austen heroines is more attractive than Elizabeth Bennet, none more clearly possessed of intelligence and warm affections, but as she develops she effectively destroys the role she is supposed to play. The result is that she begins to look too much like a heroine without a part, a real-life character, not a creature in print, and this will not do, for her extreme, and improbable, good luck in marriage is acceptable only if it is properly distanced from life by the formal requirements of plot and part. That is why Jane Austen spoke of *Pride and Prejudice* as 'too light and bright and sparkling', and why she developed new ways of dealing with the heroine's role, so that the plot should no longer turn on a major reversal of her beliefs or judgment. (92)

MR FITZWILLIAM DARCY

In *Pride and Prejudice,* Darcy and Wickham, the hero and the villain, have prominent, interesting, and convincing parts. Each is present throughout the novel, both attract the heroine, and both receive the marital fates which they deserve. Elizabeth Bennet is a complicated and penetrating heroine; the two men with whom she associates herself romantically must also be intricate and intelligent.

If Elizabeth's prejudices are views in which she takes pride, so ought it be said that Darcy's pride leads to prejudice. But even this is an over-simplification: his austerity of manner, as we learn from his housekeeper at Pemberley, stems partly from an inordinate shyness. It is impossible, however, to explain away his famous remark about Elizabeth ("...tolerable; but not handsome enough to tempt me...") on the grounds of diffidence alone—nor, indeed, the statement that "My good opinion once lost is lost for ever," nor the first proposal to Elizabeth; nor his subsequent explanatory letter. He is a proud man.

One way in which Jane Austen delineates his character is through his relationship with Bingley. It is partly through this friendship that a certain completeness is given to Darcy's character. Although we are struck, at the very beginning of the book, with Darcy's rudeness and with his pride, we may overlook the solidity of temperament implied in his affection for Bingley.

Despite his early bad impression of Elizabeth, he is soon constrained to like her better: for, ironically, the heroine by behaving disdainfully to him, does just what is necessary to captivate him. Thus at Sir William Lucas's party, her refusal to dance with him only sets him to thinking of her attractiveness; her piquancy at Netherfield leads to the famous conversation in which Elizabeth, while acknowledging that "I dearly love a laugh," insists that "I hope I never ridicule what is wise or good." When Darcy appears during Elizabeth's visiting Hunsford, where she has gone to fulfil an unwilling promise of spending some time with Charlotte and William Collins, besides the unfortunate first impression which the squire of Pemberley has made, there is now the insistent and plausible evidence against his character which Wickham has adduced. Elizabeth cannot understand the why of Darcy's repeated calls at the parsonage, nor can she comprehend the astonishing regularity of their 'unexpected' encounters in the Park. And she is stunned by his declaration of love, and proposal of marriage.

> Elizabeth's astonishment was beyond expression. She stared, coloured, doubted, and was silent. This he considered sufficient encouragement, and the avowal of all that he felt and had long felt for her, immediately followed. He spoke well, but there were feelings besides those of the heart to be detailed, and he was not more eloquent on the subject of tenderness than of pride. His sense of her inferiority—of its being a degradation—of the family obstacles which judgment had always opposed to inclination, were dwelt on with a warmth which seemed due to the consequence he was wounding, but was very unlikely to recommend his suit.

> In spite of her deeply-rooted dislike, she could not be insensible to the compliment of such a man's affection, and though her intentions did not vary for an instant, she was at first sorry for the pain he was to receive; till, roused to resentment by his subsequent language, she lost all compassion in anger. She tried, however, to compose herself to answer him with patience, when he should have done. He concluded with representing to her the strength of that attachment which, in spite of all his endeavours, he had found impossible to conquer; and with expressing his hope that it would now be rewarded by her acceptance of his hand. As he said this, she could easily see that he had no doubt of a favourable answer. He *spoke* of apprehension and anxiety, but his countenance expressed real security. Such a circumstance could only exasperate farther.... (*PP* 189)

Elizabeth's angry refusal marks the beginning of the great change in Darcy: he is humbled, though there is but one sentence in the letter which he writes to her, to indicate that he has been mollified: 'I will only add, God bless you.'

When Elizabeth first visits Pemberley, after having rejected Darcy's proposal, she is struck by the 'large handsome stone building,' and the magnificent setting in which it is situated, 'neither formal nor falsely adorned.' The natural beauty and moral character of the house and grounds makes her feel that 'to be mistress of Pemberley might be something!' (*PP* 245). When she and the Gardiners knock at the door they are received by the housekeeper, Mrs Reynolds, who has known Darcy since he was four years old. Elizabeth is surprised at her obvious fondness for her master. Personally, Mrs Reynolds says Darcy is 'good-natured.' Further he is 'the best landlord' and like his father, 'affable to the poor.' As the housekeeper is describing her employer she is conducting the guests on a tour of the house, enabling Elizabeth to see Darcy in a new light, in the midst of the surroundings in which he has grown up. Upstairs, in the picture gallery, there is a portrait of him, along with those of his ancestors. After pausing before it 'in earnest contemplation' (*PP* 250), Mrs Reynolds explains that the picture 'had been taken in his father's life time.' As if looking down at Elizabeth, with a smile that she recognized, Darcy is part of a family tradition; he is part of a continuity that is architectural, familial and social. Thinking about Darcy after finishing the tour of the picture gallery, Elizabeth realizes 'how many people's happiness were in his guardianship.' That such an 'intelligent servant' as Mrs Reynolds regards him as an ideal master and landlord makes Elizabeth think of Darcy with 'a deeper sentiment of gratitude' (*PP* 251) than ever before. "Such a landlord as this was a bulwark of a community of which he was the leading figure. Endowed with a strong sense of duty and responsibility, he cared for those in his custody. As the head of the family estate he managed the business of its operation, as indicated by his early return to Pemberley to tend to 'business with his steward' (*PP* 256). His concern for Pemberly transcended his interest in its operation, as seen in his regarding himself as a trustee who was not the 'entire master,' but the 'life-renter' of the estate—a nice Burkean conception, as Duckworth points out, just as he also notes that Darcy had a Burkean regard for his ancestors. The estate, then, was something to be carefully and well managed, and also to be handed down from generation to generation" (Roberts 48-49). The tradition that Darcy carries forward is coming to an end in the Bennet family. Not only does Elizabeth's father have no sons, but also his estate 'was entailed in default of heirs male, on a distant relation' (*PP* 28). That he could not pass on his estate to his progeny undoubtedly contributes to his detachment and cynicism, and it helps explain his retreat from the world. Mr Bennet's one achievement in life is his beloved 'Lizzy,' who unlike her sisters has his clearness of mind and verbal quickness, along with her own energy and independence, the very qualities that helps her to win over Darcy. Precisely because she has come from a different social stratum than Darcy and belongs to a family line that is running out, she is all the more capable of appreciating the tradition of Darcy's family and helping to maintain it. Darcy stands for permanence, while Elizabeth represents an energy that could translate into improvement. Through marriage the two are synthesized.

As represented by Darcy, the aristocracy is not a closed caste, but open to infusions of life from below. Not only did he marry down in the social sense, but also related easily and successfully to people of different classes than his own. When Elizabeth imagines herself as mistress of Pemberley during her first visit, and wonders if she hasn't made a mistake in rejecting Darcy's proposal, she thinks of her aunt and uncle, the Gardiners, and 'recollecting herself' decides that she has made the right decision. 'My aunt and uncle would have been lost to me: I should not have been allowed to invite them' (*PP* 246). When Darcy appears unexpectedly he is friendly and thoughtful to Elizabeth's aunt and uncle, offering Mr Gardiner the use of his stream any time he might choose, along with his own fishing tackle. Only knowing what Elizabeth has told them about Darcy they feel surprised at such generosity, and wonder afterwards if he had been serious in the offer. In fact, he has been, partly because they are Elizabeth's aunt and uncle but also because he is polite and finds them nice and agreeable people. That Mr Gardiner is a lawyer from London certainly does not prejudice Darcy; pride he certainly does have, but not the type that makes him disdainful of those beneath him socially. We read in the final paragraph of *Pride and Prejudice* that 'with the Gardeners' Darcy and Elizabeth alike 'were always on the most intimate terms' (*PP* 388). As Duckworth has said, '"the three classes of (Austen's) fictional world—nobility, gentry, and trade—come together finally in the park at Pemberley"' (Quoted by Roberts 50). But this is not all: he behaves heroically, for he hastens to London, seeks out Lydia and Wickham, makes a provision for them, and all but drags them to the altar. These things he does not out of admiration for the eloped couple, but out of love for Elizabeth—which, however, he does not again bring himself to declare, until after Lady Catherine de Bourgh's interview with Elizabeth. This "taught me to hope," and so he is able to propose again, this time with success.

For the simple-minded reader the denouement offers much enjoyment. Darcy had been encouraged by his aunt's angry report of Elizabeth's refusal to give the promise demanded; Lady Catherine had also worked on him, less effectually than he had worked on Bingley. The happy talk of the engaged pair (lviii) is surely enough—along with all that has gone before to blunt the traditional complaint about Darcy's incredible changes of character. Some of his original "pride" had been the creation of Elizabeth's prejudice. For the rest of it, he had, like Elizabeth, arrived at self-knowledge; her vehement rejection had given him a new view of himself. He had been a selfish being all his life, "in practice though not in principle" his right principle he had been left, "almost taught," to follow in "pride and conceit," and when shocked and humbled by Elizabeth, he had broken out of the social shell in which he had grown up and resolved to show that he could become a different man, a sensitive individual. Although the total characterization of Darcy has been censured as both a wooden and an inconsistent stereotype, we may think that, in such a novel, such a reformation does not overtax our belief in a character of his strength, sincerity, and devotion. It might be called a large-scale development of Lord Osborne's conscious change of attitude in *Emma* when, in talking with Emma Watson, he realizes that she is a person who has her own dignity.

Sylvia Townsend Warner observes in *Jane Austen*: "The fact that in the latter part of the story he (Darcy) behaves with magnanimity and modesty is not allowed to atone for his behaviour at the ball, where he stalks about and will not dance with Elizabeth. Indeed, he is at odds with the rest of the book, for he is the only character where the author falters in her worldly wisdom. Young persons who have recently come of age see mankind divided into three groups: those younger than themselves, who are children; those over thirty, who are elderly; those between twenty and thirty, who are grown up. An older author would have remembered to make Darcy more perceptibly a young man, whose shyness and youthful censoriousness are in alarmed revolt at a society to which he is not accustomed. This, I think, is how Jane Austen conceived him, and his development from theory to practice is an essential part of the narrative; but her failure to establish his youthfulness splits him into halves: the unamiable Darcy of the opening, the amiable Darcy of the close" (11). Although Warner attributes it to Austen's "failure to establish his youthfulness," one can think that this is how Austen invested the story of Darcy with a different level of meaning adding a new dimension.

MR BENNET

Mr Bennet, the father of the Bennet sisters, is represented as a man of abilities, but of a sarcastic humour, and combining a good deal of caprice and reserve in his composition. He possesses an estate of about two thousand a year, and lives at Longbourn, in Hertfordshire, a pleasant walk from the market town of Meryton. This gentleman's estate is made to descend, in default of male issue, to a distant relation. Mr Bennet, captivated by a handsome face and the appearance of good temper, had married early in life the daughter of a country attorney.

> A woman of mean understanding, little information, and uncertain temper. When she was discontented, she fancied herself nervous. The business of her life was to get her daughters married, its solace was visiting and news.

At a very early period of his marriage, Mr Bennet finds, that a pretty face is but sorry compensation for the absence of common sense; and that youth and the appearance of good nature, with the want of other good qualities, will not make a rational companion or an estimable wife. The consequence of this discovery of the ill effects of an unequal marriage is the defalcation of all real affection, confidence, and respect on the side of Mr Bennet towards his wife. His views of domestic comfort being overthrown, he seeks consolation for a disappointment, which he had brought upon himself, by indulging his fondness for a country life and his love for study. Being a man of abilities and sense, though with some peculiarities and eccentricities, he contrives not to be out of temper with the follies which his wife discovers, and is contented to laugh and be amused with her want of decorum and propriety.

> This, [as our sensible author remarks] is not the sort of happiness which a man would, in general, wish to owe to his wife; but where other powers of entertainment are wanting, the true philosopher will derive benefit from such as are given.

Mr Bennet has his five daughters. Jane, the eldest daughter, is very beautiful, and possesses great feeling, good sense, equanimity, cheerfulness, and elegance of manners. Elizabeth, the second, is represented as combining quickness of perception and strength of mind, with a playful vivacity something like that of her father, joined with a handsome person. Eventually, Elizabeth, the one daughter that Mr Bennet respects has to feel that her father has been incorrect in 'exposing his wife to the contempt of her own children...she had never felt so strongly...the disadvantages of so unsuitable a marriage' (*PP* 236). Mary is a female pedant, affecting great wisdom, though saturated with stupidity. 'She is a lady,' as Mr Bennet says, 'of deep reflection, who reads great books and makes extracts.' Kitty is weak-spirited and fretful; but Miss Lydia, the youngest, 'is a stout, well-grown girl of fifteen, with a fine complexion and good humoured countenance; a favourite with her mother, whose affection had brought her into public at an early age. She had high animal spirits, and a sort of self-consequence.'

If it is to be said that Mr Bennet is not the traditional patriarch, the question that is raised is what role Bennet plays in the household. In spite of his chosen position at the periphery, he is of central importance to his family. In the context of necessities it becomes unavoidable for him to stay alive as long as possible. But even in his life it becomes inevitable for Mr Bennet to face the tests of the life as he is under constant economic anxieties. As the nominal head of the family he is supposed to give his daughters the permission to marry the men of their desire. But his hold and power on family is illusory. Whenever he takes the decisions for the family as a head of the family, it is either rejected or goes completely against the wishes of the family. His authority in the family is gradually subdued by the constant protest of female members of the house. On the whole, though Mr Bennet is far from perfect as a father, his laxity is perhaps better than the other extreme—that of patriarchal tyranny, which for instance, Mr Collins' father exhibits by bringing up his son in subjugation.

Mr Bennet is essentially the eighteenth-century man of wit, a type we might expect to find in Goldsmith or Sheridan. Like Mr Burchell he is sardonic, like Honeywood, the Good-Natured man, he shows the dangers as well as the merits of his foible. But he is used as a focal character throughout the book, and only two people, the hero and heroine, are allowed to increase in stature beside him. Because he loves a fool he increases our delight in them: Mrs Bennet, Mr Collins and Wickham are all funnier because of his comments on them, and he thus sustains and increases the comic tone of the book. His relationship to Elizabeth is beautifully contrived. She alone sees his folly in allowing Lydia to go to Brighton. Whether he has any objection to Darcy, Mr Bennet replies:

> 'None at all. We all know him to be a proud, unpleasant sort of man; but this would be nothing if you really liked him.'
>
> 'I do, I do like him,' she replied with tears in her eyes. 'I love him. Indeed he has no improper pride. He is perfectly amiable. You do not know what he really is; then pray do not pain me by speaking of him in such terms.' (Ch. 59)

Elizabeth's response, which for a moment puts her love for Darcy above her life-long confederacy with her father, is a stroke of great tact and subtlety. To Jane's question how long she has loved Darcy, she answers in the old style: 'It has been coming on so gradually that I hardly know when it began; but I believe I must date it from my first seeing his beautiful grounds at Pemberly.' But with her father she is reduced to seriousness, to something more than the wit he stands for and she shares. So the implicit censure of Mr Bennet's inertia in the novel must be balanced against his important function. He sets the scale of criticism though he is criticized himself, and it is in relation to him that we recognize the heroine's good sense and her real feelings.

MRS BENNET

Mrs Bennet, the wife of Mr Bennet and mother of five children, in *Pride and Prejudice* "was a woman of mean understanding, little information, and uncertain temper. When she was discontented, she fancied herself nervous. The business of her life was to get her daughters married; its solace was visiting and news." Mrs Bennet is just opposite to Mr Bennet in manners and presentation. Mrs Bennet is a type of marriage broker, who still has a house full of unmarried daughters. Mrs Bennet comes to know that Netherfield Park, which is situated near the Longbourn estate, is let to a young single gentleman of good fortune. The intelligence puts Mrs Bennet on the *Qui vive*; or, in a more homely phrase, quite on the *high fidgets*. In her own mind, Mrs Bennet augurs not only great good from this occurrence, but secretly determines, that the said gentleman *shall and must* fix one of her girls for a wife: 'The business of her life was to get her daughters married' (*PP* 5). She therefore exhorts her husband to visit the newcomer without delay. The desired object of Mrs Bennet's wishes at length arrives; and Mr Bennet, though he continues to tease his lady, by refusing to go to Netherfield, is among the first to welcome Mr Bingley. Mrs Bennet is delighted to find, that not only her husband has complied with her wishes but that Mr Bingley is a charming handsome man, that he intends to be at the next county ball, and that he is fond of dancing, 'which was a certain step towards falling in love.' At the ball her raptures know no bounds, when Mr Bingley evidently gives the preference to her eldest daughter before any lady in the room by dancing twice with her in the course of the evening. This is not all; for Mr Bingley, according to the wishes and desires of Mrs Bennet, does really and truly fall in love with the beautiful and amiable Jane. Mr Bingley is, however, prevented from making his proposals of marriage by the interference of his friend, Mr Darcy, a man of high birth and great fortune. Mr Darcy represents to his friend the disgrace not only of being allied to a family, who had relations in trade, but particularly where the chief members of it were so wanting in the common forms of the decorum and propriety as Mrs Bennet and her younger daughters were.

It can be inferred that Mrs Bennet's main goal as a girl had been to make romantic attachments and land a husband. In an interesting comment about her two youngest daughters, Catherine and Lydia, she remembers that as a girl she had been much as they are. Just as they could talk of nothing but officers so too did she 'remember the time when I liked a red coat myself very well—and indeed so I do still at heart' (*PP* 29). Here is a woman who did not mature fully, at least in the sense that she never completely overcame deeply engrained female habits, habits that makes her frivolous and foolish and overtly interested in men, not for herself but for her daughters, and in a way that makes her irresponsible. When Lydia runs off with Wickham, Mrs Bennet is delighted, in spite of everything. "To know that her daughter would be married was enough." Knowing full well that Lydia is living with a man out of wedlock, and believing that the marriage is to take place because her brother has made settlement with Wickham, she says, "This is delightful indeed!—She will be married! ...How I long to see her!...and to see dear Wickham too! But the clothes, the wedding clothes!" (*PP* 306). That the two youngest Bennet girls are overtly concerned with men and overtly anxious to marry is not surprising; they are just as their mother has encouraged them to be, and much as she must have been. One can well imagine these girls, years later and with daughter of marriageable age, becoming brokers on the marriage market and repeating the same dreary pattern.

Noisy and foolish, Mrs Bennet is a miraculously tiresome character. Austen uses her continually to highlight the necessity of marriage for young women. Mrs Bennet also serves as a middle-class counterpoint to such upper-class snobs as Lady Catherine and Miss Bingley, demonstrating that foolishness can be found at every level of society. In the end, however, Mrs Bennet proves such an unattractive figure, lacking redeeming characteristics of any kind, that some readers have accused Austen of unfairness in portraying her—as if Austen, like Mr Bennet, took perverse pleasure in poking fun at a woman already scorned as a result of her ill-breeding.

GEORGE WICKHAM

George Wickham, the son of a manager of the Pemberly estate, is at once the most plausible and the most villainous of Jane Austen's anti-heroes: he is handsome, persuasive, personable, disingenuous, calculating, and dishonourable. He is the Godson of Fitzwilliam Darcy's father. He lost both his parents at a young age, and was raised by his Godfather, growing up alongside Darcy. He is an officer at a militia stationed near Meryton. His appearance in the story comes just as Elizabeth, smarting from Darcy's disapprobation, willingly abrogates her critical faculties in favour of a pleasant countenance and manner. She all too readily believes the militia lieutenant's defamation of Darcy's character—though we, the readers, are expected to take note of the warning signals which Elizabeth ignores. In the first place, Jane Bennet declares:

> It is impossible. No man of common humanity, no man who had any value for his character, could be capable of it. Can his most intimate friends be so excessively deceived in him? Oh! no. (*PP* 85)

In the second place, Miss Bingley plainly warns Elizabeth about Wickham, and indicates his relationship to Darcy:

> So, Miss Eliza, I hear you are quite delighted with George Wickham!—Your sister has been talking to me about him, and asking me a thousand questions; and I find that the young man forgot to tell you, among his other communications, that he was the son of old Wickham, the late Mr Darcy's steward. Let me recommend you, however, as a friend, not to give implicit confidence to all his assertions; for as to Mr Darcy's using him ill, it is perfectly false; for, on the contrary, he has been always remarkably kind to him, though George Wickham has treated Mr Darcy in a most infamous manner. (*PP* 94)

Jane Austen does not stack the cards, but she is not averse to throwing sand in her readers' eyes: both Jane Bennet and Miss Bingley are, as it happens, perfectly correct here; but Elizabeth does not believe either of them, for Jane's unwillingness ever to be unkind does sometimes blind her to people's faults, and Caroline Bingley's careless, insensitive stupidity often leads to complete misapprehension.

So Elizabeth continues to think well of Wickham, and ill of Darcy—even when the former announces his engagement to Miss King, whose dowry is £10,000. This time the heroine ignores the testimony—or rather, the conjecture—of one whose judgment she has always trusted: her aunt, Mrs Gardiner. However, Elizabeth will remember the doubts which she quashed in her early enthusiasm for Wickham—which, after all, arose partly out of her disdain for Darcy. Her big change dates from her second reading of Darcy's letter; then she excoriates herself for her blindness—though she cannot be expected to have guessed the full measure of Wickham's evil: his complete misrepresentation of Darcy, his planned elopement with Georgiana, his dissipated existence in London. He gets the fate which he deserves: he marries Lydia, after causing great distress to everyone concerned, except the foolish young girl herself. But, true to his character, he does not lose an ounce of aplomb.

JANE BENNET

Jane Austen liked Elizabeth the best of all her heroines. 'I must confess,' she wrote, 'that I think her as delightful a creature as ever appeared in print.' If, as some have thought, she was herself the original for her portrait of Elizabeth—and she has certainly given her own gaiety, high spirit and courage, wit and readiness, good sense and right feeling—it is perhaps not rash to suppose that when she drew the placid, kindly, and beautiful Jane Bennet she had in mind her sister Cassandra.

The eldest daughter of the Bennet parents, Jane Bennet, aged twenty-two at the beginning of the novel, has good understanding with Elizabeth. Her mother likes her for her beauty. The very modest and shy girl falls in love with Bingley very deeply, but hardly can express it to him. She is a true lover and continues to love Bingley, though he goes back to London without leaving any hope of coming back. Her nature is so good and genuine that she doesn't even suspect Miss Bingley that she has played an instrumental role in separating Bingley and her (Jane). The most striking feature of Jane Bennet is that she has an unshrinking faith in human goodness. Vindictiveness is alien to her nature and that is why she doesn't feel any revenge for Bingley's sister even after she gets proof that she played ill with Jane.

In the first ball of the novel when Darcy rejects Bingley's proposal to dance with Elizabeth, Jane is the only one to support Darcy speaking in his favour while others criticized him as haughty and proud. It is also seen when she supports Wickham even after revelation of his crookedness. As a matter of fact she is not in a situation to disbelieve either Darcy or Wickham. Her comment on Darcy's letter to Elizabeth about the nature of Wickham is that "interested people have perhaps misinterpreted each to the other."

We feel that she is neither boring nor uninteresting in the novel; instead her appearance in the novel appears very cozy and sweet. This has come out of her great concern and her respect for her parents and has a great understanding and love for her sister Elizabeth. They both are very loyal to their parents; they are very supportive and take the full responsibility of the family at the situation of Lydia's elopement. Although all the confusions in the romantic relationship between Bingley and Jane are resolved through Darcy, we can think that it is of course Jane's pure heartedness that works for her relationship. Thus at the end we see Jane joining Darcy-Elizabeth wedding at Derbyshire, as husband and wife.

At first glance, perhaps the two elder Bennet sisters may seem to vie with each other for primacy in *Pride and Prejudice*; but Elizabeth is definitely the heroine. It is Elizabeth who quite thoroughly dominates the action—and, by comparison, Jane is a shadowy accessory. The relationship of Jane Bennet to Bingley, which parallels that of Elizabeth and Darcy, is treated much less fully, partly because it is much simpler, but partly because it is intended to be a comment on that of Elizabeth and Darcy. Yet Jane, throughout the book, has the unqualified approbation of Elizabeth, author, and reader—though we may, with Elizabeth, wish to speak to her with the following affectionate mock-exasperation:

> My dear Jane!...you are too good. Your sweetness and disinterestedness are really angelic; I do not know what to say to you. I feel as if I had never done you justice, or loved you as you deserve. (*PP* 134-35)

Indeed it is because of—not despite—her perfection that we must reject Jane as the heroine: the author's concern is with the complexity, the interrelationship, of good and bad—the mixture which cannot be unmixed. Jane is a simple character, but "intricate characters are the most amusing," and Jane, like Bingley, is not intricate: she is heroic but minor—she is not a heroine.

MARY BENNET

Mary Bennet, the third daughter in the Bennet family, "in consequence of being the only plain one in the family, worked hard for knowledge and accomplishments, was always impatient for display. Mary had neither genius nor taste; and though vanity had given her application, it had given her likewise a pedantic air and conceited manner, which would have injured a higher degree of excellence than she had reached." Mary is interested in reading books and accomplishing knowledge rather than partying. Although she feels she is intelligent, she is as silly as her sisters, Catherine and Lydia. She says to herself: 'What say you, Mary? For you are a young lady of deep reflection, I know, and read great books and make extracts....' She tries to prove sensible enough and not always at a loss of words, though she seems to express herself at the wrong moments.

Although we are told that Mary's collection of quotations is to be admired, the irony is that she asks for, rather than deserves, admiration. Her pedantic affectation to show off her erudition by quoting from the books she has read makes her an object of burlesque in the novel. She fails to develop social relations and feels at ease by retreating in the world of books. Her unsociable character and pompous and sententious platitudes help to round out the repulsiveness of the Bennet family.

LYDIA BENNET

Lydia is a stout, well-known girl of 15 years, with a fine complexion and good-humoured countenance. In the novel she is presented as the "youngest of the Bennet girls." She is a "favourite with her mother, whose affection had brought her into public at an early age." Always flirting with the officers of militia and interested in partying, she is a girl of unusual height, giddy laughter and animalistic spirits. She is sensually charged and contrary to her sisters and friends her choice of marriage is based on physical attractions. She was just sixteen when she is married. She was brought up in the environment where her mother had no other topic to discuss except marriages. There are indications that her superficial and flirtatious character is not unlike what her mother was at her age. Her elopement with Wickham is boosted by this family environment and thus she loses her morality and causes threat for her family honour because of her irresponsibility. She has no sense of remorse or shame. Lydia's conduct is expressed in the following words in the novel 'that loss of virtue in a female is irretrievable—that one false step involves her in endless ruin-that her reputation is no less brittle than it is beautiful' (*PP* 234).

Lydia plays an important role in the development of the plot, though indirectly, by her elopement with Wickham as it gives Darcy occasion to come gallantly to the aid of the Bennet family and to show how he can curb his pride and deal with hated Wickham for the sake of his love of Elizabeth.

CATHERINE BENNET

Catherine, also called Kitty, is the fourth daughter of Mr and Mrs Bennet and is only seventeen. She is of delicate health and a little bit tense: "What is the matter, mama? What do you keep winking at me for? What am I to do?" According to her father, Kitty is as silly as her younger sister Lydia. She is the close friend and confidant of Lydia. She will follow wherever Lydia leads her. She seems to be completely devoted to dancing, gossiping, flirting and dressing. Her especial liking is for men in uniform. Vain, ignorant, idle, and absolutely uncontrolled, but "she was not of so ungovernable a temper as Lydia: and, removed from the influence of Lydia's example, she became, by proper attention and management, less irritable, less ignorant, and less insipid." In fact, under the influence of Jane and Elizabeth, she gradually improves.

MR COLLINS

Mr Collins, the clergyman in *Pride and Prejudice,* is shown as a person of his profession as neither Henry Tilney nor Edward Ferrars had been. As Rector of Hunsford he lives in the parsonage house, delivers sermons every Sunday, and expresses opinions that are consistent with his clerical office. When visiting the Bennets he is asked to 'read aloud to the ladies' after tea, and a book was duly handed him for that purpose. When it happened to be a novel, 'he started back' and 'protested that he never read novels.' Finally, 'Other books were produced,' and he chooses one of sermons, from which he begins his recitation, in a tone of 'monotonous solemnity.' Bored by it, Lydia interrupts him by relating some local gossip, which provokes this man of the cloth, 'much offended,' to put down his book and say, 'I have often observed how little young ladies are interested by books of a serious stamp, though written solely for their benefit. It amazes me, I confess,—for certainly, there can be nothing so advantageous to them as instruction. But I will no longer importune my young cousin' (*PP* 69).

Mr Collins' solemn and scrupulous ways lead Elizabeth to assume that he would refuse to dance and therefore decline Mr Bingley's invitation to the Netherfield Ball. Even as he was assured that the host is 'a young man of character' and that the guests are 'respectable people,' he feels that attending can have no 'evil tendency,' and under the circumstances he is 'far from dreading a rebuke' from either his archbishop or patron, Lady Catherine de Bourgh. What he reveals in making a demonstration of his scruples in the same moment that he accepts the invitation is a mixture of sanctimoniousness and deference to his social betters. He would show those same tendencies again a short time later when he explains that the 'very noble lady whom I have the honour of calling my patroness' has told him he has to marry. In Mr Collins, Austen depicts a clergyman whose 'good opinion of himself, of his authority as a clergyman, and his rights as a rector, made him altogether a mixture of pride and obsequiousness, self-importance and humility' (*PP* 70). A comic figure, his cowing to his patroness in one moment and assuming pious airs in the next makes him an object of ridicule. Here is a clergyman to be laughed at.

When Mr Collins has annoyed Mrs Bennet by supposing that one of her daughters has helped with the cooking, he begged pardon for having displeased her. In a softened tone she declared herself not at all offended; but he continued to apologize for about a quarter of an hour. D.W. Harding observes in "Character and Caricature in Jane Austen": "If we were to object that this surely is rather unlikely—two or three minutes perhaps but hardly a quarter of an hour—it would be a misreading; we should be missing the fact that this is a convention of joking exaggeration" (Southam, *Critical Essays on Jane Austen* 83). As to the character of Mr Collins, Gilbert Ryle in "Jane Austen and the Moralists" comments: "Mr Collins is the incarnation of vacuous complacency. He glories in what are mere reflections from the rank of his titled patroness and from his own status as a clergyman. He is a soap bubble with nothing at all inside him and only bulging refractions from other things on his rotund surface" (Southam 109).

Austen takes a feminist position by having Mr Collins read from Fordyce's sermons after tea and in the presence of the Bennet family. He did so by choice and after rejecting a novel that had been handed him. Dr Fordyce's *Sermons to Young Women* appeared in 1766 and became one of the more popular courtesy books, running to eleven editions by 1798 and fourteen by 1814. It contains typical genteel advice: the feminine ideal was one of modesty, 'bashful beauty,' 'shamefacedness,' 'sedate manners,' and attentiveness to husbands. 'Sprightliness' and a 'love of shining' leads to dissipation. Wit is inappropriate to the gentle sex. Needle-work is an ideal pastime, and drawing is recommended because it promotes elegance and grace. And so on. This is a book that indeed appeals to Mr Collins, whose view of women seems to have agreed with that of Dr Fordyce. When he proposes to Elizabeth he refuses to accept her negative decision, assuming that she is going through the usual motions of young ladies who 'reject the addresses of the man whom they secretly mean to accept, when he first applies for their favour' (*PP* 107). Repeated reassurances by Elizabeth that her refusal is genuine had little effect. 'I know it to be the established custom of your sex to reject a man on the first application, and perhaps you have even now said as much to encourage my suit as would be consistent with the true delicacy of the female character' (*PP* 108). Charlotte Lucas married Collins with a "pure and disinterested desire of an establishment." His view of the female character and his acceptance of the genteel code is exactly what Austen satirizes and ridicules.

To a critic like Mrs Oliphant, Jane Austen seems too harsh in her treatment of Mr Collins, who, coming nearest to a 'humorous' character, appears to have had a particular attraction for nineteenth century readers. Rachel Trickett observes in "Jane Austen's Comedy and the Nineteenth Century": "...but Jane Austen's fools are to be delighted in, not detested. The sentimentalizing of Mr Collins and the moral earnestness revealed...are interesting examples of the coarsening of comic sensibility in the nineteenth century" (Southam 173).

MR CHARLES BINGLEY

Aged 22, Charles Bingley is a character whose distinguishing feature is his readiness "to yield to the persuasion of a friend." Charles Bingley is equally handsome and rich with his friend Mr Darcy but not as clever as him. He is to rent Netherfield park, and his neighbours soon find him "good looking and gentlemanlike: he had pleasant countenance, and easy, unaffected manners." His manners recommend him to the assembly at the Meryton ball. He "had soon made himself acquainted with all the principal people in the room; he was lively and unreserved, danced every dance, was angry that the ball closed so early." At the ball he finds Jane Bennet as the loveliest creature in the room and she later confides to Elizabeth: "he is just what a young man ought to be...sensible, good-humoured, lively, and I never saw such happy manners!—so much ease, with such perfect good breeding!" Elizabeth also agrees with her and remarks: "His character is thereby complete."

Although Bingley is a very generous and unselfish character, he is somewhat weak-willed and irresolute. We see that at the insistence of Darcy, and his sister Caroline he leaves Jane and goes to London. He allows Darcy to decide what is good for him, even in matters so vital as love and marriage. He suspends his courtship with Jane as Darcy objected to it and resumes it only when Darcy gives his consent to it. But he sincerely refuses to be led into another love and remains completely indifferent to the charms of Darcy's sister. Although Bingley's role is mostly confined to his relationship with Jane in the novel, in his love for Jane we realize the true worth of the relationship of Elizabeth and Darcy. It may be said that the simple and docile Bingley serves as a foil to the complex and authoritative Darcy in the novel.

CAROLINE BINGLEY

The 'proud and conceited' and the most transparent sort of snob, Miss Caroline Bingley has pretensions to aristocratic refinement and good taste. She is a girl having physical charm, proper education and the social accomplishments considered suitable in a young lady of her class. But she is very keen to rise higher in society and so she desperately tries to marry Darcy. She takes Elizabeth to be a rival and seizes every opportunity to show in front of Darcy her imagined superiority over Elizabeth.

It is useful to look at Caroline Bingley when Elizabeth Bennet goes to Netherfield to look after her ailing sister, Jane. After dinner Elizabeth and Jane join Caroline and Mrs Hurst in the drawing room, where they had an hour of conversation. Before Bingley and Darcy arrived, Caroline's and Mrs Hurst's "powers of conversation were considerable. They could describe an entertainment with accuracy, relate an anecdote with humour, and laugh at their acquaintance with spirit. But when the gentlemen entered, Jane was no longer the first object. Miss Bingley's eyes were instantly turned towards Darcy..." (*PP* 54).

When Darcy starts reading, Caroline picks out a book, but her 'attention was quite as much engaged in watching [his] progress through his book, as in reading her own' (*PP* 55). Unable to strike up a conversation and bored with her book, she declares that there 'was no enjoyment like reading,' hoping to catch Darcy's attention. The ruse fails, so she turns to her brother and brings up the question of the ball that he had been discussing. Darcy keeps reading, so Caroline decides on another strategy. She gets up, starts walking about the room, and invites Elizabeth to join her, which she does. When 'Mr Darcy looked up' Caroline asks him to join their promenade. After he declined, a discussion between Caroline and Elizabeth follows that perfectly reveals the chasm that separates these two women. By turns Caroline is coy and mentally helpless, professing to be unable, or unable, to understand one of Darcy's remarks. When Darcy himself explains the meaning Caroline says, in her archly female way, 'Oh! shocking!... I never heard anything so abominable. How shall we punish him for such a speech?' (*PP* 56-57). When Elizabeth suggests to Caroline that she punished him by teasing him this genteel—and designing—young lady tries her female best to achieve her goal through flattery. 'But upon my honour I do *not* [think Darcy should be teased]. I do assure you that my intimacy has not yet taught me *that*. Teaze calmness of temper and presence of mind! No, no—I feel he may defy us there, and as to laughter, we will not expose ourselves, if you please, by attempting to laugh without a subject' (*PP* 57). This speech is the capstone of Caroline Bingley's strategy. All evening long her goal has been to win Darcy's attention. Ever resourceful, she discovers an expedient, after several failures, that worked. Finally, she is able to use her female skill, which she does in telling Elizabeth that she has achieved a certain measure of intimacy with Darcy, but not so much that she could make light of him.

Miss Bingley's haughty artificial wiles and flattery cannot win Darcy who feels attracted towards Elizabeth. She even tries to lead her brother into loving Darcy's sister so as to improve her chances of marrying Darcy. She abominably criticizes Elizabeth behind her back and is a treacherous friend of Elizabeth. Being unaware of Darcy's growing fondness for Elizabeth, her short-sighted attempts like criticizing Elizabeth before Darcy only alienates Darcy from her more and more. Her immodesty, insincerity and snobbery may be assumed to serve as foils to the virtues of the two eldest Bennet girls, Jane and Elizabeth.

LADY CATHERINE

Lady Catherine de Bourgh is an aristocrat who upholds marriages, superior breeding, and limitless snobbery. Lady Catherine is a tall, large woman with strongly marked features. Although Lady Catherine is convinced that social position automatically confers individual distinction, Elizabeth cannot detect in her any individual virtue or quality. She is a caricature of all that is worst in rank and privilege. She thinks that she has a moral duty to intrude into the lives of people socially inferior to her. As Elizabeth notes, 'nothing was beneath this Lady's attention, which could furnish her with an occasion of dictating to others.' In XIV chapter of the novel we see that Mr Collins eloquently talks about her "affability" and "condescension," though he admits that she is reckoned proud by a number of people. Even Wickham tells Elizabeth that Lady Catherine's manners are dictatorial and insolent. She is used to adulation and flattery. That is why she cannot tolerate any criticism or opposition.

Darcy comes to recognize that his aunt, Lady Catherine, and Mrs Bennet are sisters under the skin. Lady Catherine has much in common with Mrs Bennet, for both are equally ill-bred, mercenary and over-bearing. Again, she is as ridiculous in her endeavours at match-making as Mrs Bennet. She deliberates an alliance between her sickly daughter and her nephew Mr Darcy so that both of their estates might be joined. She visits Elizabeth to persuade her that Darcy is not meant for her. It is a new experience for her when Elizabeth refuses to be cowed down by her over-bearing inquisitiveness and answers all her queries with profound dignity. When Elizabeth refuses to listen to her she gives a strong warning in the following words: "very well, I shall know how to act." Her efforts to asunder Darcy and Elizabeth actually misfire and unite them.

There is perhaps some exaggeration in the drawing of Lady Catherine, but little more than comedy allows. Comedy sees life in a light more sparkling, but colder, than that of common day and a touch of exaggeration, that is of farce, is often no disadvantage. A discreet admixture of farce, like a sprinkle of sugar on strawberries, may well make comedy more palatable. With regard to Lady Catherine one must remember that in Jane Austen's day rank gave its possessors a sense of immense superiority over persons of inferior station, and these persons accepted the position without resentment. If Lady Catherine looks upon Elizabeth as so much white trash, let us not forget that Elizabeth looked upon her Aunt Phillips, because of her being the wife of an attorney, as very little better.

CHARLOTTE LUCAS

An 'intricate' character, Charlotte Lucas, in *Pride and Prejudice*, is a woman who has reached an age—twenty-seven—that dims her marital chances. Charlotte Lucas, the daughter of Sir William and Lady Lucas, is seven years older than Elizabeth and they are good friends. She is sensible and intelligent and completely conscious of her modest fortune and plain appearance. She knows well about her getting old and also about her social and economic insecurity.

She responds to her position by scaling down her expectations, which she does through rationalising a view of marriage that would enable her to accept almost any one. She feels that happiness in marriage is 'entirely a matter of chance,' and that however well husband and wife know one another at the beginning they are bound to 'grow sufficiently unlike afterwards to have their share of vexation.' That being the case, it is 'better to know as little as possible of defects of the person with whom you are to pass your life' (*PP* 23). Elizabeth Bennet's response is to say 'You make me laugh, Charlotte; but it is not sound. You know it is not sound, and that you would never act in this way yourself' (*PP* 23). But she acts exactly in that way. With such a view of marriage she was prepared—unflinchingly ready—for Mr Collins. The hard reality is that she was motivated by a 'pure and disinterested desire of an establishment...' (*PP* 122). Her family's response to the engagement indicates the intense pressure that she was under to marry. Lady Lucas immediately thinks about the economic consequences of her daughter's moving into Longbourn. Once Charlotte had time to think over her decision she feels 'tolerably composed'. True, Mr Collins is irksome and his attachment to her is 'imaginary,' but 'still he would be her husband. Without thinking highly of men or matrimony, marriage had always been her object.' For a 'well-educated young woman of small fortune' it is the only 'honourable provision' and it is a 'preservative from want.'

Although her manipulation of Collins to marry her has been defended on the ground of her poverty and her family situation, Austen herself satirizes Charlotte for accepting a fool and caricature like Collins 'from the pure and disinterested desire of an establishment.' We feel pity for her when we think that she chooses a future in which she is aware that she will have to suppress all her qualities that constitute her self and pretend affection and respect hypocritically for a husband she despises, but at the same time when we feel that as she has acted 'with her eyes open,' she stoically refuses 'to ask for compassion.' It is evident from charlotte's life that middle class woman had less fortunes in life with regards to marriage and are left with few possibilities. In the case of Charlotte it was at least possible for her to get the benefits of a wife of a rich man through her marriage. Thus Charlotte thinks and acts practically in making her decision to marry Collins. Charlotte is more pragmatic, rational and mature than Elizabeth as she finds that marrying Collins would ensure a comfortable life for herself whereas Elizabeth is shocked on being told that

Charlotte would be marrying Collins. Elizabeth, after visiting Charlotte in Hunsford after their marriage, finds Charlotte leading a happy life with Collins.

THE GARDINERS

A man of good sense and taste, Mr Gardiner is a living proof to Darcy that being in trade is no disqualification to be a gentleman. The part he plays after Lydia's elopement proves his integrity as well as practical sense. Like Mr Gardiner, Mrs Gardiner is also practical as well as discreet. She perceives Elizabeth's feelings and she supports her through a tough phase of life, and later copes sensibly and firmly with Lydia after her elopement. Her practical wisdom is manifest in her remarks about marriage. With her husband, she makes a very favourable impression on Darcy when they meet at Pemberly, and Elizabeth feels pride in her uncle and aunt.

8 Critical Responses

Susan J. Wolfson

Not for nothing is *Pride and Prejudice* about reading, brimming with letters, the language of manners and behaviour, conversations and chance remarks, reports and gossip, and a vast sign-system of family and connections, estates, homes, carriages, furnishings, and décor. All become objects of implied or provoked reading. A sympathy of readings proves telling, and so does openness to rereading. This is a novel in which the adage "first impressions are lasting impressions" proves a test rather than a truth: Austen's original title was *First Impressions*.

("Re: Reading *Pride and Prejudice*: What think you of books?" in *A Companion to Jane Austen.*)

Mary Poovey

Identifying the Restriction Act in the background of *Pride and Prejudice* also helps me explain the tone in which the novel's famously fantastic conclusion is cast. Like the novel's narrative system, its tone is complex and multilayered, but each of its resonances, like the dynamics of the narrative, can be referred to the Restriction. Most obviously, the novel's conclusion is gratifying and would have reassured the novel's readers: if three broken promises could bring about Elizabeth's marriage to Darcy (Lydia's promise not to disclose that Darcy attended her wedding, Mrs Gardiner's promise not to reveal Darcy's payment of Wickham's debts, and the "promise" Elizabeth breached in thanking Darcy), then surely the Bank's violation of its promise would bring no harm to the nation.

Beneath this reassurance, however, the conclusion also sounds a second tone, the irony for which Austen is justifiably famous. As the signal of an author's awareness that a gap always separates words from the meanings they convey, irony is the signature of representation-made-visible—that is, of the very fact about representation that the Restriction made visible. And third, the nostalgia the conclusion conveys, as the tonal mark of lost possibilities, expresses what passage of the Restriction Act made clear and what must have grown more obvious as the Restriction period dragged on: the power associated with landed gentlemen like Darcy was beginning to wane in favour of the power exercised by the moneyed men who backed the Restriction. Whatever its other effects, after all, the Restriction Act and its prolongation made it clear that the Bank of England's directors were successfully equating the interests of the Bank—and not the landed gentry—with the welfare of the nation as a whole. Thus the gentle rebuke Elizabeth deals to herself…"what becomes of the moral, if our comfort springs from a breach of promise"—preserves what Darcy represents in a kind of historical aspic, memorializing the comfort he can confer in the novel as an appealing, but increasingly distant, possibility for Austen and her readers. The way in which Austen memorializes the possibility associated with Darcy is also deeply ironic, of course, for sanctioning the violation of Lydia's and Mrs Gardiner's and Elizabeth's promises can clear the way for Elizabeth to know, and for Darcy to act upon, their mutual love, but sanctioning the Bank's violation of its promise to pay, as this resolution implicitly does, acceded to the transformation of political power that was already beginning to marginalize Britain's actual landed gentry.

The anxieties that we know the Bank Restriction Act to have provoked in many of Jane Austen's contemporaries register in *Pride and Prejudice*, if they do at all, in a muted and indirect way through the complex dynamics of narrative that forecloses reference, the thematic and formal treatment of representation, and the ambiguous register of tone. But this makes sense, too, for, unlike her more radical peers, Austen did not want literary writing to be a political engine, nor did she want simply to provide escapist fantasies for her readers. The aesthetic she developed, which curtails reference by raising, then dismissing, the issue of representation, constituted an engagement with the social situation that her readers could experience, but not find distressing. That this engagement was complex as well as enjoyable should come as no surprise—given the complexity by which Austen made Elizabeth Bennet's engagement to Darcy so pleasurable for readers to share.

("From Politics to Silence: Jane Austen's Nonreferential Aesthetic." *A Companion to Jane Austen.* 259-60.)

Sylvia Townsend Warner

In 1811, *Sense and Sensibility* 'By a Lady', was published at Jane Austen's own expense. *Pride and Prejudice* followed in the New Year of 1813. In a letter she tells of getting her first copy of *Pride and Prejudice*, 'my own darling child', and goes on to say: 'Now I will try to write something else. And it shall be a complete change of subject—ordination.' This threat was not substantiated. Ordination is not the main issue of *Mansfield Park*, though enough is made of it, perhaps, to account for the fact that Mr Gladstone found this the most enjoyable of her books. Of all Jane Austen's unthematic works, *Mansfield Park* is the least thematic, and the most completely unified. Its characters are presented so convincingly that they are sufficient in themselves to hold the reader's attention—what happens to them is of less interest than how they will adapt themselves to circumstances. [...]

By November 1815, when Jane Austen was staying with her brother Henry in London seeing *Emma* through the printer's hands, *Sense and Sensibility* was in a second edition, *Pride and Prejudice* in a third, and *Mansfield Park* (published in 1814) sold out, with a second edition in contemplation. Her anonymity was lost in something like celerity—Henry had been too proud not to boast a little of his kinship to the *Lady* of the title page. Among her admirers was the Prince Regent. Learning that she was in town he sent her an invitation to visit the library of Carlton House; and during her visit the librarian, a Mr Clarke, intimated that His Royal Highness would be very willing to receive the dedication of her next book. H.R.H. was modestly content to suggest nothing beyond a dedication page. Mr Clarke's patronage was more searching. He hoped that she would 'delineate in some future work the life, character and enthusiasm of clergyman', and 'describe him burying his own mother—as I did'.

(*Jane Austen* 20-24)

Marilyn Butler

Elizabeth and Darcy take a properly pessimistic view of human liability to err, and, rightly applied, their perceptiveness will be a great moral quality: for Jane Austen insists that the scrupulous self-knowledge which she prizes is the product of their kind of sceptical intelligence...the different beliefs that divide Elizabeth and Jane are not fundamental, for they concern the proper application of principles which they both share. Elizabeth's satire versus Jane's candour is a very different polarization from nature versus art, and it can never suggest to us that over the novel as a whole Jane Austen compromises between two views of human nature. Her moral ideal is clear: it is most nearly approached by Darcy and Elizabeth at the point when they have acknowledged the necessity of Jane and Bingley's humility and candour. In their ultimate state of enlightenment, Jane Austen's hero and heroine illustrate a view of human nature that derives from orthodox Christain pessimism, not from progressive optimism. The theme of the moral education of Elizabeth, which is paralleled by that of Darcy, does not sanction but rebukes the contemporary doctrine of faith in the individual.

An explanation of *Pride and Prejudice* based on the theme of Elizabeth's moral enlightenment accounts for about three quarters of the novel; and like most other obvious explanations, it leaves a number of problems unresolved. What for example, of the theme so beautifully established in the first sentence—'It is a truth universally acknowledged, that a single man in possession of a good fortune, must be in want of a wife'? It is a topic which brings Darcy's relative and Elizabeth's, Lady Catherine de Bourgh and Mrs Bennet, unexpectedly together, since both are venal about marriage and blind to its moral significance for the individuals concerned. If we make this theme important, we perceive that there is after all some social criticism in the novel. The progress of the two central couples towards matrimony shows what the state ideally means. But for representative people of very different classes in society, it is a transaction involving merely money and status.

If Jane Austen meant to enforce the moral contrast between her ideal couples and her matchmakers, it is strange that she allowed Elizabeth's intermittent reflections on the subject of prudent marriage to be so disconnected and (from the general ideological point of view) so pointlessly inconsistent. It is true that she is appalled by Charlotte's loveless marriage for financial security. (She is equally shocked by Lydia's reckless pursuit of passion). But Elizabeth's readiness to condemn Charlotte operates more as a means of throwing light on her own wavering judgement than as an insight into marriage-in-society: for the next time we hear of the subject is in relation to Wickham, whose plans for a prudent marriage to Miss King Elizabeth is so inconsistently ready to condone.

The marriage-and-money theme operates in an even more baffling way when Elizabeth herself comes to marry. Walter Scott has been teased for declaring that Elizabeth decides to marry Darcy because when she sees Pemberley 'her prudence' begins to subdue her 'prejudice.' Of course we are not supposed to take so literally her own joke to Jane that she must date her love for Darcy from first seeing his beautiful grounds. The fact remains that Elizabeth *does* make what from the materialistic point of view is a glorious match, the most glorious of any Austen heroine, and that its material splendor is pointedly put forward....

Marriage at the end of a conservative novel should be, and is, the fulfillment of a personal moral quest. An impulsive or mistaken protagonist, frequently someone whose first choice in love was rash, now uses sober judgment and external evidence to select a partner in marriage. Usually it is a girl, a Marianne or a Camilla, who wisely chooses a guardian-like husband;

occasionally, for the point is not a sexist one, an Edward Ferrars or an Edmund Bertram arrives at his second choice, to find a wise mentor in an Elinor or a Fanny. The personal implication in every case, given the prudence of the partner, is that by the act of choice the erring lover gives up his or her youthful waywardness; all at once, it seems time to grow up. The 'true' marriage which follows close and skeptical analysis of the self is also the marriage which commits a couple to a responsible leading role in society. Jane Austen's heroines have a tendency to end up married to clergy or landowners, the spiritual or material leaders of a local community.

Unquestionably the marriage of Elizabeth's and Darcy in *Pride and Prejudice* suggests all these traditional aspects. For both, but in our eyes more essentially for Elizabeth, it represents the arrival at true criticism of the self via correct, humbling assessment of another. Pemberley is significant in this inward process, but not because it means money and status. Darcy's grounds teach Elizabeth that his taste is 'neither formal, nor falsely adorned,' and thus refute her preconceived notion of his pomposity. The good opinion of his housekeeper and tenants is precisely the objective proof of character that she neglected to look for in the case of Wickham. And of course the existence of Pemberley hints at a future life of active social involvement for both Darcy and Elizabeth, a role of far more real dignity than the self-important and selfish patronage of a Lady Catherine de Bourgh.

Knowing the other five Austen novels, and a whole genre of lesser works by novelists of similar ideals, we can guess at a properly inward reading of the denouement. It would have been obvious to her first readers, who were well schooled in the ideological significance of marriage and of the processes leading up to it. But the meaning is not precisely or not sufficiently written into the text. If we return to the issue of Elizabeth's ideas about marriage in general, or to her own marriage with Darcy in particular, we find something of a vacuum. The elements in the novel which convey its meaning are the antithetical patterning, and a series of incidents; *Pride and Prejudice* tends to externalize its action, even though that action is a history of changing attitudes. The most striking omission from the novel's stylistic techniques is continuous free indirect speech, the simulated flow of the heroine's consciousness which is the narrative vehicle of the other mature novels.

What makes *Pride and Prejudice* especially baffling is that the form taken by intelligence in the novel is so seductive. The reader cannot help admiring Elizabeth's wit and sharing her lively and satirical vision. He enjoys *Pride and Prejudice* largely for its caustic portraits of the servile Mr Collins, the foolish Mrs Bennet, the sublimely insolent Lady Catherine de Bourgh—which means that he looks out on the world of the novel with the eyes of an Elizabeth, even of a Mr Bennet. The *action* may imply that this is morally a defective outlook. But, granted that the reader cannot identify himself either with Darcy or Jane, where is his alternative? Elizabeth's reformation is not complete until near the end (and everyone notices that the second, less satirical and extrovert half of *Pride and Prejudice* is less enjoyable than the first). The Gardiners, the only characters in the greater part of the novel who combine sceptical intelligence with good nature, do not offer a persuasive alternative to Elizabeth's consciousness, because during most of the action they do not know enough about what is really happening. The result is that in *Pride and Prejudice* the reader tends to feel himself in a moral limbo. The intention never was a statement about contemporary society which was 'militantly anti-snob' or 'anti-Church'. But the mistake is understandable. The inadvertent impression left by *Pride and Prejudice* is, literally, a negative one.

(From *Jane Austen and the War of Ideas*. 212-17)

9 Chronology

1764	
26 April	Marriage of Revd George Austen, Rector of Steventon, and Cassandra Leigh; they go to live at Deane, Hampshire, and their first three children—James (1765), George (1766) and Edward (1767)—are born here.
1768	
Summer	The Austen family move to Steventon, Hampshire. Five more children—Henry (1771), Cassandra (1773), Francis (1774), Jane (1775) and Charles (1779)—are born here.
1773	
23 March	Mr Austen becomes Rector of Deane as well as Steventon, and takes pupils at Steventon from now until 1796.
1775	
16 December	Jane Austen born at Steventon.
1781	
Winter	JA's cousin, Eliza Hancock, marries Jean-Francois Capot de Ferillide, in France.

1782	
	First mention of JA in family tradition, and the first of the family's amateur theatrical productions takes place.
1783	
	JA's third brother, Edward, is adopted by Mr and Mrs Thomas Knight II, and starts to spend time with them at Godmersham in Kent.
	JA with her sister Cassandra and cousin Jane Cooper, stays for some months in Oxford and then Southampton, with kinswoman Mrs Cawley.
1785	
Spring	JA and Cassandra go to the Abbey House School in Reading.
1786	
	Edward sets off for Grand Tour of Europe, and does not return until autumn 1790.
April	JA's fifth brother, Francis, enters the Royal Naval Academy in Portsmouth.
December	JA and Cassandra have left school and are at home again in Steventon. Between now and 1793 JA writes her three volumes of *Juvenilia*.
1788	
Summer	Mr and Mrs Austen take JA and Cassandra on a trip to Kent and London.
December	Francis leaves the RN Academy and sails to East Indies; does not return until winter 1793.

1791

July	JA's sixth and youngest brother, Charles, enters the Royal Naval Academy in Portsmouth.
27 December	Edward Austen marries Elizabeth Bridges, and they live at Rowling in Kent.

1792

27 March	JA's eldest brother, James, marries Anne Mathew; they live at Deane.
	Cassandra becomes engaged to Revd Tom Fowle this year.

1793

23 January	Edward Austen's first child, Fanny, was born at Rowling.
1 February	Republican France declares war on Great Britain and Holland.
8 April	JA's fourth brother, Henry, becomes a lieutenant in the Oxfordshire Militia.
15 April	James Austen's first child, Anna, born at Deane.
3 June	JA writes the last item of her *Juvenilia*.

1794

22 February	M de Feuillide guillotined in Paris.
September	Charles leaves the RN Academy and goes to sea.
	JA possibly writes the novella *Lady Susan* this year.

1795

	JA probably writes 'Elinor and Marianne' this year.

3 May	James's wife Anne dies, and infant Anna is sent to live at Steventon.
Autumn	Revd Tom Fowle joins Lord Craven as his private chaplain for the West Indian campaign.
December	Tom Lefroy visits Ashe Rectory—he and JA have a flirtation over the Christmas holiday period.

1796

	JA starts writing 'First Impressions'.

1797

17 January	James Austen marries Mary Lloyd, and infant Anna returns to live at Deane.
February	Revd Tom Fowle dies of fever at San Domingo and is buried at sea.
August	JA finishes 'First Impressions' and Mr Austen offers it for publication to Thomas Cadell-rejected sight unseen.
November	JA starts converting 'Elinor and Marianne' into *Sense and Sensibility*.
	Mrs Austen takes her daughters for a visit to Bath.
	Edward Austen and his young family move from Rowling to Godmersham.
31 December	Henry Austen marries his cousin, the widowed Eliza de Feuillide, in London.

1798

	JA probably starts writing 'Susan' (later to become *Northanger Abbey*).
17 November	James Austen's son James Edward born at Deane.

1799

Summer	JA probably finishes 'Susan' (*Northanger Abbey*) about now.

1800

	Mr Austen decides to retire and move to Bath.

1801

24 January	Henry Austen resigns his commission in the Oxfordshire Militia and sets up as a banker and army agent in London.
May	The Austen family leave Steventon for Bath, and then go for a seaside holiday in the West Country. JA's traditionary West Country romance presumably occurs between now and the autumn of 1804.

1802

25 March	Peace of Amiens appears to bring the war with France to a close.
Summer	Charles Austen joins his family for a seaside holiday in Wales and the West Country.
December	JA and Cassandra visit James and Mary at Steventon; while there, Harris Bigg-Wither proposes to JA and she accepts him, only to withdraw her consent the following day.
Winter	JA revises 'Susan' (*Northanger Abbey*).

1803

Spring	JA sells 'Susan' (*Northanger Abbey*) to Benjamin Crosby; he promises to publish it by 1804, but does not do so.
18 May	Napoleon breaks the Peace of Amiens, and war with France recommences.

Summer	The Austens visit Ramsgate in Kent, and possibly also go to the West Country again.
November	The Austens visit Lyme Regis.

1804

	JA probably starts writing 'The Watsons' this year, but leaves it unfinished.
Summer	The Austens visit Lyme Regis again.

1805

21 January	Mr Austen dies and is buried in Bath.
Summer	Martha Lloyd joins forces with Mrs Austen and her daughters.
18 June	James Austen's younger daughter, Caroline, born at Steventon.
21 October	Battle of Trafalgar.

1806

2 July	Mrs Austen and her daughters finally leave Bath; they visit Clifton, Adlestrop, Stoneleigh and Hamstall Ridware, before settling in Southampton in the autumn.
24 July	Francis Austen marries Mary Gibson.

1807

19 May	Charles Austen marries Fanny Palmer, in Bermuda.

1808

10 October	Edward Austen's wife Elizabeth dies at Godmersham.

1809

5 April	JA makes an unsuccessful attempt to secure the publication of 'Susan' (*Northanger Abbey*).
7 July	Mrs Austen and her daughters, and Martha Lloyd, move to Chawton, Hants.

1810

Winter	*Sense and Sensibility* is accepted for publication by Thomas Egerton.

1811

February	JA starts planning *Mansfield Park*.
30 October	*Sense and Sensibility* published.
Winter	JA starts revising 'First Impressions' into *Pride and Prejudice*.

1812

17 June	America declares war on Great Britain.
14 October	Mrs Thomas Knight II dies, and Edward Austen now officially takes surname of Knight.
Autumn	JA sells copyright of *Pride and Prejudice* to Egerton.

1813

28 January	*Pride and Prejudice* published; JA half-way through *Mansfield Park*.
July	JA finished *Mansfield Park*.
November	*Mansfield Park* accepted for publication by Egerton about now.

1814

21 January	JA commences *Emma*.
5 April	Napoleon abdicates and is exiled to Elba.
9 May	*Mansfield Park* published.

24 December	Treaty of Ghent officially ends war with America.
1815	
March	Napoleon escapes and resumes power in France; hostilities recommence.
29 March	*Emma* finished.
18 June	Battle of Waterloo finally ends war with France.
8 August	JA starts *Persuasion.*
4 October	Henry Austen takes JA to London; he falls ill, and she stays longer than anticipated.
13 November	JA visits Carlton House, and receives an invitation to dedicate a future work to the Prince Regent.
December	*Emma* published by John Murray, dedicated to the Prince Regent (title page 1816).
1816	
Spring	JA's health starts to fail. Henry Austen buys back manuscript of 'Susan' (*Northanger Abbey*), which JA revises and intends to offer again for publication.
18 July	First draft of *Persuasion* finished.
6 August	*Persuasion* finally completed.
1817	
27 January	JA starts *Sanditon.*
18 March	JA now too ill to work, and has to leave *Sanditon* unfinished.
24 May	Cassandra takes JA to Winchester for medical attention.
18 July	JA dies in the early morning.

24 July	JA burid in Winchester Cathedral.
December	*Northanger Abbey* and *Persuasion* published together, by Murray, with a 'Biographical Notice' added by Henry Austen (title page 1818).
1869	
16 December	JA's nephew, Revd James Edward Austen-Leigh (JEAL), publishes his *Memoir of Jane Austen*, from which all subsequent biographies have stemmed (title page 1870).
1871	JEAL publishes a second and enlarged edition of his *Memoir*, including in this the novella *Lady Susan*, the cancelled chapters of *Persuasion*, the unfinished *The Watsons*, a precis of *Sanditon*, and 'The Mystery' from the *Juvenilia*.
1884	JA's great-nephew, Lord Brabourne, publishes *Letters of Jane Austen*, the first attempt to collect her surviving correspondence.
1922	*Volume the Second* of the *Juvenilia* published.
1925	The manuscript of the unfinished *Sanditon* edited by R.W. Chapman and published as *Fragment of a Novel by Jane Austen*.
1932	R.W. Chapman publishes *Jane Austen's Letters to her sister Cassandra and others*, giving letters unknown to Lord Brabourne.
1933	*Volume the First* of the *Juvenilia* published.
1951	*Volume the Third* of the *Juvenilia* published.

1952	Second edition of R.W. Chapman's *Jane Austen's Letters* published, with additional items.
1954	R.W. Chapman publishes *Jane Austen's Minor Works*, which includes the three volumes of the *Juvenilia* and other smaller items.
1980	B.C. Southam publishes *Jane Austen's Sir Charles Grandison*, a small manuscript discovered in 1977.
1995	Deirdre Le Faye publishes the third (new) edition of *Jane Austen's Letters*, containing further additions to the Chapman collections.

Bibliography

Aczel, Richard. "Throwing Voices." *New Literary History*, 32: 5 (2001): 703-05.

Aiken, Joan. *Mansfield Revisited: A Novel*. Doubleday & Co., 1984.

——. *Jane Fairfax: A Novel to Complement Emma by Jane Austen*. Gollancz, 1990.

——. *Eliza's Daughter: Sequel to Sense and Sensibility*. St. Martin's Press, 1994.

Alexander, Christine, and Juliet McMaster, eds. *The Child Writer from Austen to Woolf*. Cambridge: Cambridge University Press, 2005.

Allestree, Richard. *The Whole Duty of Man*. London: Printed for John, Francis, and Charles, 1719.

Anderson, Benedict. *Imagined Communities: Reflections on the Origin and Spread of Nationalism*. London: Verso, 1991.

Anderson, Chris. *The Long Tail: How Endless Choice is Creating Unlimited Demand*. Random House Books, 2009.

Anon. *Brief Remarks on English Manners, and an Attempt to Account for Some of Our Most Striking Peculiarities*. London: John Booth, 1816.

Appadurai, A. ed. *The Social Life of Things: Commodities in Cultural Perspective*. Cambridge, UK: Cambridge University Press, 1986.

Appadurai, Arjun. *Modernity at Large: Cultural Dimensions of Globalization*. Minneapolis: University of Minnesota Press, 1996.

Aravamudan, Srinivas. "The Return of Anachronism." *Modern Language Quarterly*, 62 (2001): 331-53.

Armstrong, Nancy. "The Nineteenth-century Jane Austen: A Turning Point in the History of Fear." *Genre* XXIII, 1990.

——. *Desire and Domestic Fiction*. Oxford: Oxford University Press, 1987.

——. *How Novels Think: The Limits of Individualism from 1719-1900*. New York: Columbia University Press, 2005.

Auerbach, Emily. *Searching for Jane Austen*. Madison: The University of Wisconsin Press, 2004.

Austen, Frank. "Letter." *The Times*, May 12. (1880).

Austen, Henry Thomas. "Biographical notice of the Author." *Northanger Abbey and Persuasion*. London: John Murray, 1817.

Austen, James. *The Loiterer* 39. 13 March 1790.

Austen, Jane. *Mansfield Park*. 3rd edn. Ed. R.W. Chapman. Revised by Mary Lascelles. *The Novels of Jane Austen*. Vol. 3. London: Oxford University Press, 1932-4/1965-6.

——. *Minor Works*. Ed. R.W. Chapman. Revised by B.C. Southam. *The Works of Jane Austen*. Vol. 6. London: Oxford University Press, 1954/1969.

——. *Northanger Abbey and Persuasion*. 3rd edn. Ed. R.W. Chapman. Revised by Mary Lascelles. *The Novels of Jane Austen*. Vol. 5. London: Oxford University Press, 1818/1932-4/1965-6.

——. *The History of England*. Eds. Jan Fergus *et al*. Edmonton: University of Alberta Press, 1995b.

——. *Emma*. 3rd edn. Ed. R.W. Chapman. Revised by Mary Lascelles. *The Novels of Jane Austen*. Vol. 4. London: Oxford University Press, 1815/1932-4/1965-6.

——. *Jane Austen's Letters*. 3rd edn. Ed. Deirdre Le Faye. Oxford, New York: Oxford University Press, 1995a.

——. *Jane Austen's Letters to Her Sister Cassandra and Others*. 2nd edn. Ed. R.W. Chapman. London: Oxford World's Classics University Press, 1964/1979.

——. *Pride and Prejudice*. 3rd edn. Ed. R.W. Chapman. Revised by Mary Lascelles. *The Novels of Jane Austen*. Vol. 2. London: Oxford University Press, 1813/1932-4/1965-6.

——. *Pride and Prejudice*. Eds. Claudia L. Johnson and Susan J. Wolfson. London: Longman/Pearson, 1813/2003.

——. *Catharine and Other Writings*. Eds. Margaret Anne Doody and Douglas Murray. Oxford: Oxford University Press, 1993.

——. *Juvenilia*. Ed. Peter Sabor. Cambridge, UK: Cambridge University Press, 2006.

——. *Mansfield Park*. Ed. John Wiltshire. Cambridge: Cambridge University Press, 2005.

——. *Northanger Abbey*. Eds. Barbara M. Benedict and Deirdre Le Faye. Cambridge: Cambridge University Press, 2006.

——. *Persuasion*. Eds. Janet Todd and Antje Blank Cambridge: Cambridge University Press, 2006.

——. *Pride and Prejudice*. Ed. Pat Rogers. Cambridge: Cambridge University Press, 2006.

——. *Sense and Sensibility*. 3rd edn. Ed. R.W. Chapman, Revised by Mary Lascelles. *The Novels of Jane Austen*, Vol. 1. London: Oxford University Press, 1811/1932-4/1965-6.

——. *Sense and Sensibility*. Ed. Edward Copeland. Cambridge: Cambridge University Press, 2006.

——. *Emma*. Eds. Richard Cronin and Dorothy McMillan. Cambridge: Cambridge University Press, 2005.

Austen-Leigh, Caroline. *My Aunt Jane Austen: A Memoir*. London: Jane Austen Society, 1952.

Austen-Leigh, James Edward. *A Memoir of Jane Austen*. Ed. R.W. Chapman. Oxford: Oxford University Press, 1967.

Austen-Leigh, Mary Augusta. *Personal Aspects of Jane Austen*. London: J. Murray, 1920.

Austen-Leigh, William, and Richard Arthur Austen-Leigh. *Jane Austen: Her Life and Letters, A Family Record*. London: Smith, Elder & Co., 1913.

Austin, Linda. *Nostalgia in Transition 1780—1917*. Charlottesville: University of Virginia Press, 2007.

Bader, Ted, and Marilyn Bader. *Desire & Duty: A Sequel to Jane Austen's Pride and Prejudice*. Revive, 1997.

Baker, Ernest A. *The History of the English Novel*. London: H.F. & G.W., 1942.

Bal, Mieke. *Travelling Concepts in the Humanities: A Hough Guide*. Toronto: University of Toronto, 2002.

Balibar, E. and I. Wallerstein. *Race, Nation, Class: Ambiguous Identities*. Trans. Chris Turner. London: Verso, 1991.

Barker-Benfield, G.J. *The Culture of Sensibility: Sex and Society in Eighteenth-Century Britain*. Chicago: University of Chicago Press, 1992.

Barthes, Roland. *The Pleasure of the Text*. Trans. Richard Miller. New York: Farrar, Straus and Giroux, 1975.

——. "The Death of the Author." *The Rustle of Language*. Trans. Richard Howard. Berkeley and Los Angeles: University of California Press, 1989.

Bate, W.J. and Albrecht B. Strauss, eds. *The Yale Edition of the Works of Samuel Johnson*. Vol. 3. New Haven, CT: Yale University Press, 1969.

Battaglia, Beatrice, and Diego Saglia, eds. *Re-Drawing Austen: Picturesque Travels in Austenland*. Naples: Liguori, 2004.

Baudrillard, J. *The System of Objects*. trans. James Benedict. London and New York: Verso, 1996.

Baum, L. Frank. *The Wonderful Wizard of Oz*. In Michael Patrick Hearn, Ed. *The Annotated Wizard of Oz*. New York: Clarkson N. Potter, 1975.

Behrendt, S.C. "Sibling Rivalries: Author and Artist in the Earlier Illustrated Book." *Word & Image*, 13:1 (1997): 23-42.

Bell, G.H. *The Hamwood Papers of the Ladies of Llangollen and Caroline Hamilton*. London: MacMillan, 1930.

Benedict, Barbara M. "Sensibility by the Numbers: Austen's Work as Regency Popular Fiction." In Deidre Lynch, ed. *Janeites: Austen's Disciples and Devotees*. Princeton, NJ: Princeton University Press, 2000.

Benjamin, Jessica. *Like Subjects, Love Objects, Essays on Recognition and Sexual Difference*. London: Yale University Press, 1995.

——. *Shadow of the Other: Intersubjectivity and Gender in Psychoanalysis*. London and New York: Routledge, 1998.

——. *The Bonds of Love, Psychoanalysis, Feminism and the Problem of Domination*. New York: Pantheon Books, 1988.

Berg, M. *Luxury and Pleasure in Eighteenth-Century Britain*. Oxford: Oxford University Press, 2005.

Berlant, Lauren. "Evidences of Masturbation." Eds. James Chandler, Arnold I. Davidson, and Harry Harootunian. *Questions of Evidence: Proof, Practice, and Persuasion Across the Disciplines*. Chicago and London: University of Chicago Press, 1994.

——. "Love, a Queer Feeling." Eds. Tim Dean and Christopher Lane. *Homosexuality and Psychoanalysis*. Chicago and London: University of Chicago Press, 2001.

Berman, Russell A. "Politics: Divide and Rule." *Modern Language Quarterly*, 02 (2001): 317-30.

Bettelheim, Bruno. *The Uses of Enchantment: The Meaning and Importance of Fairy Tales*. New York: Alfred A. Knopf, 1976.

Bhattacharyya, Jibesh. *Jane Austen's Pride and Prejudice*. New Delhi: Atlantic, 2005.

Bing, Just. *Verdens-litteraturhistorie: grunnlinjer og hovedverker*. Vol. 2. Oslo: Aschehoug, 1929.

Binhammer, Katherine. "The Sex Panic of the 1790s." *Journal of the History of Sexuality* 6:3 (1996): 409-34.

Birtwistle, Sue and Susie Conkin. *The Making of 'Pride and Prejudice.'* London: Penguin Books, BBC Books, 1995.

Blackwall, Anthony. *Introduction to the Classics*. 3rd edn. London: C. Rivington and W. Cantrell, 1717/1725.

Blair, Hugh. *Lectures on Rhetoric and Belles Letters by Hugh Blair, D.D.* 3 vols. Dublin: Whitestone, 1783.

Booth, A. *How to Make It as a Woman: Collective Biographical History from Victoria to the Present*. Chicago: University of Chicago Press, 2004.

Boucher, David, Wendy James, and Philip Smallwood, eds. *The Philosophy of Enchantment: Studies in Folktale, Cultural Criticism, and Anthropology*. Oxford: Clarendon Press, 2005.

Bourdieu, Pierre. *The Rules of Art: Genesis and Structure of the Literary Field*. Trans. Susan Emmanuel. Stanford, CA: Stanford University Press, 1878/1996.

Bradbrook, Frank W. *Jane Austen and Her Predecessors*. Cambridge, England: Cambridge University Press, 1966.

Bromley, Eliza Nugent. *Laura and Augusta*. 3 vols. London: W. Cass, 1784.

Brophy, Brigid. "Jane Austen and the Stuarts." In Brian Southam ed. *Critical Essays on Jane Austen*. London: Routledge and Kegan Paul, 1968.

Brown, Julia Prewitt. *Jane Austen's Novels: Social Change and Literary Form*. Cambridge, MA: Harvard University Press, 1975.

Brown, Marshall. "Periods and Resistances." *Modern Language Quarterly* 62 (2001): 309-16.

Brown, P. *The Cult of the Saints: Its Rise and Function in Latin Christianity*. Chicago: University of Chicago Press, 1981.

Burgett, Bruce. *Sentimental Bodies: Sex, Gender, and Citizenship in the Early Republic.* Princeton University Press, 1998.

Burke, Edmund. *A Philosophical Enquiry into the Origin of Our Ideas of the Sublime and Beautiful.* 9th edn. London, 1782.

Burney, F. *The Wanderer; or. Female Difficulties.* Eds Margaret Anne Doody and Robert I. Mack. Oxford: Oxford University Press, 1991.

——. *The Journals and Letters of Fanny Burney.* 12 vols. Eds. Madame D'Arblay, Joyce Hemlow *et al.* Oxford: Clarendon Press, 1972-84.

Burrows, John. *Computation into Criticism: A Study of Jane Austen's Novels, and an Experiment in Method.* Oxford University Press, 1987.

Burton, John. *Lectures on Female Education and Manners.* London, 1793.

Bury, Lady Charlotte. *The Devoted.* 3 vols. London: Richard Bentley, 1836.

Bush, Douglas. *Jane Austen.* London: Macmillan, 1975.

Butler, Eleanor. *Journal.* July 18. Dublin: Wicklow Collection, National Library of Ireland, 1819.

Butler, J. *Bodies that Matter: On the Discursive Limits of "Sex."* New York: Routledge, 1993.

Butler, Marilyn. *Jane Austen and the War of Ideas.* Oxford: Clarendon Press, 1975.

Byrne, Paula. *Jane Austen and the Theatre.* London: Hambledon and London, 2002.

——. *Jane Austen and the Theatre.* London and New York: Continuum, 2002.

Cafarelli, A.W. *Prose in the Age of Poets: Romanticism and Biographical Narrative from Johnson to De Quincey.* Philadelphia: University of Pennsylvania Press, 1990.

Cambridge, Ada. *Thirty Years in Australia.* London: Methuen, 1903.

Cannadine, David. *Aspects of Aristocracy: Grandeur and Decline in Modern Britain*. London and New York: Penguin, 1995.

——. *The Rise and Fall of Class in Britain*. New York: Columbia University Press, 1999.

Cardwell, Sarah. *Adaptation Revisited: Television and the Classic Novel*. Manchester, UK, 2002.

Chapone, Hester. *Letters on the Improvement of the Mind*. Vol. 1. In *Works*. 4 vols. London: Murray, 1807.

Chesterton, G.K. "Preface" *Love and Freindship and Other Early Works by Jane Austen*. London: Chatto and Windus, 1922.

——. *The Victorian Age in Literature*. New York: Henry Holt, 1913.

Clery, E.J. *The Rise of Supernatural Fiction 1762-1800*. Cambridge, UK: Cambridge University Press, 1995.

Cohn, D. *Transparent Minds: Narrative Modes for Presenting Consciousness in Fiction*. Princeton University Press, 1978.

Collins, Irene. *Jane Austen and the Clergy*. London: Hambledon Press, 1994.

Copeland, Edward, and Juliet Me Master, eds. *The Cambridge Companion to Jane Austen*. Cambridge, UK: Cambridge University Press, 1997.

Copeland, Edward. *Women Writing about Money: Women's Fiction in England* 1790-1820.

Craik, W.A. *Jane Austen in Her Time*. London: Nelson, 1969.

——. *Jane Austen: The Six Novels*. London: Methuen, 1966.

Crawford, Robert. *Devolving English Literature*. Oxford: Clarendon Press, 1992.

Crusie, Jennifer. *Flirting with Pride and Prejudice: Fresh Perspectives on the Original Chick Lit. Masterpiece*. Dallas, TX: Benbella Books, 2005.

Gilson, D. *A Bibliography of Jane Austen*. Winchester: St Pauls Bibliographies, 1997.

Gisborne, Thomas. *An Enquiry into the Duties of the Female Sex*. London: Cadell, 1799.

Grey, J.D. ed. *The Jane Austen Handbook*. London: Athlone, 1986.

Grey, J. David, A. Walton Litz, and Brian Southam, eds. *The Jane Austen Companion*. New York: Macmillan, 1986. 190-208.

Halperin, John. *The Life of Jane Austen*. Baltimore, Md.: Johns Hopkins, 1984.

Harding, D.W. "Character and Caricature in Jane Austen." Ed. Monica Lawlor. *Regulated Hatred and Other Essays on Jane Austen*. London: Athlone Press, 1998, 80-105.

Hardy, Barbara. *A Reading of Jane Austen*. London: The Athlone Press, 1997.

Johnson, Claudia L. and Clara Tuite, eds. *A Companion to Jane Austen*. West Essex: Willey-Blackwell, 2012.

Johnson, Claudia L. *Jane Austen: Women, Politics and the Novel*. Chicago, III: University of Chicago Press, 1988.

Kirkham, Margaret. *Women, Writing, and Revolution: 1790-1827*. Oxford: Clarendon Press, 1993.

——. *Jane Austen, Feminism and Fiction*. Brighton: Harvester Press, 1983.

Knox-Shaw, Peter. *Jane Austen and the Enlightenment*. Cambridge: Cambridge University Press, 2004.

Lane, Maggie. *Jane Austen and Food*. London: Hambledon Press, 1995.

Laplanche, J. and J.B. Pontalis. *The Language of Psychoanalysis*. London: Karnac, 1973.

Lascelles, Mary. *Jane Austen and Her Art*. Oxford: Oxford University Press, 1966.

Le Faye, Deirdre, ed. *Jane Austen's Letters*. Oxford: Oxford University Press, 1995.

Leavis, F.R. *The Great Tradition: George Eliot, Henry James, Joseph Conrad*. London: Chatto & Windus, 1960.

Liddell, Robert. *The Novels of Jane Austen*. London: Longmans, 1964.

Littlewood, Ian, ed. *Jane Austen: Critical Assessments*. 4 vols. East Sussex: Helm Information, 1998.

Locke, John. *Some Thoughts Concerning Education*. Eds. John W. and Jean S. Yolton. Oxford: Clarendon Press, 1989.

Looser, Devoney, ed. *Jane Austen and Discourses of Feminism*. New York: St. Martin's Press, 1995, 35-50.

McDonald, Edward D. ed., *Phoenix, the Posthumous Papers of D.H. Lawrence*. London: Heinemann, 1961.

McKillop, Alan D. *The Early Masters of English Fiction*. Lawrence: University of Kansas Press, 1956.

Moiooka, Wendy. *The Age of Reasons: Sentimentalism. Quixotism and Political Economy in Eighteenth-Century England*. London: Routledge, 1995.

Oliphant, M. *The Autobiography of Margaret Oliphant: The Complete Text*. Ed. E. Jay. New York: Oxford University Press, 1990.

Pittock, Murray, ed. *The Reception of Sir Walter Scott in Europe*. New York: Continuum, 2006.

Polhemus, Robert M. "The fortunate fall; Jane Austen's *Pride and Prejudice*." *Erotic Faith, Being in Love from Jane Austen to D.H. Lawrence*. London: University of Chicago Press, 1990.

Rague, Kate, and Paul Rague. *Jane Austen*. Paris: Bloud et Gay, 1914.

Raven, James. *Judging New Wealth: Popular Publishing and Responses to Commerce in England, 1750-1800*. Oxford: Clarendon Press, 1992.

Rivington, *Publishers for the Society for Promoting Christian Knowledge*, 1658/1784.

Robinson, Lilian S. "Why Marry Mr Collins?" *Sex, Class and Culture*. London: Methuen, 1986. 178-99.

Sales, Rogei. *Jane Austen and Representations of Regency England*. London: Routledge, 1996.

Shaw, Harry E. *Narrating Reality: Austen, Scott, Eliot.* Ithaca: Cornell University Press, 1999.

Siskin, Clifford. *The Historicity of Romantic Discourse.* Oxford: Oxford University Press, 1988.

Southam, B.C. *Critical Essays on Jane Austen.* London: Routledge & Kegan, 1968.

Southam, Brian and Anthony Mandal, eds. *The Reception of Jane Austen in Europe.* New York: Continuum, 2007.

——. *Jane Austen and the Navy.* London: Hambledon and London. 2nd edn. 2005.

——, ed. *Jane Austen: The Critical Heritage*, Vol. I. London: Routledge and Kegan Paul, 1968.

——, *Jane Austen: The Critical Heritage.* Vol. II. London: Routledge, 1987.

——, *Jane Austen's Literary Manuscripts.* 2nd edn. London: Athlone, 2001.

Spacks, P.M. *Novel Beginnings: Experiments in Eighteenth-Century English Fiction.* New Haven: Yale University Press, 2006.

Stokes, Myra. *The Language of Jane Austen.* London: Macmillan, 1991.

Sulloway, Alison G. *Jane Austen and the Province of Womanhood.* Philadelphia: The University of Pennsylvania Press, 1989.

Sutherland, Kathryn. *Jane Austen's Textual Lives: From Aeschylus to Bollywood.* Oxford: Oxford University Press, 2005.

Tanner, Toney. *Jane Austen.* London: Macmillan, 1986.

Tave, Stuart M. *Some Words of Jane Austen.* London: University of Chicago Press, 1973.

Taylor, A. *A Treatise on the Anaas or Pine-Apple.* Devizes, UK: Printed by T. Burrough for the Author. (1769). Thompson, J. "Jane Austen and history." *Review* 8 (1986): 21-32.

Todd, J. ed. *Jane Austen in Context.* Cambridge: Cambridge University Press, 2005.

——. ed. *Jane Austen: New Perspectives.* London: Holmes and Meier, 1983.

——. *Sensibility: An Introduction.* London: Methuen, 1986.

Troot, Linda, and Sayre Greenfield, eds. *Jane Austen in Hollywood.* Lexington: University of Kentucky Press, 1998.

Tuite, Clara. *Romantic Austen: Sexual Politics and the Literary Canon.* Cambridge: Cambridge University Press, 2002.

Waldron, M. *Jant Austen and the Fiction of her Time.* Cambridge: Cambridge University Press, 1999.

Warner, Sylvia Townsend. *Jane Austen.* Longmans: The British Council, 1961.

Watt, Ian. *The Rise of the Novel.* Los Angeles: University of California Press, 1957.

White, Hayden. *The Content of Form: Narrative Discourse and Historical Representation.* Baltimore: Johns Hopkins University Press, 1987.

Williams, Raymond. *Keywords: A Vocabulary of Culture and Society.* rev. edn. New York: Oxford University Press, 1983.

——. *The English Novel: From Dickens to Laurence.* London: Chatto & Windus, 1970.

Wilt, Judith. *The Ghosts of the Gothic.* Princeton: Princeton University Press, 1980.

Wiltshire, J. *Jane Austen: Introductions and Interventions.* London: Palgrave Macmillan, 2006.

——. *Recreating Jane Austen.* Cambridge: Cambridge University Press, 2001.

Wollstonecraft, Mary. *A Vindication of the Rights of Woman.* Vol. 5. Eds. Janet Todd and Marilyn Butler. *The Works of Mary Wollstonecraft.* 7 Vols. London: William Pickering, 1989. 61-266.

——. *Thoughts on the Education of Daughters.* London: J. Johnson, 1787.

Woolf, Virginia. "Jane Austen." Ed. Andrew McNeillie. *The Common Reader: First Series.* London: Harcourt Brace Jovanovich, 1984. 137-49.

——. *The Common Reader*. London: Hogarth (1925/1937).

——. *The Essays of Virginia Woolf.* 4 vols. Ed. A. McNeillie. London: Hogarth, 1986.

Wright, Andrew H. *Jane Austen's Novels: A Study in Structure*. London: Chatto & Windows, 1957.

Young, B.W. *Religion and Enlightenment in Eighteenth-Century England: Theological Debate from Locke to Burke*. Oxford: Clarendon Press, 1986.

Young, E. *Conjectures on Original Composition.* London: A. Millar and R. and J. Dodsley, 1759.

Zimmerman, Everett. *The Boundaries of Fiction: History and the Eighteenth-Century British Novel.* NY: Cornell University Press, 1996.

Index